DEEDS NOT WORDS

David Robertson

Dedicated to all Irishmen
who served and died
in two World Wars

Distributed by
Easons Wholesale Ltd
Furry Park
Santry
Dublin 9

Tel: 01 8622111
Fax: 01 8622672

First published 1998 by
David Robertson
Portnashangan
Multyfarnham
County Westmeath

Tel.: 044 71178
Fax: 044 71563

ISBN 0 9533911 0 8

Printed by
Turner Print Group
Convent Road
Longford

CONTENTS

PART 1

THE GREAT WAR
1914 - 1918

PART 2

The Second World War

APPENDICES

LIST OF MAPS AND PHOTOGRAPHS

CREDITS FOR PHOTOGRAPHS

Foreword

by

Kevin Myers

It is in our little platoons that we find ourselves, our community, and our true humanity; and the first of the little platoons we find outside our own families is in our schools, within those fraternities and sororities of assembly, class and playground. Wilson's Hospital School has been the home of one of those little platoons of Irish Protestants for a quarter of a millennium. It is perhaps not surprising that it is from such a quarter that we should hear the first publicly enquiring voice from any Irish school in the Republic. Just what did the sons of our little platoon do in two World Wars?

Over the past twenty years, and increasingly in more recent ones, voices throughout Ireland have been moved to ask the same question. An awareness has been growing that a vast and terrible veil of secrecy has been drawn over the truth of what Irishmen and indeed a good few Irish women - did in the cause of European freedom in two World Wars this century. And the answer has been coming, in a steady and unmistakable voice; a great deal, as this timely volume makes clear,

The boys of Wilson's Hospital School eighty or ninety years ago belonged to a class which is now almost entirely unknown - poor rural Protestants, presumably as unionist as their poor Catholic neighbours were nationalist. Even at this juncture at the end of the 20th century, and with the Island of Ireland having voted overwhelmingly in favour of a peace settlement, it is still not easy for people of the Republic to accept the legitimacy of the unionist aspiration, and hard, too, for many people of unionist extraction who are no longer unionist, to accept that that is indeed the stock from which they come.

But if we are to be true to ourselves and our history, we must accept other greater historical truths - unionism was and is as legitimate a political position as nationalism; and it was as unionists that many of the old boys of the school volunteered during The Great War. They were more than unionist; of far greater import is that they were free men and Irishmen, who as free men and Irishmen chose to fight German aggression in Belgium, and who as free men and Irishmen gave their lives, their liberty, their health, their future.

Wilson's Hospital School owes a great debt of gratitude to David Robertson for the pioneering work he has done in compiling a record of what those boys did eighty years and more ago - including, happily, of how one former pupil made good the Mark Twain quip that "reports of my death are greatly exaggerated". Such reports, alas, were invariably unexaggerated. It would be a hard heart even at this remove not to be touched by the tragedy of, say, the Savage family of Donaghpatrick, County Meath, who lost two of their sons, killed in action, with the third, Charles, both an ex-pupil and an apprentice gardener at the school, being seriously injured.

Yet their fates were not as utterly consumed by the fog of war as were those of the Thompson brothers of Moate. All three enlisted, and two were killed - yet their regiments, place and date of death are unknown; how suitably symbolic of those thousands of other Irishmen who vanished from history, not from lack of documentary evidence, but from amnesia, from terrorist-inspired shame and by the self-imposed historical denial by a nation emerging into independence, an amnesia which was fostered by government after government. And still today, as David Robertson points out, no question about Ireland in The Great War has ever been asked in the Leaving Certificate - yet Ireland was a lawful combatant and sent nearly a quarter of a million men and women into the armed and nursing and medical services.

The war was truly an Irish war. The first shots fired by a British soldier were fired by an Irishman. An Irishman from near Multyfarnham won the very first Victoria Cross of The Great War. The first army chaplain to die was Irish. The youngest soldier to die was Irish. The highest-scoring British fighter pilot was Irish. The battalion with the greatest losses in a single campaign was Irish. The first tank VC was to an Irishman. And in the middle of these hibernian superlatives, one might see the humble lads of Wilson's Hospital doing their humble duty unseen, and too often in the humble doing of it, dying.

As with so many Irish schools, Wilson's Hospital saw a great number of its pupils off to service in the greater and the greatest war which followed, and which again had an imperishably Irish dimension. The first RAF, army and Fleet Air Arm Victoria Crosses went to Irishmen. The first Victoria Cross in North Africa went to an Irishman. The youngest RAF Wing Commander was an Irishman. The last naval Victoria Cross winner was Irish - and the city which suffered the greatest casualties in a single night's bombing, apart from London and Liverpool, was Belfast.

It was from that city that a former pupil of the school, Stafford Vigors - presumably kin of the two Vigors brothers killed with the Dublin Fusiliers in the Great War - collected the corpse of his brother, and fellow ex-Wilsonian, Forbes in a wheelbarrow on their terrible journey back to the family home in Carlow after the blitz there in May 1941. By that time, many of the former pupils of Wilson's Hospital had joined the British armed forces, and one of them, Teddy Whittle, age 21, was in the RAF, where, remarkably (or maybe not) he served in an all-Irish crew in a Blenheim bomber. He survived the war - but another ex-Wilsonian RAF man, Noel Kerr did not.

Perhaps no Multyfarnham story compares with that of the Tottenham family, both for its extraordinary coincidences, and as a parable of what happened to so many rural Irish Protestants of relatively high status (though you will have to resort to the text to find the rest of the Tottenham tale). For what lifts the story of the lads of Wilson's Hospital above the norm is the forgotten truth about the boys it educated; these were poor Protestant boys from poor Protestant homes in southern Ireland.

So they were not born with their tongues touching silver spoons. They were plain Irish lads, and as plain Irish lads they followed the call of duty, of clan, of loyalty, of peer pressure, of family habit or of money. Come what may, they were and they are Irish. They served in the two great wars for freedom; and after decades of neglect, we in Ireland are better and wiser for now taking them in our broad embrace. David Robertson deserves our thanks for his splendid, wide-ranging scholarship into the sacrifices and the service of one small platoon. Out of such small platoons grew the generous freedom of this earth.

The Irish Times,
November 1998

Introduction

It all began in the classroom. Why, my Leaving Certificate history class wanted to know, did so many Irishmen enlist for The Great War? I endeavoured to explain. The class wasn't convinced; the formal reasons lacked a vital ingredient, human interest. We went across to The Chapel and studied the Roll of Honour. From such a small school - it numbered only 35 pupils in 1912 - there were 78 names on the list. Who were these men? Where did they live? Where did they fight? How had so many come to be killed or wounded? The questions fell over one another; they had to be answered.

We took the School Register from the archives and began to work our way through the names. Bit by bit, a picture began to emerge. Names which gathered dust on the walls of The Chapel for eight decades came alive, took shape and substance. It was at this point that my attention was drawn to an article by Kevin Myers in The Irish Times about an exhibition by the Royal Dublin Fusiliers Association in The Civic Museum. Two weeks later, my history class spent a day in Dublin. We began at the War Memorial at Islandbridge, trying to come to terms with the vast numbers who had enlisted. From there to Kilmainham, to place the questions in a different perspective. And finally to the Civic Museum where our guide was Pat Hogarty of the Royal Dublin Fusiliers Association. In the ensuing months, Pat became my friend and mentor.

From such small beginnings, this book has emerged. I have tried to set the story in its historical perspective and to make it accessible to the general reader as well as to friends of Wilson's Hospital. The Irish soldiers, sailors and airmen who fought and died in the two World Wars have been airbrushed out of our history books as if they had never existed. They are Ireland's forgotten men, swept aside by an exclusive view of Irish history. Such prejudice diminishes our integrity as a nation. This book is one small endeavour to restore the balance. I hope that by shedding light on this fragment of Irish history in Wilson's Hospital, our understanding of the larger canvas will be enhanced.

Publication of the book is timed to coincide with the dedication of the Island of Ireland Memorial at Messines Ridge in Belgium. Let us hope that this marks a new beginning in our understanding of Irish history; that parity of esteem will now be accorded to all who fought and died in two World Wars and who aspired to the common name of Irishmen.

David Robertson
Wilson's Hospital School

11th November 1998

Acknowledgements

This book could not have been written without help, advice and support from a considerable number of individuals and organisations. Any errors or omissions in the text are due to my oversight, not theirs. Similarly, all opinions or interpretations of fact in the text are the sole responsibility of the author.

Those to whom my thanks are due fall into six categories:

First, to the authorities in Wilson's Hospital who gave me access to the school archives and every encouragement: The Chairman of the Board of Governors, Mrs Pearl Holt; The Warden, Mr Adrian Oughton; The Bursar, Mr Liam Coyle.

Second, to former servicemen, their families and friends who readily supplied service records, contributed articles, and loaned photographs and memorabilia.

Third, to regimental associations, museums and record offices. Foremost among these is Pat Hogarty and the Royal Dublin Fusiliers Association. Pat Hogarty was an unfailing source of help and advice, initiating research into the service records of many former pupils of Wilson's Hospital. Others who readily provided information include:

The War Graves Commission, London and Ieper (Ypres)
The Royal Irish Fusiliers Regimental Museum, Armagh
The Somme Heritage Centre, Newtownards
The Public Records Office, Kew
National Archives of Canada
National Office of Australian Archives
The Records Office, Islandbridge War Memorial.

Fourth, to a host of friends of Wilson's Hospital whose extensive knowledge of the school was an unfailing source of help. Principal among these was Dr Trevor Winckworth, Mullingar.

Fifth, to Joe Weafer and a battalion of volunteers in Wilson's Hospital who enlisted in the computer room and prepared the text for publication. Foremost among these were Elaine Champ, Kieron Garland and Laura Ryder. This book could never have been produced without their dedication and enthusiasm.

Finally, to Kevin Myers for readily agreeing to write the Foreword and for the care which he has taken

D.S.R.

PART ONE

THE GREAT WAR

1914 - 1918

Chapter One

<u>The lamps go out; Europe before The Great War.</u>

At 11.30 a.m. on June 28th 1914, pistol shots rang out in the streets of Sarajevo. The heir to the throne of the Empire of Austria-Hungary, Archduke Franz Ferdinand, slumped forward in his open car. A bullet had severed his jugular vein and lodged in his spine. Beside him, Sophie, his Czech wife, lay dying; a bullet had penetrated her right side. Within minutes, both were dead. Within days, Europe was plunged into the greatest crisis in its history. Within a fortnight, all the major European Empires were at war. Within four years, 9,000,000 soldiers were dead and 21,000,000 wounded. It was the greatest calamity which the world had ever seen.

The map of Europe before The Great War reveals many differences to the world we know at the end of the twentieth century. The whole of Ireland was part of the United Kingdom and subject to the British rule of Westminister. France was a republic dominated by one soaring political issue; the loss of the Provinces of Alsace and Lorraine. They had been seized in the Franco-Prussian War of 1870-71 and incorporated into Bismarck's Germany. The German Empire extended as far as Russia and included large parts of Western Poland. It was presided over by Kaiser Wilhelm II, King of Prussia. Russia was ruled over by the last of the Romanov family, Tsar Nicholas II.

The last and greatest difference in Europe a hundred years ago lay in the south-east. The great Empire of Austria-Hungary was the dominant power. It was a dual monarchy with separate parliaments in Vienna and Budapest, ruled over by Emperor Franz Joseph, the last of the Hapsburg monarchs. The Empire of Austria-Hungary extended far into central and southern Europe. It contained eleven nationalities of which nearly 40% were Slavs. It was here that the spark was lit which started the Great War in 1914. The rising tide of nationalism in the Balkans, led by the Serbs, threatened to overwhelm the Hapsburg dynasty. In her determination to hold onto a crumbling Empire, Austria-Hungary relied on her principal ally, Germany. Fear of isolation in the event of war drove the major Empires into two armed camps. By 1914, the Triple Alliance of Germany, Austria-Hungary and Italy was opposed by the Dual Alliance of Russia and France. Britain was not formally committed to a European alliance, but had made it clear that her interests lay with France. If a war were to start, the peoples of every major country in Europe would become embroiled.

The pistol shots which signalled the start of this catastrophe were fired by a Serbian nationalist, Gavrilo Princip. He was a member of a fanatical revolutionary organization, the Unity or Death Society. Better known as the Black Hand, this secret society aimed to unite Serbia with all the Slav nationals who were living within the Empire of Austria-Hungary. Such a policy, if successful, would have meant the end of the Empire. Franz Ferdinand's assassination was seen as a deliberate attempt to precipitate this collapse. The Austrian government, having obtained a guarantee of support from Germany, issued an ultimatum to Serbia. When the Serbs refused to accept all the points in the ultimatum, Austria-Hungary declared war. On July 29th 1914, Belgrade, the capital of Serbia, was bombarded by Austrian artillery.

Archduke Franz Ferdinand and his wife on the day of their visit to Sarajevo

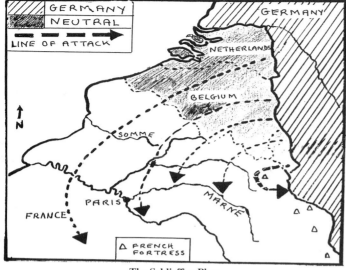

The Schlieffen Plan

The main cause of the First World War was German militarism. Walter Hines, Ambassador of The United States of America in London, said in August 1914 "The German militarism, which is the crime of the last fifty years, has been working for this for twenty-five years. It is the logical result of their spirit and enterprise and doctrine. It had to come."

Otto von Bismarck, Chancellor of Germany from 1871 to 1890, used war as an extension of diplomacy. The unification of Germany was achieved by three wars fought successively against Denmark, Austria and France. Each war was decisive. Each brought the gains Germany sought. Moreover, each war was short. The myth was created in German political consciousness that this would be the outcome of any future war which Germany precipitated.

While Bismarck remained Chancellor, the peace he had imposed on Europe was maintained by a series of alliances. This diplomatic network was destroyed when Bismarck was forced to resign by the new Kaiser, Wilhelm II. German imperial ambitions now dominated political considerations. From 1891 to 1914, German militarism held sway over the government. The ultimate consequence was the "blank cheque" given by the German government to Austria-Hungary to deal with Serbia as she wished. German military thinking had calculated that both France and Russia could be defeated. The Schlieffen Plan was the basis of German's aggressive diplomacy. This plan had two key elements; Russia would be contained on Germany's Eastern front by a holding operation; France would be defeated in six weeks by a lightning invasion through Belgium. Victorious German troops would then be transferred by train to the Eastern front to defeat Russia.

By now, the train of events was racing out of control. Russian troops mobilized in support of Serbia. Germany demanded an end to this mobilization within 24 hours and went on to demand that France, Russia's ally, declare her neutrality. When both refused, Germany declared war on Russia and France. In order to attack France, Germany invaded Belgium. The following day, Britain declared war on Germany in defence of Belgian neutrality which had been guaranteed by Britain, France and Germany in 1839. By August 4th 1914, all the major Empires of Europe were at war.

This may explain how the war started, but it does not explain why. Ever since the guns ceased firing on November 11th 1918, historians have argued about the causes of the war. It is now the politically correct view of history to state that all the major Empires must accept some responsibility; it was their economic, imperial, colonial and military rivalries which caused the war. This view of history lays the blame at all their doors. Or perhaps at none. It is the view of this historian that by failing to pinpoint the principal cause of the war, truth is submerged in generalizations. Truth may be the first casualty of war; it would be ironic if political correctness were also to make it a casualty of history.

This military plan was bold, simple and seductive. In the highly charged political atmosphere of 1914, it matched Germany's mood of arrogance, ambition and aggression. This was the most important factor in the diplomatic equation which plunged Europe into war in 1914. Failure to appreciate this results in failure to understand the settlement imposed on Europe at Versailles in 1919. The failure of that settlement was to lead directly to the Second World War in 1939.

All this was a long way from Ireland, further still from the tranquillity of Wilson's Hospital, Multyfarnham. Within weeks, however, the consequences of the assassination in Sarajevo had made themselves felt in almost every town and village in Britain and Ireland. It was the events of June 28th, 1914, in Sarajevo which brought a political crisis in Ireland to a halt. Young men who been preparing to fight on opposite sides in a civil war, now took up arms to fight side by side in a wider and far more terrible conflict in Europe.

On August 4th 1914, the British Foreign Secretary spoke the words which were to have a prophetic resonance; "The lamps are going out all over Europe and we shall not see them lit again in our lifetime".

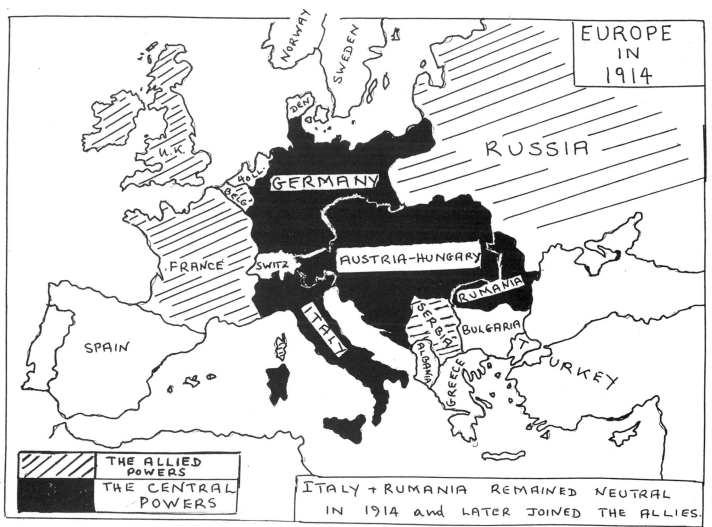

The European Powers 1914

Chapter Two

Ireland Before the first World War

One hundred years ago, Ireland was a very different country from the one we know today. Since the Act of Union in 1800, the whole of Ireland had been under direct rule from Westminster. The United Kingdom of Great Britain and Ireland was governed by a single parliament at Westminster. Queen Victoria was entering the 64th year of her reign as sovereign. The Union Jack flew over Dublin and Belfast. The British Empire was at the height of its power and prestige. Dublin was one of the most prized jewels in its crown.

However, beneath this facade of imperial might, political developments within Ireland were far from tranquil. Demands for Home Rule had found a sympathetic ear in the great Prime Minister, William Ewart Gladstone. In 1886 and 1893, he had introduced two Home Rule Bills in parliament. Either of these Bills would have provided a parliament in Dublin for the whole of Ireland, which would have remained part of the British Empire. Their defeat by Conservatives and Unionists at Westminster served to stoke the fires of political antagonism within Ireland.

In the years which followed, both Unionists and Nationalists endeavoured to consolidate their political support. Unionists, most of whom were Protestants, numbered about 25% of the population of Ireland. In the three southern Provinces of Leinster, Munster and Connacht, they were in a small minority. They formed the Irish Loyal and Patriotic Union. However, apart from the two MP's elected to represent Trinity College, then a Unionist stronghold, they had no significant support. In Ulster, the position was very different. Protestants and Unionists were in a majority. They determined to defend their position within the Union by all means within their power. In the years immediately before the First World War, they found a ready ally in the Conservative and Unionist Party at Westminster.

Nationalist opinion within Ireland was divided into two main groups. The Home Rule Party represented moderate

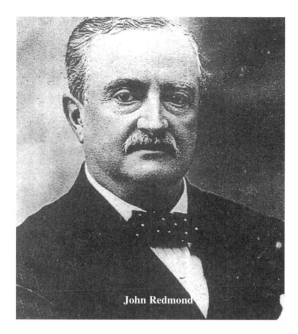

John Redmond

nationalism. It sought a parliament in Dublin for the whole of Ireland, but was willing to remain within the Empire and to accept Westminster control over foreign affairs and defence. By 1900, John Redmond had emerged as the leader of this party. His principal aim was to pressurise the British Government into introducing a third Home Rule Bill.

The more radical element within Irish nationalism was republican. The foundation of Sinn Fein in 1905 revived the aims of the Irish Republican Brotherhood, to sever all political links with Britain and establish an independent state governed by Dublin. Arthur Griffith differed from the I.R.B. in that he hoped to establish a Republic by boycotting British rule in Ireland rather than planning armed rebellion.

The first ten years of the new century witnessed little prospect of Home Rule for Ireland. A Conservative Government in London offered no prospect of devolved government. Its successor was a Liberal government with a landslide majority whose priorities lay elsewhere. Unionists felt safe and were content to consolidate their position by normal democratic processes. Republicanism grew in this context. The political and cultural appeal of Sinn Fein flourished as long as there was no realistic prospect of progress through parliament.

In 1911, the position changed dramatically. A radical budget, introduced by a fiery young Welshman, David Lloyd George, was defeated in the House of Lords by Conservative peers. This forthright challenge to the democratically elected House of Commons was regarded as intolerable by the Liberal government. Two General Elections followed. The Liberals survived, but with a greatly reduced number of MP's. The Prime Minister, Asquith, needed the support of John Redmond's Home Rule Party to retain an overall majority in the House of Commons.

In Ireland, Unionists reacted with alarm. It would not be long before Redmond would claim the reward for his support. This, indeed, was Redmond's finest hour. Support for him swelled in nationalist circles in Ireland; Sinn Fein waned as the prospect grew of progress by democratic means. In 1911, Redmond's MP's supported the Government when a Parliament Bill was introduced. When this became law, the veto of the House of Lords was removed; any Bill which was passed by the House of Commons in three successive sessions would become law automatically. Intended as an Act to prevent the Lords rejecting major legislation (such as a budget) the implications for Ireland were clear. Any future Home Rule Bill could no longer be prevented from becoming law by the Conservative and Unionist peers in the House of Lords.

The following year, 1912, the Third Home Rule Bill for Ireland was introduced into the House of Commons. It was certain to become law in 1914. Redmond's supporters were jubilant; victory was in sight; a parliament would be restored to Dublin within two years with a substantial degree of independence. Unionists, on the other hand, viewed developments with alarm. To them, Home Rule meant Rome Rule. They saw a parliament in Dublin with a Catholic, nationalist majority as a potential threat to their civil and political liberty. They feared for their jobs and economic prosperity. They felt that their place within the British Empire would be in jeopardy. They concluded that if the Home Rule Bill could not be defeated within parliament, it must be prevented from becoming law by other means. Thus began the descent into one of Ireland's darkest hours.

The Home Rule crisis lasted for two years, 1912 to 1914. In that time, two rival armies were formed. Ireland came very close to civil war. The turmoil might well have spilled over into major British cities where the loyalties of Irish immigrants were also sharply divided. It was from the core of these two politically opposed armies that two Divisions were to be raised to fight in the First World War. Men from Wilson's Hospital were to enlist in regiments which made up both these Divisions.

The first of the two armies was formed in Ulster. Even before the Third Home Rule Bill had been introduced into the House of Commons, the leader of H.M. Opposition had pledged his support to Unionists in unequivocal terms. Speaking at Blenheim, Bonar Law, who came from Ulster Presbyterian stock, proclaimed "I can imagine no length of resistance to which Ulster will go which I shall not be ready to support."

The leader of the Ulster Unionists was Sir Edward Carson, a Dublin lawyer and M.P. for Dublin University. He was to prove a formidable advocate for his cause. "We shall yet defeat the most nefarious conspiracy which has ever been hatched against a free people" he had declared in 1911 in Belfast. Carson's plan was simple and uncompromising. If Home Rule were to become law, Ulster would ignore it and establish its own government. His policy was, ironically, very similar to Sinn Fein's concept of "Ourselves Alone" advocated by Arthur Griffith from the opposite side of the political spectrum.

In January 1912, the formation of the Ulster Volunteers began. A retired General, Sir George Richardson, was appointed Commander. Over £1 million was raised to purchase arms. In April 1914, a shipment of 35,000 rifles and 5,000,000 rounds of ammunition were successfully landed in Ulster from Germany. In a carefully planned operation, the arms were distributed to the U.V.F. throughout the Province under cover of darkness. Unionists now had the military muscle to put their opposition to Home Rule to the test.

Meanwhile, nationalists had also set about forming their own army to protect Home Rule when, as they confidently expected, it became law. In November 1913, the Irish National Volunteers were formed with Eoin MacNeill, a Professor of Irish at U.C.D., as their Commander. By May 1914, the Irish Volunteers numbered some 75,000 men. A year later, this had risen to 180,000. On July 24th, arms and ammunition were landed at Howth on Erskine Childer's yacht, Asgard.

As the political crisis deepened in 1914, the prospects of civil war in Ireland loomed very large. The Home Rule Bill was set to pass through its final stages in parliament and seemed certain to become law in August. Desperate attempts were made to find a compromise. King George V summoned a Conference at Buckingham Palace on July 21st. Unionist and nationalist leaders faced each other across the table. Three days later, the Conference ended in failure. Neither side would compromise. The Prime Minister, Asquith, described the situation as "an impasse with unspeakable consequences".

It is one of the great ironies of Irish history that Civil War in 1914 was only prevented by the outbreak of a war of far greater magnitude in Europe. On August 4th, 1914, Britain declared war on Germany. This brought the Home Rule crisis to a dramatic end. Both Carson and Redmond pledged their support for the war effort. Home Rule was to be allowed to become law, but was to be accompanied by a Suspensory Act which prevented its implementation for the duration of the war.

The motives of Carson and Redmond were very similar. Both men hoped that their pledges of loyalty to Britain in time of war would bring their reward at the end of hostilities. No one thought that the war would last long. "The boys will be home by Christmas" was the universal belief. The Home Rule crisis was set aside. For the time being, unionists and nationalists united in response to the call to march to the defence of Belgium. During the course of the next five years 250,000 Irishmen of all political and religious persuasions - and none - were to become embroiled in the conflict. Why, when and where the soldiers of Ireland enlisted for the war will now be examined.

Unionist poster

Chapter Three

The Call to Arms 1914

On September 20th 1914, at Woodenbridge, County Wicklow, John Redmond urged the Irish Volunteers to enlist in the British Army and be prepared to go "Wherever the firing line extends". This speech split the Irish Volunteers. About 11,000 refused to follow Redmond's leadership and formed a separate nationalist force under the leadership of Eoin MacNeill, still calling themselves the Irish Volunteers. The majority, however, responded to Redmond's call. Approximately 170,000 men formed a military organisation under the command of Colonel Maurice Moore, known as the National Volunteers. At least 25,000 of these men were to enlist for war in Europe.

It was Redmond's hope that one new Army would be raised in Ireland. He suggested it should be recruited in Belfast, Dublin and Cork. It should be used for the defence of Ireland and in Europe. However, the Secretary of State for War, Lord Kitchener, was not prepared to countenance any "private armies" and Redmond's proposals were not accepted. This left a legacy of considerable resentment in Ireland.

In Ulster, enlistment in the British Army was not as immediate as might have been expected. Carson's pledges of support for the war effort were hedged with anxieties about the situation in Ireland. For some time, Carson remained afraid that if all the Ulster Volunteers were to leave to fight in France, then Ulster would be defenceless. If a Home Rule Act were suddenly to be implemented, there might be no military opposition left behind to oppose it in Ulster. However, these reservations were overcome by the political necessity for Carson to prove the loyalty of the Volunteers to the Crown.

At first, the War was popular in Ireland. There was genuine enthusiasm for the Allied cause. Belgium was a small, Catholic country. It had been invaded by a powerful aggressor. The rights of a small nation to independence and protection had been flagrantly violated by Germany. Moreover, war meant jobs and money. The Irish economy grew quickly. The war at sea cut Britain off from many of its traditional suppliers of food and raw materials. Irish farmers were only too delighted to supply beef and butter to Britain. In the North, Belfast enjoyed an economic boom. The shipyards flourished as demand rose during the expansion of the Royal Navy. Linen was needed for uniforms and army tents. Throughout Ireland, the departure of men to join the army left jobs open to women. Money sent home by the soldiers, together with separation allowances paid to their wives, boosted domestic incomes.

The reasons for enlisting in the army varied. Many responded to the joint call from Redmond and Carson to prove they were loyal to the Crown - though from opposite political motives. Others signed on because it was a job. It meant a steady income, a uniform, free bed and board. To the poor and unemployed in Ireland in 1914, these were real incentives. The army offered a break from routine and boredom. It offered adventure. It was exciting, romantic, a chance for man to prove himself. The enthusiasm for the war was contagious. Men signed on to be with their friends and workmates. They didn't want to be left at home while others obtained all the glory. Teenagers lied about their age in order to enlist. The war was going to be over by Christmas. Optimism prevailed. All was to be for the best in the best of all possible worlds. The total number of Irishmen enlisted eventually exceeded 250,000- some historians have even suggested a figure of 300,000. All of these men were volunteers, unlike Britain, where conscription was introduced after 1915. Throughout the history of the British Army, Irish regiments had enjoyed a long-standing tradition. They featured in almost every campaign which had been fought in the history of the British Empire.

In 1914, there were four Irish Cavalry Regiments -
4th Royal Irish Dragoon Guards
6th Inniskilling Dragoons
5th Royal Irish Lancers
8th King's Royal Irish Hussars

Recruiting Poster 1914

And nine Irish Infantry Regiments-
The Irish Guards
The Royal Irish Regiment
The Royal Inniskilling Fusiliers
The Royal Irish Rifles
The Connaught Rangers
The Leinster Regiment
The Royal Munster Fusiliers
The Royal Dublin Fusiliers

It was into these Regiments that the great majority of Wilsonian Volunteers were to enlist. All of these Irish Regiments were represented in the British Expeditionary Force (B.E.F.)which went to France in August 1914. When the orders came to mobilise, they responded with exhilaration. War would be the climax of their professional training. Moreover, war in Europe was infinitely preferable to the prospect of war in Ireland. This is not to say that these regular Irish soldiers were under any illusions about the nature of war against such a powerful enemy as Germany. They did not share the jingoistic attitudes of the British press or the naivety of the general public. They recognised that the war would result in considerable bloodshed. The professional soldier left bombast and braggodacio to the politicians.

The Irish Regiments which were stationed in Ireland in July 1914, left in good spirits when they were mobilised. Tom Johnston has recorded the scene in "Orange, Khaki and Green." When the Royal Irish Regiment left Clonmel, the National Volunteers provided it with an honorary escort. The 2nd Battalion, Leinster Regiment was given a rousing send-off in Cork. They were known by the nickname of the "40-10s". Legend had it that when on a tour of duty in India, they were called out on parade for an emergency one night. Troops were instructed to "number" from the right. In the front rank, the men shouted out their number from one to forty-nine. When it came to the fiftieth man, who "had drink taken", he shouted "forty-ten". The incident gave rise to the nick-name which the Leinster Regiment was proud to carry wherever it served.

The regular regiments were not sufficient for the needs of war on a European scale. Lord Kitchener was placed in charge of raising an extra 500,000 men. Of these, three Divisions were to be raised in Ireland. The regular soldiers in existing Irish Cavalry and Infantry Regiments formed the basis of the 10th (Irish) Division. The Ulster Volunteer Force formed the basis of the 36th (Ulster) Division. The Irish Volunteers formed the basis of the 16th (Irish) Division. During the course of the war, many soldiers transferred from one regiment to another, often when they were offered commissions. Wilsonians were to serve in each of the three Divisions raised in Ireland and there are many cases of these men being transferred.

The 10th (Irish) Division was the first Irish Division to leave for France. It contained a complete cross-section of the

Irish community, both in term of class and religion. It was supplemented by old soldiers returning to the ranks. Recruits were sent to Irish regimental depots through the country. After initial training, these recruits were sent on to their Battalions on active service. Later in the war, they were often sent out before their training had been completed - the casualties were so great, this was considered "necessary".

On 16th April 1915, just seven months after it had been formed, the 10th (Irish) Division left for France. The 7th battalion, Royal Dublin Fusiliers was part of this Division. As they marched through the streets of Dublin, they sang the regimental song-

"Left, right, left, right, here's the way we go
Marching with fixed bayonets, the terror of every foe.
A credit to the nation, a thousand buccaneers,
A terror to creation are the Dublin Fusiliers".

Three months later, the 10th (Irish) Division prepared to embark for the Dardanelles. Most sailed from Liverpool on ships of the Cunard Line. En route, they stopped in Egypt at Alexandria. Here, some of the problems they were to face became immediately apparent. Intense heat, to which they quite unaccustomed, took a severe toll. Disease spread rapidly. There was a shortage of water. The food became infected by swarms of flies. Enteritis was rife. To this was added the soldiers' perennial nightmare - boredom. On August 7th, 1915, the 10th (Irish) Division reached its destination at dusk. During cover of darkness, they disembarked on the Dardenelles' Peninsular. Nearly 25% were never to return to Ireland.

The second of the Irish Divisions to be raised for the war was the 16th Division. This began in September 1914. It was to this Division that the National Volunteers turned to enlist, with the full support of the leader of the Home Rule Party, John Redmond. The 6th Battalion Royal Irish Regiment included in its ranks Captain William Redmond, M.P. for Waterford. The 7th Battalion, Leinster Regiment, included Stephen Gwynn, also a Nationalist M.P. who insisted on enlisting as a Private. The 9th Battalion, Royal Munster Fusiliers, included Captain Tom Kettle

K.C., former Nationalist M.P. for East Tyrone. He was also Economics' Professor at U.C.D and a poet.

Captain William Redmond shared his brother's vision of what the advent of war in Europe could mean for the future of Ireland. It was his hope that Unionist and Nationalist could unite in a great cause in Europe and thereby solve the problems at home. "Used with the wisdom which is sown with tears and blood", he wrote, " This tragedy of Europe may be and must be the prologue to the two reconciliations of which all statesmen have dreamed, the reconciliation of Protestant Ulster with Ireland, and the reconciliation of Ireland with Great Britain."

Recruiting Poster 1914

SALUTING OF OFFICERS.

Warrant Officers, Non-Commissioned Officers, and men will salute all Commissioned Officers whom they know to be such, whether dressed in uniform or not, including Officers of the Royal Navy, Royal Marines, Royal Indian Marine when in Uniform, Special Reserve of Officers, Militia, Honourable Artillery Company, Yeomanry, Volunteers and Territorial Force, and such Warrant Officers of the Royal Navy as have rank corresponding to that of the Commissioned Officers in the Army.

The salute, except when swords are worn, will always be with the hand further from the person saluted. When a Soldier passes an Officer he will salute on the third pace before reaching him, and will lower the hand on the third pace after passing him ; when swords are worn the salute will be with the right hand.

A Soldier, if sitting when an Officer approaches, will rise, stand at attention, and salute ; if a number of men are sitting or standing about, the senior Non-Commissioned Officer or oldest Soldier will call the whole to "Attention," and salute. When a Soldier addresses an Officer he will halt two paces from him and salute. He will also salute when withdrawing. When appearing before an Officer in a room, he will salute without removing his cap.

A Soldier without his cap, or who is carrying anything that prevents him from saluting properly, will, if standing still, come to attention as an Officer passes ; if walking, he will turn his head slightly towards the Officer in passing him.

Excerpt from the Soldiers' Rule Book

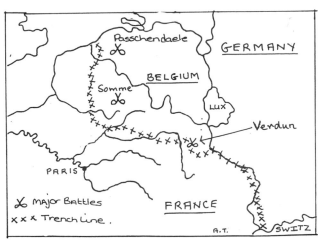

The trenches on the Western Front

When war broke out in 1914, Tom Kettle was in Belgium. He witnessed the advance of German troops into Louvain and atrocities committed by German troops. When he returned to Ireland, he encouraged enlistment in the 16th Division. "We started the National Volunteers to defend the liberties of Ireland", he said. "Well, if you are engaged on a work of defence, you must carry that out in the proper place, and the proper place now is not in Ireland, but on the plains of France and Flanders". It is one of the tragedies of the First World War that neither William Redmond nor Tom Kettle survived the War. They were both to die in action. With them, their hopes of peace and reconciliation in Ireland also perished in the trenches and mud of the Western Front.

The 16th (Irish) Division trained in Ireland between September 1914 and September 1915. Recruits to its ranks were often drawn into the 10th (Irish) Division which was seen as a greater priority. After a year of mandatory instruction in " The Manual of Infantry Training and Field Service Regulations", route marches of some 70/80 miles in 4 days, and simulated battle exercises around Dublin, the 16th (Irish) Division sailed

for England. Further training followed at Aldershot and it was not until February 1916 that the 16th (Irish) Division sailed for France.

The third Division raised in Ireland was the 36th (Ulster) Division. It was the most territorial of all the three Divisions. This was to have appalling consequence at town and village level when the carnage in battle took its toll. Whole male communities of eligible age enlisted together. The small towns and villages in the North were to be inflicted with mass casualties which wiped out most of their young men.

Because the 36th Division was based on the Ulster Volunteers it had already received initial training in the North before the war started. Indeed, two days after Lord Kitchener was appointed Secretary of State for war, he said, " I want the Ulster Volunteers". The Division was authorised on 28th October 1914 and by July 1915, it was ready to sail for England. In October 1915, it crossed to France and received more training near Amiens. In March 1916, the 36th Division occupied the sector between Thiepval and Beaumont Hamel. In those spring days, this was one of the quietest sectors on the Western Front. As rumours of an Allied attack grew, spirits were high, confidence was supreme. Within weeks, the name given to the battle in this sector was to be engraved forever on the North of Ireland; the Battle of the Somme.

A war is often best understood if one small detail is enlarged and examined closely. The study of one section of a canvas leads to a greater appreciation of the painting as a whole. It is to one school in the Midlands of Ireland that our attention will next be drawn. An extraordinary number of young men who were educated at this school enlisted for the war. What kind of school was it? What sort of education did it provide? What can we learn from this school about the young Irishmen who enlisted in their tens of thousands in 1914? These questions will now be considered.

Chapter Four

<u>Wilson's Hospital Before The Great War</u>

On Wednesday, 27th May 1914, the Trustees and Guardians of Wilson's Hospital met in the Representative Church Body at 12 noon. Those present were His Grace the Primate and Archbishop of Dublin; The Most Reverend The Lord Bishop of Meath; The Chaplain and Warden, The Reverend Henry de Vere White.

The report of the Chaplain and Warden showed that, after providing for an extraordinary expenditure of £219/14/0d, there was a credit balance of £371/12/5 in the Hospital account. As Mr. Micawber might have said, "Result - happiness". It was resolved that after the summer vacation, the number of boys be increased from 55 to 60. The final decision of the Trustees was to elect two boys to join the school ; Victor Weir from Tinahely, Co. Wicklow and Hugh Nummy from Newry, County Down. In their last meeting before The Great War, the Trustees had elected the last boys from the school who were to enlist for The Great War.

All was not happiness, however, at Wilson's Hospital. The Reverend Henry de Vere White had become Warden and Chaplain on the death of his father, the Reverend Hill Wilson White in August 1912. Indeed, for some years before that, he had been Warden in all but name. At the date of his formal appointment as Warden, there were only 36 boys in the school. This is a remarkable statistic bearing in mind that 90 boys and 3 masters were to enlist in the course of The War. A glimpse of the state of the Hospital can be found in a report which he made in 1912; the buildings were too big for proper care and maintenance; the staff accommodation was inadequate; the sanitary arrangements were insufficient; the lack of a proper lighting system was a serious drawback; the task of meeting ever increasing costs from a fixed income was a major problem. More than a few years were to pass before all these problems were entirely overcome.

By the time of the outbreak of The Great War, Wilson's Hospital had been in existence for some 150 years. It was founded under the Will of Andrew Wilson of Piersfield, County Westmeath, who had died in 1725 and was buried at Leney Church. It was his wish that the Hospital would care for aged men, being Protestants, and decayed housekeepers, of the County Westmeath, or of other adjacent Counties if it be deemed proper, not exceeding the number of forty. He also wished that a number of Protestant male children, not exceeding 150, be also cared for here. Wilson's Hospital started life as a National School. It was not until 1932 that a Secondary Department was opened. Before that date, no fees were charged. The Hospital's income came from the Endowed land.

The building was completed in 1761. To qualify for entry, a boy or old man had to have a certificate from the Rector and Church Warden of the parish from which he came, detailing his place of residence, an account of his poverty, his name and his religion. The boys remained for five or six years in the school. Each year, twelve or fourteen were apprenticed to various trades. A suit of clothes was given to a boy who became an apprentice, and a fee of £5 was paid to his master after the boy had served

Wilson's Hospital

two years with him. Andrew Wilson's Will directed that a Chaplain be appointed to read prayers according to the Established Church of Ireland once every week-day and on Sunday. The boys were to wear blue shirts, turned up or faced with orange; the same with badges and hats for the men. The old men, who were nearly all former soldiers, remained a feature of Wilson's Hospital for nearly two hundred years, though their numbers fell steadily. By 1934, there were only four left. The last was Tom Macauley who died in 1957.

This is not the place in which to provide a detailed history of Wilson's Hospital from the Foundation to The Great War. Suffice it to say that the basic principles on which the Hospital had been founded remained intact. Not even the events of 1798, in which The Hospital had been occupied both by the Militia and by the United Irishmen - and the Warden, Mr. Radcliff, had nearly been hanged - upset the continuity of tradition unduly. We can gain an accurate glimpse of what life was like in Wilson's Hospital for many of those who enlisted for The Great War from an article written by a former pupil in about 1960. Unfortunately, we cannot be certain who he was. The most probable author is James Wheatley from Killucan, County Westmeath, who entered The Hospital in November 1897 aged 9 years.

Two old men from the Hospital

"I remember well the time I went to Wilson's Hospital School. It was after the summer vacation in the year 1897. I was taken there by my father and I had my first glimpse of the school buildings from the train as we came near Multyfarnham Station."

"We were received by the Warden, The Reverend H.W. White, and after entering my name in a big book, he called for a boy and asked him to show me around. When my father went away, I felt very lonely and unhappy. I had never previously been away from home and I was only 9 years old."

"What I had seen of the place did not impress me. It looked to me like a prison, rather dismal. Soon, however, a lot of the boys gathered around and tried to make me welcome. On my first night, I was terrified of the large dormitory with its rows of beds. I lay awake a long time, thinking of my own little room at home."

"I was awakened by a voice calling, "Everyone up smartly." It was the Head Master, Mr. O'Neill, and the time was 7 a.m. Then down to the wash-house where there was a large swimming bath. Every boy was expected to go into the bath, winter and summer. Many lads would sit shivering on the ladder but a push from the other boys would send them in. Fortunately, I was very fond of the water and could already swim, but I pitied other lads who were really afraid."

"We then went to Chapel and thence to breakfast. It consisted of porridge and milk. We got plenty of this but nothing else. For dinner, we had potatoes, meat and vegetables and sometimes, rice pudding. For tea, we had dry bread and cocoa. Butter was unknown as far as we boys were concerned. We often gathered around the stoves and pressed our bread on the hot metal to make it more palatable. We never got tea except on breaking up day."

"There were three masters when I went to Wilson's. Mr. O'Neill was the Head Master. We called him "The Dad". I remember him very vividly. He was a fair man and never punished a boy unjustly. I have recollections of his many kindnesses. Our greatest pleasure was to be asked to tea in his study. There were boys who worked and learned their lessons and others who wasted their time. Mr O'Neill did not like slackers and treated them accordingly."

"We had our leisure time and plenty of games, soccer, rugby, cricket in summer and handball. In the playroom, there were horizontal bars and a long ladder on which we used to swing."

"There was an old men's home attached to the school and an infirmary. The matron was Mrs Gillespie, and I have very pleasant recollections of her kindness to us boys when we were ill. In winter, boys were often taken to a shed to cut timber. Ropes were attached to the handles of a saw. A team of boys would draw the saw on each side. They often vied with each other who could saw most and the logs piled up."

"In the summer, the boys would be taken to help in the hay field. Mr Mason, the Steward, would be in charge while we were at these jobs. There was also the school tailor, John Griffith; the coachman, Nugent Sprinks, and the carpenter, Billy Spence. The latter was a bit of a character, fond of a joke. A good deal of his time was spent repairing glass broken by the boys with catapults. John Trenier was the gardener."

"I imagine that few people know that Wilson's Hospital was then a National School. It was at this time that two or three girls attended the school as day pupils. They were daughters of the workers on the estate. An institution of the school in my time was a jennet * we called Billy Wax. We boys used to torment him. He would chase us with open mouth. It was also a problem to harness him but, when we did, he would work without trouble."

"We also had a school band (Fife and Drum). It was rather a makeshift affair, but the enthusiasm of the boys made up for the lack of instruments. A boy named Nelson was the big drummer. A boy called McKenzie played the kettle drum which was a round hat box belonging to one of the boys. We used to take

periodic walks down the back avenue but a local farmer complained that the music set the cattle galloping, so the band was prohibited from leaving the playground."

"In summer, we were often taken to the lake. Lord Greville gave permission to go through his estate which was a walk through the woods. We had bathing and Mr O'Neill had a boat in which he took the boys out in their turn for a row."

"On Sundays, we marched to Bunbrosna to the local parish church and we had evening Service in our own Chapel. At that time, most boys were put to some trade. I recollect boys going to harness making, shoe making and gardening. Looking back on the time we spent in Wilson's, it was on the whole a happy time. There were plenty of hard knocks. The boys did most of the work, washing dishes, sweeping up."

A group of boys 1895

"Many parents who keep their boys at home these days would be wise to seriously consider sending them to a boarding school. Boys learn self-reliance, they learn how to give and take,

* a small horse

- 15 -

they learn discipline and they learn how to do things for themselves. Above all, they receive a sound education and are away from many of the temptations which beset boys kept at home, especially in our large cities and towns."

James Wheatley does not mention one aspect of life at Wilson's in those years. Dr. White fought a battle with the rodent population of the Hospital and enlisted Wilson's boys in support of this campaign. He offered the sum of 1d for every rat tail brought to him. However, in the interests of hygiene, such tails had to be coated with tar before being brought to the Warden to be counted. The story goes that one enterprising boy tarred the tails of half a dozen parsnips and presented these for payment. He was not detected and collected his 6d - a large reward; but one which was certainly commensurate with the risk he had taken.

Such was life in Wilson's Hospital 100 years ago. The education which they received equipped them for the essential rudiments of life. Indeed, considering how many were to obtain Commissions during The Great War, James Wheatley's comments about learning self-reliance and discipline seem well founded. The political sympathies of boys at this time were almost certainly Unionist. They came from Church of Ireland families, the great majority of whom were opposed to Home Rule. Two or three glimpses of the light hearted way in which the loyalties of the boys expressed themselves at this time have been recorded.

James Gillespie, son of the school matron, went on to become the "Mr. Chips" of Wilson's Hospital. He served for many years as master of the Junior Department, remaining on the staff when a secondary department was opened in 1932. He was something of a poet, too. He has left behind verses written to celebrate the last visit of Queen Victoria to Dublin in April 1900:

"Welcome! Great and Mighty monarch
To our island green.
We are proud to have among us
Once again, our noble Queen."

During the days of The Boer War, James Gillespie wrote verses to celebrate major victories by Her Majesty's armies. The relief of Mafeking in February 1900 was cause for celebration in Wilson's Hospital. The Warden granted a holiday and the boys marched round the roads bearing the Union flag, as James Gillespie recorded :

"Oh very pleasant was the sight
That here took place that day,
When news came that the Boers took flight
From Mafeking away.

James Gillespie

We first did give a lusty cheer
In honour of B-P*
When we the glorious news did hear
Of his great victory.

And then The Warden gave command
That we upon that day,
Should for a walk go with our band
And bring our banners gay.

And so we marched both proud and gay
Along the road to Bun,
And on us gloriously that day
Did shine the summer's sun."
*(Baden-Powell)

Similar verses were written to celebrate the Relief of Ladysmith in May 1900. "Show the people roundabout, boys, that we're not pro-Boer here", wrote James Gillespie. These sentiments would have been common to most Church of Ireland families at that time and should neither surprise -nor shock - anyone to-day. Attitude to the Boer War was a litmus test for loyalty to the Crown.

The last piece of evidence indicating allegiance is attributed to a boy who was to enlist for the war, Victor Weir, elected by the Trustees in May 1914. In a letter written to his brother in 1917, James Wheatley recorded that on a return visit to the school, he noticed a tricolour flying over Donegan's in Bunbrosna, "Something of a Sinn Fein stronghold." Whether he commented on this to any of the boys during his visit, we do not know. However, several nights later, the flag was taken down in the middle of the night and replaced by a Union Jack. The deed was attributed to Victor Weir who, a year later, enlisted with two of his friends for The Great War. No doubt, their expertise in raising and lowering flags was put to good use there.

Political allegiance was not a primary motive for the Wilson's boys who were to enlist for the war; it was almost certainly something much deeper and more instinctive. What is of particular interest here to the historian is humanitarian. Who were the young men from Wilson's Hospital who enlisted for the War? Where did they live? What occupations did they leave behind? Where did they serve? Where and how did so many come to be wounded or killed? These questions will now be examined in detail.

Chapter Five

Wilson's men in The Great War
A broad survey - and a case of mistaken identity

A total of 90 boys and three members of the teaching staff from Wilson's Hospital served in The Great War. Of these, 20 lost their lives and 27 were seriously wounded. Seven decorations for bravery were awarded.

When one surveys the list of these men, the first aspect which one notices is how ordinary and humble their lives were. These are men drawn from the ranks of apprentices and clerks, gardeners and servants. They did not come from wealthy or famous families.They were not the sons of the landed gentry or the professional middle classes. They were the sons of the working class. Before The Great War, they earned their living by the sweat of their brow.They were not the heirs apparent to Anglo-Irish estates ; they were destined to serve on those estates. They have much in common with their counter-parts in Ulster.They came from the same class as the infantry men from the north of England and Scotland. They would have shared the same hopes and aspirations as the young men from all over the world, from Australia, Canada and New Zealand who enlisted to fight when war broke out. They shared a common humanity in life and in death.

Very few traces remain of the families or descendants of these men from Wilson's Hospital. Had they come from prestigious, well established families, the line of descent might have been more readily traced. They came from working class,

Church of Ireland families in the south of Ireland; a social class which has largely ceased to exist in the Irish Republic today. This is not the place to analyse the reasons for the decline of the Protestant population of the Irish Republic, but one or two aspects are relevant. After Independence, many of the Anglo-Irish estates were divided up and their owners never returned. This must have reduced, if not removed, many employment opportunities for working-class Protestant boys. Equally the notorious "Ne Temere" decree which required children of mixed marriage to be brought up as Roman Catholics dramatically reduced the Protestant population. To this must be added the consequences of The Great War itself. Historians often talk of "The lost generation". However, this term is rarely applied to the Church of Ireland members who were killed in The Great War. We know that nearly 50,000 Irishmen were killed in the War. We do not know what proportion of these were Church of Ireland. However, we do know that 20% of Wilson's boy's who enlisted were killed. If this figure were representative of the Church of Ireland as a whole it would go a long way to explaining why the Protestant population in the Republic has declined so dramatically. Finally, emigration took its toll. All these factors added together explain why so little trace can be found of Wilson's families from the era of The Great War.

The School Register, painstakingly maintained since the Foundation, records the destinations of Wilson's boys when they

Entry in school register - William Wilson

left the school. It is immediately apparent how many of the men who enlisted were working on the great estates. Clover Hill in County Cavan was an estate which regularly offered employment to Wilson's boys. Frederick Brady, Georges Schoales and Frederick Armstrong were all apprenticed to that estate as gardeners. They enlisted for war at different times and in different Services, but one wonders what tradition of enlistment existed on the estate. John Piggott, Francis Hassard, Charles Savage and Richard Wilson all became gardeners - Piggott and Wilson at Loughcrew, Co. Meath. Many more went into "service". This could mean as houseboys, working in the kitchens, general labour or maintenance. George Pakenham and William Walker (both from Killucan), George Martin, Henry Needham and Robert Morrow all went to service after they left Wilson's.

Many boys served apprenticeships in trade. Joseph Hodgins became a saddler. Francis Hourigan was a motor mechanic. Joseph Leahey was a chauffeur. Victor Weir became a plumber. Jeremiah Leahey and David Wilson went to The Kildare Club in Dublin. Thomas Nelson and William Wilson found employment on the railways as clerks. Charles Harvey and Harold Woods became bank clerks. Arthur Wackett became a stud groom. These boys were employees at the foot of the ladder; ordinary working class boys doing ordinary working class jobs.

When war broke out, they enlisted for much the same reason as working class boys throughout the British Empire. A search for adventure, for glory, for comradeship were all motives. In Ireland there were political motives. The 36th (Ulster) Division and the 16th (Irish) Division were largely recruited from opposite sides of the great divide in Ireland. The 10th (Irish) Division recruited from all sections of the community. The interesting point to note about Wilson's boys is that they served in all three of these Divisions. It would be therefore be quite wrong to ascribe to them any particular motive for enlistment. Rather, one senses from the records that their motives were more due to instinct. It would have been part of their tradition to respond to a call from the Crown. They would have inherited a sense of belonging to a wider community, one far beyond their own small school or village. The history they studied would have placed them as members of part of that community; the British

Empire. When the call to arms came, they responded. They enlisted, as far as one can judge, at the recruiting office nearest to their place of employment or their home. This explains how they came to serve in different Divisions; Wilson's boys came from all four Provinces. The wide diversity of regiments in which they served is largely explained by the widespread net of the Church of Ireland from which they came.

To study the list of regiments which Wilson's boys joined is to study a cross-section of the three Irish Divisions which fought in the War. To them must be added those Wilson's boys who enlisted in regiments in England or further overseas. Emigration breaks ties with home and family as well as country; there may be some who enlisted about whom we know nothing. Indeed, of those whom we know served in the War, not all service records are given. The Register in Wilson's Hospital did not always include details of regiment; army records cannot always supply service details unless the regiment is named. For many of the Wilson's boys who served, their records remain incomplete; an added reflection of the concept of lost generation.

The Great War brought casualty lists to Ireland which were on a scale never witnessed before. Families waited in constant fear for the telegram which might bring news of fatalities. There was, regrettably, confusion. Men listed as "missing" might subsequently be found. On the battlefields, tens of thousands of bodies were never recovered for burial. As news filtered back from the front, schools and parishes searched the casualty lists for names they might recognise. In Wilson's Hospital, The Warden, The Reverend Henry de Vere White made copious notes in the School Register. Occasionally, mistakes were made. Identities were confused. The task of the historian, eighty years after The Great War ended, is made easier by access to computerised records. Nothing, however, is more gratifying in the course of research than to discover a family link with the past which can shed new light on forgotten events; or enable mistakes to be corrected. Such is the case with the record of Joseph William Wilson.

On the original Roll of Honour in the Chapel at Wilson's Hospital are inscribed some 78 names. Among these is "Wm

William Wilson at his daughter's wedding 1950

A search began through the School Register to identify all boys by the name of Wilson in the relevant years. There were over twenty, but among them, one name stood out. Arthur William Wilson entered Wilson's Hospital in 1905 aged 11 years. The Royal Dublin Fusiliers Association confirmed that he had enlisted in the 8th Battalion and had been killed in 1916. There was no such record in the school. A clear case of mistaken identity had been made by the Warden. How the error had been made must be speculation. However, both boys were known by the name of William; they were separated by only two years in the school and both had enlisted in the same regiment. Moreover, both had left the school at least five years before The Reverend Henry de Vere White had taken over as Warden. In such circumstances, the confusion is understandable. It is one poignant illustration of the chaos of war and the agonies which families must have suffered when names were published.

It is also a story with a happy ending, at least for one family. Joseph William Wilson, born in Killaduff House, Billis, County Cavan, enjoyed a career which illustrates very well the kind of boy who attended Wilson's Hospital a century ago. He was born on January 15th 1893, the youngest son of William and Jane Wilson. His father died a year later and in 1903, Willie (as he was known) arrived in Multyfarnham. From there, he won an assisted scholarship to Ranelagh School, Athlone. Among the prizes that Willie won there was a bound volume of the weekly Edwardian magazine entitled "Boys of our Empire". In September 1911 he joined the Midland Great Western Railway as a probationer at £39 a year. He served at a number of stations before being transferred to Claremorris at £65 per annum. The following month, he enlisted in the Royal Dublin Fusiliers.

Very little is known about William Wilson's period in the army. His grandson writes that "It was not something he spoke about". In that short sentence, a dreadful truth about the war is conveyed. The unspeakable horrors of the war traumatised thousands of soldiers. The memories haunted them for years to come. Very few wanted to talk about what they had experienced. Their first instinct was to try to forget. Many also felt that noone

Joseph Wilson". His name is preceded by a Cross, indicating that he had been killed in action. In the School Register, the note "killed in France in 1918" appears alongside his name. Clearly, The Warden had received information which left him in no doubt as to the fate of this young man in the war. During the course of research, this writer received a letter from Mr Robert D. Marshall, enquiring whether the school had the name of his grandfather, Joseph William Wilson, on the Roll of Honour.

The delight that a direct link with 1918 had been established was overtaken by Mr. Marshall's subsequent information; his grandfather survived the war and went on to a successful career on the railways. Careful checking of the name, date and place of birth, left no room for doubt. The Roll of Honour in the Chapel contained one serious error. How could such a thing have happened? Moreover, if this man had survived the war, had another Wilson been killed?

would understand; a chasm separated those who survived from those to whom they returned.

It is known that Corporal William Wilson was awarded the Victory Medal and the British European Medal. It is also known that he refused the initial requests to go to Cadet School, both for financial reasons (life as an officer was expensive), and because the casualty rates amongst subalterns was high. However, on St. Patrick`s Day 1919, he was commissioned as a Second Lieutenant into the 6th (Service) Battalion, Royal Dublin Fusiliers. Returning to Ireland in 1919, William Wilson was appointed Clerk in charge of the Mullingar parcels office at a salary of £90 per annum; during the War of Independence this rose to £250. Ireland was changing and in April 1923 he went to Belfast as goods clerk with the Great Northern Railway at a reduced salary of £210 per annum. In 1958, William Wilson was presented with a gold watch by his colleagues to mark his retirement. He died in December 1961 aged 68 years; exactly 43 years after his name had been recorded on the Roll of Honour in Wilson`s Hospital. The case of William Wilson is one which reveals much about the chaos of war. The history of some of his comrades will now be considered.

William Wilson at Ranelagh School 1908 (Standing, right, 2nd row)

Chapter Six

Wilson's boys in the War - individual case histories

Among the Irishmen who enlisted for The Great War, astonishing disparities in age can be found. It is believed that the youngest soldier of the War was Private John Condon, 2nd Battalion, Royal Dublin Fusiliers, killed in action, aged 14, near Ypres in 1915. Close by his grave lies one of the oldest soldiers of the War, Private Thomas Carthy, aged 56, 2nd Battalion, Royal Irish Regiment. Anyone who visits their graves at Poelcapelle, just north of Ypres, will be immediately struck by the poignancy of their deaths.

Wilson's did not lose men as young or as old as these two soldiers. However, men almost the same ages as Condon and Carthy were enlisted. The oldest enlisted soldier from Wilson's Hospital was William J. Little. He was born in St. Peter's Parish, Athlone, in June 1868. It was the year when Mr. Gladstone became Prime Minister for the first time. Little entered Wilson's Hospital on December 15th, 1876. When he left just over five

Pte George Cox

years later, January 1st 1882, it was to be apprenticed to Porteus and Gibbs in Wicklow Street, Dublin. He was a member of the Australian Expeditionary Force in France in September 1916. We do not know any further details of his service career, but the Warden recorded a visit by him to the school while on leave, on August 29th 1917. At that time, William Little would have been just one year short of his fiftieth birthday. There is no record of his death in the war; we can only hope that he survived to return home safely. By any standards, this man was one of the oldest soldiers of the Great War.

The details of the youngest men in the war make disturbing reading. The youngest age permitted for enlistment for active service was 18 years. Yet in a country where enlistment was voluntary, boys lied about their age in order to enlist. Wilson's boys were to deceive recruiting sergeants in several instances. George Cox, born in Almoritia, County Westmeath, entered Wilson's Hospital School on November 9th 1908 aged 10 years 2 months. He was apprenticed to a drapery business in Belfast on April 8th 1913. He succeeded in enlisting for War in 1915, at least nine months short of his eighteenth birthday. Charles Anderson from Clonfadoran, Co.Westmeath joined the school in July 1909 aged eight. Seven years later, he was apprenticed to Belvedere House to work in the gardens. He enlisted in the King's Royal Rifles in January 1918; he, too, was only seventeen years old.

Victor Weir was born in Tinahely, County Wicklow on November 3rd 1901. He entered Wilson's Hospital aged twelve years and nine months in August 1914. He left school two years later, to be apprenticed to Halleck and Best, plumbers, Lombard Street, Dublin. By February 1917, he was a qualified Master Plumber. Seven months later, he succeeded in enlisting in enlisting in the Royal Field Artillery. He was then 15 years and 10 months. A year later, he was on active service in France and was wounded the same year (1918); he was still only seventeen

Pte Robert McCreddin RAMC

Pte Francis Hassard,
Royal Irish Rifles

years of age. After the War was over, Victor Weir joined the U.S. Navy in November 1919.

Henry Tilson was born in Rathaspic, Co. Westmeath in 1899. He entered Wilson's Hospital on May 12th, 1910, aged 11 years. He left two years later, on January 6th 1912 to be apprenticed to the gardens at Beleveder House. This apprenticeship should have lasted at least a year. However, in June 1913, he broke his apprenticeship and succeeded in enlisting in the Royal Field Artillery. Henry Tilson was 15 years old at the time.

The case of these four young men needs further comment because there was a tradition of "Boy Soldiers" in the army. Boys could join the Royal Hibernian School in Phoenix Park as boy soldiers at that time. This was intended for the sons of soldiers serving overseas. There they would learn a trade until they were old enough to enlist, if they so chose. The Royal Field Artillery was permitted to take on boys as young as 14 years old. They could learn to play the bugle and join the military bands. However, they were not permitted by law to see active service

until they were 18 years old. Often as not, this might depend on how physically mature they appeared to be; on the disposition of the recruiting Sergeant-major; and on the need for men as the casualty lists mounted.

By the law of the day, Henry Tilson was old enough to become a boy soldier with the Royal Field Artillery in 1914. Unfortunately, we have no record of when he saw active service, if at all. However, George Cox, Charles Anderson and Victor Weir appear to have been enlisted and, in Weir's case, wounded, when they were still underage. Such are the diverse characteristics of war; young men enlisting under false pretences and recruiting officers prepared to be hoodwinked.

The Royal Navy also recruited boy sailors. They undertook training until the age of 18, the minimum age for active service. Several boys from Wilson's Hospital undertook naval training on H.M.S. Impregnable. Among these was Robert McAllister from Mullingar who entered the school on September the 9th 1912 aged 10 years and 3 months. He joined H.M.S. Impregnable at Devonport on January 28th 1918 aged 15. It is recorded that he qualified in Advanced Gunnery.

Edward Villiers Montserrat was born in Tullamore on September 22nd 1901. He entered Wilson's Hospital aged 12 and left in December 1917 to join the Royal Navy training ship in February 1918 aged 17. He qualified in Advanced Wireless Telegraphy.

Hugh Nummy came from Howth, County Dublin, where he was born on March 7th 1902. He entered Wilson's Hospital in August 1914. Four years later, he joined H.M.S. Impregnable at Devonport - January 28th 1918. He qualified in Wireless Telegraphy as well.

There is a striking similarity to the decisions which these three boys made. They all joined in January and February 1918, straight from school. There is no record of many boys from Wilson's Hospital joining the Royal Navy before that; Frederick Armstrong (1913) and Daniel North (1909) are the only two others. The Senior Service was the choice of a very small minority until 1918. The reason for the change can only be surmised. The three boys were all contemporaries at school ; it may have been an agreement made between them. It may also have been the influence of the Warden, Dean Henry de Vere White. Over the intervening three and a half years, he would have followed reports on the war; read the obituaries ; announced to the school the names of former pupils on the casualty lists. It is not beyond bounds of probability that The Warden may have exercised his influence in persuading boys still within his charge to enlist in the Royal Navy rather than the army. The Navy had been in action in The Dardanelles (1915) and at the Battle of Jutland (1916) but losses in that branch of the Services were markedly less than in the army.

Those who served in the armed forces of Australia and Canada are an interesting commentary both on the School and on the Country. No school is an island; it is a microcosm of the society it serves. Emigration has been a constant feature of Irish history for centuries. It is to be expected, therefore, that Wilson's pupils, like many of their contemporaries in Ireland, would have emigrated after leaving school. The reasons for this were, no doubt, similar to those which drew so many into the army during the war years; duty, adventure and a regular wage. It is ironic, though, that these same motives may have drawn them back from the other side of the world to fight in a European War.

William Little has been mentioned already. At the age of 48, when he landed in France with Australian troops, he was Wilson's oldest serving soldier in the war. In addition to Little, there were three boys serving with Canadian troops. George Strong was born in Mount Nugent, County Cavan in 1894. He entered Wilson's Hospital on August 4th 1902 aged 10 years and 10 months. Six years later, he is recorded as having emigrated to Quebec, his passage of £10 being paid by the Warden, The Rev. Hill Wilson White. He enlisted for war in 1915 in Canada and served with the 13th Canadian Highlanders. In the course of action, he was awarded the Military Medal. After the armistice in 1918, he visited the school before returning to his own farm in Canada.

Thomas Nelson was born in Mullingar in 1887. He entered Wilson's on July 6th 1896 at the age of 9 years 8 months;

before obtaining a free scholarship to Ranelagh School, Athlone. The Warden supplied him with the necessary uniform. Wilson's Hospital did not have a Secondary Department until 1932; this transfer would have enabled him to take his education further. In 1903, Nelson obtained a Clerkship with the G.S.G.R by open competition- the outfit for his first position again being supplied by Wilson's Hospital. Nine years later, he is recorded as being a Stationmaster with the Canadian Pacific railway (1912). He enlisted in 1915 into the Canadian 202 regiment and had reached the rank of Sergeant in 1916. He was killed in action a year later on the Western Front.

The third Canadian from Wilson's Hospital to enlist for war was Percy Wainwright Carleton. He was born in 1892, the son of Dr. William Carleton and Charlotte M. Carleton of Delvin, Co. Westmeath. A year later, he was elected as a free pupil of the Masonic Orphan school in Dublin. This can only mean that Percy was the adopted son of the Carletons; the doctor's profession leads us to guess at the circumstances in which he came to be adopted. The probability is that Percy was placed in Wilson's until such time as a place became available at the Masonic School. At some date after 1901, Dr. and Mrs. Carleton emigrated from Delvin to Canada. They settled in Montreal at 377, Mance Street where Dr Carleton set up a medical practice. Percy, who had emigrated to Canada with them, enlisted for war in the Princess Patricia's Canadian Light Infantry, Eastern Ontario Regiment. His unit was involved in fighting on the Belgian sector of the western front close to the French border. The date of his death there carries a terrible poignancy; 10th of November, 1918; the day before the guns ceased firing at the end of the war. There is no information on his military service record as to the circumstances of his death. However, the register in Wilson's Hospital records that he died as a result of exposure in France - here the date is given as January 1919. One may take the date given by the military authorities as the correct one, but the record in Wilson's provides evidence to the circumstances. One is forced to the conclusion that he may have been wounded or concussed in action and was stranded on the field of battle, perhaps in no man's land, until he could be brought back to the trenches. By that time, he would have been suffering from exposure and shock, from which he never recovered. Or, he may

Sergeant Harold Woods, Royal Dublin Fusiliers

There are several instances where a boy's career before the war was a strong indication of the regiment in which he would enlist. Francis Hourigan, born in Mullingar in 1896, entered Wilson's Hospital in February 1907 aged 11 years. In 1909, he won the Gibson Hall Scholarship to Ranelagh School. From there he was apprenticed to a Motor Garage in Mullingar. When he enlisted in September 1916, it was in the Mechanical Transport Corps.

Arthur Wackett was one of the oldest Wilson's boys on active service. He was born in Navan in 1879, and entered the school in January 1891. When he left five years later, he went to England and became a stud groom at Oakham in Rutland. He went on to serve with a cavalry regiment, 5th Lancers, from 1915 to 1918, by which time he would have been nearly 40 years of age.

Joseph Hodgins from Ardbraccan, Co. Meath, became a saddler in Killeshandra, Co.Cavan when he left Wilson's in 1898. He enlisted in the Inniskilling Dragoons. He was listed as missing in action in 1915. Like tens of thousands of soldiers of the war, his body was never recovered for burial. Similarly, other boys who had peacetime jobs in stables also joined cavalry regiments. David Pratt from Agher and John Thompson from Moate both joined the Royal Horse Artillery. Both were professional soldiers long before the war broke out. David Pratt enlisted in 1899 and John Thompson in 1908. As far as records show, both men survived the war.

It has been said in the last chapter that virtually no trace remains of the families of the men from Wilson's who served in the war. A second exception to that is Thomas Stotesbury from Almoritia, County Westmeath. Thomas entered Wilson's Hospital on May 12th 1910, aged 9 years and five months. He was the fourth of five brothers to attend the school. The eldest was Robert (born 1894), then George (1897), Richard (1899) and the youngest Edward (1903). In 1916, Thomas Stotesbury left Wilson's to go into service with Mr. Sanderson at Clover Hill, County Cavan. He enlisted in the army at the earliest permitted age in September 1918. Thomas survived the last few months of the war and joined the Royal Irish Constabulary when he was

simply have been exposed to severe winter weather in the trenches, with fatal consequences for his health. Percy Carleton's death, aged 26, on the battle fields of Flanders only 24 hours before the Armistice, serves as a sad and pitiful epitaph to this terrible war.

As a footnote to this episode, a detail can be added a detail about Percy Carleton's birthplace. Many young men from Delvin enlisted for the war in 1914. Most joined the Royal Dublin Fusiliers and were involved in the fighting in Gallipoli. When those soldiers who survived returned to Delvin after the war, they were given grants of land by the local landlord. To this day, that land is known locally as "The Dardanelles".

Able Seaman Hugh Nummy

when Robert Stotesbury left Wilson's Hospital in 1971, he joined the Garda Siochana, and is now based in County Wexford.

From the records which exist in the school, one can determine the dates and campaigns of serving soldiers. Photographs add a third dimension. The faces from The Great War look straight out at the historian. They carry their own message. The expressions of the young men who posed in those photographic studios eighty years ago are calm, collected and serious. One senses the pride they felt, the sense of duty as they set out for Europe and, perhaps, the wish to leave behind an image of which their families could be proud.To the modern eye, however, many of these photographs strike a discordant note. The faces are too youthful; too innocent of the horrors they were about to face. Each successive generation since The Great War has reached maturity earlier. It is probable that the voices of some soldiers of this war had not broken when they enlisted.

Barney McCreddin from Longford and Frank Hassard from Moyne, County Westmeath, appear calm and collected. There is a certain wistfulness in their expressions, carrying messages of love and remembrance to their families. The photograph of Sergeant J.T.H. Woods is the most remarkable of all. He, too, came from Moyne. When he enlisted in the Royal Dublin Fusiliers in 1914, he was aged 18. Three years later, when the photograph was taken, he had been wounded and promoted to Sergeant. His stance, one hand on hip, the other holding his walking stick, right leg thrust forward, a uniform which appears oversized; these images are surmounted by a young and purposeful face which had already witnessed three years of war. But it is a face which today one would expect to see in Vth form, not in the uniform of a seasoned soldier. Harold Woods was one of those fortunate to serve throughout the entire war and return safely home. When he did so, it was with the rank of 2nd Lieutenant.

demobilised. After Partition, Thomas moved to County Down, where he joined the Royal Ulster Constabulary. He served there until his retirement and is buried in the Church of Ireland graveyard at Killyleagh. Sixty four years after Thomas entered Wilson's, his nephew, Robert Stotesbury, joined the school (1965). Robert records that the name of one of his uncles was to be found carved into the walls above the Concert Hall. Sadly, such is progress, that part of the school has since been replastered. It is an interesting comment on changing times that

The concept of families in war is an emotive one. It is to that aspect of Wilson's pupils in The Great War that attention will next be turned.

Chapter Seven

Brothers In Arms

One of the reassuring aspects of an old established school is tradition and continuity. Sons and daughters follow where their parents have trodden before them. A school which has existed since 1761 and, moreover, one which has remained on the same site in the original eighteenth century buildings, has an aura which no modern buildings can replicate. To walk up the front steps of Wilson's Hospital, through the front hall and look down into the courtyard, is to look back in time. To sit in the peace and tranquillity of the chapel, uniquely set in the heart of the school, is to absorb an atmosphere which nurtured previous generations.

The central part of the old school remains today exactly the same as it was one hundred years ago when the future soldiers of The Great War were in their formative years. It must have been a cold and forbidding place, not least in winter. Moreover, before the era of modern transport and communications, it was an isolated place. No cars to whisk the pupils away for weekends, no television or Internet to bring news of the outside world, no telephones, fax machines or electronic mail to make instant cries for help in some real or imagined crisis. When the pupils arrived at Wilson's Hospital and the great door closed behind them, many must have felt not so much cut off, as imprisoned.

In such circumstances, close ties and friendships would have been formed. We can only guess at the extent to which these friendships affected attitudes to the war in 1914. How many former pupils remained in contact and encouraged each other to enlist we shall never know. The one piece of evidence which suggests this may have happened has already been mentioned; six boys who went into service at Clover Hill in County Cavan all enlisted.

However, when one studies the names of the enlisted men from Wilson's Hospital, one aspect stands out very clearly.

Thirteen families sent thirty young men to the war; nine pairs of brothers, and four families where three brothers went to the war. One can only imagine the mixture of emotions which their parents must have gone through; pride turning to anxiety; fear turning to grief as news filtered back from the front.

The Martin brothers came to Wilson's from Roscommon. The eldest by some distance was William who came to the school in 1896. Three years later he was "put to business" in Dublin. He enlisted for the war in 1915, but no further details are known. Frederick Martin entered the school in 1905 and remained for three years before his parents undertook to provide for him in 1908. He enlisted for war in 1914, was awarded the D.C.M.[Distinguished Conduct Medal] in 1916 and the Military Medal at the end of the war. The third brother was George, who came to Wilson's in 1907. Five years later he went into service with William Gibbs Esquire, Westmeath. George enlisted in the Royal Army Medical Corps in 1915. All three brothers returned home safely at the end of the war.

The three Savage brothers came from Donaghpatrick, County Meath. George was the second, entering Wilson's in 1899. At the outbreak of war, he enlisted in the Royal Army Medical Corps in Dublin, later transferring to the 1st Battalion, Royal Irish Rifles. He was killed in action in France on March 4th, 1917 aged 26. Robert Savage was George's elder brother, entering Wilson's in 1896 aged 9. When he left the school some four years later, he was sent to a general merchant's in County Carlow to learn the trade. Robert enlisted in the 1st Battalion, Royal Dublin Fusiliers. He, too, was killed in action. The date of his death is recorded as August 8th, 1918, only three months before the war ended. Ironically, Robert Savage was killed when his Battalion, by then part of the 29th Division, was advancing steadily towards victory in the final stages of the war. Robert Savage is buried in Northern France, in the British Military Cemetery at Borre. Grave number 11.G.13.

The Courtyard, Wilson's Hospital

George and William Schoales were born in Clara, King's County. George came to the school in October 1899 aged 9 and, after four years, was sent to Clover Hill, County Cavan, as a gardener. In 1912, both brothers went to work in England. George enlisted in the East Lancs Regiment which met heavy fighting in the Ypres salient in the spring of 1915. The first battle of Ypres has become synonymous with the use of gas as a means of warfare. There is no recorded evidence that George Schoales met his death in this way. What we do know is that he was killed in the course of this battle, on May 9th 1915. His body was never recovered for burial. George Schoales' name can be found on the Ploegsteert Memorial, 12.5 kilometers south of Ypres. William Schoales, who was two years younger than George, left school in 1903. At the time he was reported as being "unfit for school", though it is not clear what The Warden meant by this. In 1915, he enlisted in the Royal North Lancashire Regiment. One is left wondering whether this was before or after the news of George's death at Ypres. William went on to be commissioned. 2nd Lieutenant William Schoales returned home safely in 1918.

There were three brothers in the Thompson family from Moate, County Westmeath at Wilson's Hospital before the War. All three were to enlist, only one brother was to return home in 1918. William was the second, entering the school on August 19th, 1901 aged eight. He enlisted in 1914 and was killed two years later; no details are known as to the place or regiment. John, the eldest brother, was more fortunate. He left school in 1904, enlisted in the Royal Horse Artillery and survived the war. The youngest brother was Edward. He entered Wilson's in 1905 aged 8 years and 9 months. Two years later when Edward was only ten, his father kept him at home in Moate to train for work with the horses. Like William, Edward also enlisted in 1914. He did not survive. Regrettably, the date, place and regiment were not recorded.

George and Stephen Strong came from Mount Nugent, County Cavan. George, who was the elder brother, entered Wilson's in 1902 when he was ten years old. Six years later, he emigrated to Canada and settled in Quebec. His fare of £10 was paid by the Warden. He served with the 13th Canadian Highlanders in the war, gaining the Military Medal. At the

The youngest of the three brothers was Charles who had joined the Hospital in 1904 aged 11. He went on to become an apprentice gardener in County Mayo. He survived the war; enlisting in 1915, but returning home wounded. Of the three Savage brothers from Donaghpatrick, County Meath, two had been killed in the war and the third seriously wounded. The grief and pain which their parents, Robert and Frances, must have had to bear for the rest of their lives provides a grim insight into the realities of "the war to end all wars."

conclusion of hostilities, George paid a visit to the school in 1918 before returning to his own farm in Canada. Stephen Strong, who was four years younger than George, did not enter the school until 1905. When he was fourteen, he emigrated to Canada on November 26th 1910. Eight years later, he is recorded as enlisting in the American Flying Corps. Stephen Strong also visited the school after he left, on May 15th 1920. He was later reported to be making a good career for himself as a railway clerk in San Francisco.

The Gilmore Brothers from Derryhew, County Cavan, also survived the war. Francis joined Wilson's when he was eleven in 1906. Two years later, he left to join his mother in England- the circumstances are not recorded, but one might speculate that the boys' father had died. The elder of the brothers, William, was eleven when he joined the school in 1904. Three years later, he left to become a gardener. Both brothers enlisted for the war in 1915 and both survived.

Harold McCormack was born in Drumcree, in County Westmeath. Together with his younger brother, James, they became pupils at Wilson's Hospital in 1906 and 1907 respectively. Harold was nine years old at the time and after three years, he obtained an Assisted Scholarship to Sligo Grammar School. (It is to be remembered that Wilson's Hospital had no secondary department until 1932). In 1916, Harold enlisted in the cavalry regiment, the North Irish Horse. Horses were used to draw heavy artillery at the front - as well as maintaining the Commanders' fantasies of carving through enemy lines as in days of old. The same year, he was transferred to the 1st Battalion, Royal Irish Rifles. Two years later, when the 16th (Irish) Division was reorganised, Harold McCormack was commissioned into the Royal Irish Fusiliers.

2nd Lieutenant McCormack was now part of the 50th Division which in October 1918 launched an attack on the Hindenburg line (known to the Germans as the Siegfried Line); a heavily fortified defensive line which was intended to withstand any attack on its sector at Le Cateau. The Germans regarded this as critical to their final defences and the German High Command ordered that it was to be held at "all costs". The 2nd Battalion

Royal Irish Fusiliers marched on compass bearings in the fog that early morning and completely surprised the Germans' defences. However, nearly all the officers were killed or wounded in the attack. Harold McCormack was one of the officers seriously wounded, but he survived and returned home a few months later.

James McCormack, the elder of the two brothers, was aged twelve years and one month when he arrived at Wilson's Hospital School on January 8th 1907. By that time, Harold, who was eighteen months younger, had already been in the school for a year. In view of James' subsequent service record in the War, the explanation for his late arrival at Wilson's is remarkable. The Warden records that James was "too delicate when first sent for". Four years later, on June 30th 1911, James was apprenticed to a watchmaker in Ballybay, County Monaghan. He enlisted for the war in 1915, was wounded in action in 1916 and invalided home. The following year, he was out in France again. In the final stages of the war, James McCormack, once considered "too delicate" for school, was wounded at the front for a second time. The date was April 1918. This time, James returned home for good.

The Lougheed brothers came from Ballyboy, King's County. Richard was ten when he arrived at Wilson's in January 1907. Three years later, he won an Assisted Scholarship. In 1915, he enlisted in the Royal Army Medical Corps. Walter Lougheed was a year younger than his brother, coming to Wilson's in August 1908. Five years later, on July 15th 1913, he entered the hardware business - the location is not known. Two years later, he was reported to be working on the Midlands Railway, near Sheffield, employed in the Engine Shed. In the same year, Walter Lougheed enlisted in the West Yorkshire Regiment. He was wounded in action on May 3rd 1917 and gained the Military Medal in 1918. The story has a happy ending. In 1920, Walter was back at work with the Midland Railway, employed as an engine driver.

Joseph and Jeremiah Leahey entered Wilson's Hospital on the same day, January 12th 1909. They were twin brothers, aged ten years and four months. When he left school on December 11th, 1913, Jeremiah went into service with the Kildare Street

Club, Dublin. The Warden records him as being "a very good boy". Two years later, when he was still four months short of his 17th birthday, he tried to enlist in the Royal Inniskilling Fusiliers, but was too young for active service. Jeremiah went to England and in December 1915, he was employed by the Tramway Company in Burnley, Lancashire. He enlisted in the Royal Field Artillery in January 1917, survived the War and was still serving with the Army in India in 1923.

Joseph Leahey stayed on at Wilson's almost two years longer than his twin brother. In September, 1915, he left school to be trained as a chauffeur, but the Warden reports that five months later, "He came back to me". Joseph would by that time have been 18 years of age. The presumption is that he was employed in Wilson's Hospital as a gardener, handyman - or chauffeur. A year later, Joseph, described by the Warden as "A very reliable, straightforward boy", left Wilson's for the final time. He enlisted in the Motor Transport Corps on March 26th 1917 and survived the War.

Altogether, 13 families from Wilson's Hospital saw 30 brothers set out for the War, of whom 6 never returned. Two particular brothers who lived very close to the school provide us with a very good insight into different aspects of the War. It is towards Kilbixy and the Somersett brothers that our attention is next directed.

Pte Gerry Leahey, Royal Field Artillery

Chapter Eight

<u>William and Henry Somersett</u>

Occasionally it happens that a simple entry or pencilled note in a historical record can be the source of a much longer story than might appear at first sight. Such is the case with two brothers who entered Wilson's Hospital in the first few years of the century. Their story brings us images of the War which reveal both gallantry and bravery, carnage and death.

Isaiah Somersett was the younger of the two brothers. Both are entered in the Register as coming from Kilbixy, Co. Westmeath, just a few miles from the school. However, there are no such names recorded in the baptismal register in that parish; perhaps they moved to Kilbixy in the early years of their lives. Isaiah entered Wilson's on January 16th 1904 aged nine years and ten months. Six years later, he left school and went as a clerk to a land agent's office in Limerick on July 31st 1910. Isaiah enlisted in the Army Pay Department in 1914. A year later, he was transferred to the King's Royal Rifles while he was at the Western Front. In 1916, he had been promoted to Sergeant. In May 1917, he was commissioned into the Royal Irish Rifles and held the rank of Second Lieutenant. He was wounded in action in 1916 and again in 1917. In that year, Isaiah Somersett won the Military Cross. After that award, he wrote a remarkable letter to the Warden in which he describes the circumstances:

H6 Clifton Park,
Clifton,
Bristol

29.3.18

Rev Sir,

I hope that you and Mrs. White are well and enjoying the best of health. No doubt you will be surprised to learn that I have been awarded the Military Cross for service rendered during the Cambrai Push. At the time of my good luck I had been wounded

and just then the Bosch launched a heavy counter-attack and I had to take two platoons and face him. In doing so I secured three enemy machine guns and a number of prisoners, including three officers. I was very lucky to get off so easily.

My brother Willie is now in France and I fear in the present launch by the enemy.

I am transferred to the Indian Army and am awaiting embarkation orders.

I really must conclude
I am
Your Obd servant
I.S.S.

Rev. H. de Vere White,
Wilson's Hospital.

The scene of the action, Cambrai, was on the northern sector of the Western Front, 60 miles south of Ypres. The Third Battle of Ypres had just concluded amidst appalling slaughter. Ten days later, on November 20th, the Allies launched another offensive in an attempt to breach the German defences. The primary objective was the city of Cambrai. The attack was noteworthy because it was the first time tanks had been employed. 324 tanks lumbered through the barbed wire, across defensive trenches and dug-outs before finally being halted by German artillery and, in many cases, by the break-down of the tank tracks. Nevertheless, on the first day of the Battle of Cambrai, the German lines had been decisively breached; five miles of territory had been taken; over 4,000 German soldiers had been taken prisoner.

Within three days of the initial attack, the Allied advance was halted at Bourlon Wood, 6 miles west of Cambrai. General

Haig insisted that this objective should be captured to enable the attack to be renewed. It is probable that it was in this sector of the Battle of Cambrai that 2nd Lt. Isaiah Somersett was wounded and subsequently decorated for bravery. In an attack south-west of Bourlon Wood, three Irish Battalions succeeded in driving German defenders out of most of the village of Moevres, only to come under intense machine gun fire from German defences. A pilot of the Royal Flying Corps witnessed what was happening and dived low to attack the German machine-gun position; he was shot down and killed. The Irish soldiers remembered his bravery. A few weeks later, the following note appeared in "The Times":

"To an unknown airman, shot down on November 23rd 1917, whilst attacking a German strong-point south-west of Bourlon Wood, in an effort to help out a company of Royal Irish Fusiliers when other help had failed".

It is an interesting comment on the international nature of the war in 1917, that the pilot was Lt. A. Griggs, an American who was flying with No 68 (Australian) Squadron. Also of note is that, above the Battle of Cambrai, the German ace pilot, Baron von Richthofen and his squadron were patrolling the skies.

By November 27th, Allied commanders were forced to break off the attack. The following day, the Germans launched a counter-offensive. The use of heavy artillery, gas shells and low flying aircraft drove back Allied troops; over 6,000 of their soldiers were taken prisoner as the retreat began. On December 2nd, General Haig ordered that a secure line be dug in for the winter. The stalemate of trench warfare settled down over Cambrai. As the snow began to fall, the carnage of the battlefield was covered by a white blanket. Not even this, however, could disguise the casualty list at the end of the two weeks' fighting. The Allies had lost 44,000 dead and wounded; the Germans 53,000. The ground gained was negligible.

As the wounded were sent towards England to convalesce, among whom was Isaiah Somersett, the British nurse, Vera Brittain was working at the No.24 General Hospital at Etaples. She witnessed the traumatic aftermath of the Battle of

Letter from Lt Isaiah Somersett to The Warden

Cambrai. On December 5th, she wrote to her mother: "I wish those people who write so glibly about this being a Holy War, and the orators who talk so much about going on, no matter how long the war lasts and what it could mean, could see a case - to say nothing of ten cases - of mustard gas in its early stages - could see the poor things burnt and blistered all over with great mustard - coloured suppurating blisters, with blind eyes - sometimes temporarily, sometimes permanently - with voices a mere whisper, saying that their throats are closing and that they know that they will choke. The only thing which one can say is that the severe cases don't last long; either they die soon or else improve, usually the former."

We know that Isaiah Somersett was one of the fortunate. He survived the battle, albeit wounded. After the war was over, he emigrated to South Africa. The last report of him was made by the Warden of Wilson's Hospital. "He is now a rich man, in the Stock Exchange in Johannesburg."

The German Offensive at Cambrai, March 1918

The story of the Somersett family does not end there, however. Isaiah's letter made reference to his brother. William Henry Somersett was four years older. He had entered Wilson's Hospital on August 8th, 1902 when he was eleven years old. We know that when he left, he obtained an Assisted Scholarship from the Incorporated Society. The only clue to his service in the war in the School Register is that he enlisted for the war in 1915.

However, Isaiah's letter to the Warden provides us, unfortunately, with evidence as to his fate. "My bro Willie is now in France and I fear in the present launch by the enemy". Since the date on the letter is March 29th 1918, there can be only one plausible interpretation.

In the early hours of March 21st 1918, the German armies launched an offensive on the Western Front which was intended to end the stalemate in the trenches, break through Allied Lines and march on Paris. Since March 3rd 1918, Russia had withdrawn from the war as a result of the Treaty of Brest - Litovsk. The Germans no longer had to fight a war on two fronts. Ludendorff gambled all on a massive assault in the West before the full weight of American troops could bolster depleted Allied forces. Between November 1917 (after the Russian Revolution) and March 1918, German Divisions in the West rose from 150 to 192, totalling 137,000 officers and 3,400,000 men. An indication of how much the war had swollen the size of the armies is that the number of German officers preparing for this assault in March 1918 was greater than the total size of the British Expeditionary Force in 1914.

At 05.00 hours on March 21st 1918, in conditions of thick fog, the German bombardment began over the whole Allied Front. Over 6,000 heavy German guns, and 3,000 mortars were brought into action. In the course of the next two weeks, over 2,000,000 gas shells fell on the Allied lines. The 16th (Irish) Division and the 36th (Ulster) Division were to bear a major brunt of this assault. The German forces advanced up to forty miles between March and July 1918, suffering a total of 800,000 casualties. Allied casualties were almost as high as they retreated. The 16th Division lost 6,435 men killed and wounded. The 36th Division lost 6,109. Both these figures include nearly 4,500 men "unaccounted for".

It is in the last figure that the name of William Henry Somersett, Kilbixy, County Westmeath, must lie. In the register, there is no record of his fate. On the original Roll of Honour in the School Chapel, he is listed as "missing". The war was in its closing stages. The family must have hoped against hope that William had been taken prisoner, or been injured and unable to locate his unit in the retreat. Many families clung on to this faint hope for years, forever reluctant to accept the dreadful finality of their sons' deaths. The English novelist, Rudyard Kipling, was one such father. He trailed the battlefields after the war, interviewing every surviving soldier he could find in his son's regiment, The Irish Guards, in an exhausting and vain attempt to avoid the finality of the military record, "missing in action".

William Somersett, like tens of thousands of soldiers of The Great War, has no known grave. The poet Siegfried Sasoon, who served as an officer with the Royal Welch Fusiliers, wrote lines which seem appropriate;

"You smug faced crowds with kindling eyes
Who cheer when soldier lads march by,
Sneak home and pray you'll never know
The hell where youth and laughter go."

But it was not only the pupils of Wilson's Hospital who enlisted for the war, "The hell where youth and laughter go"; masters were also to serve on the Western Front. And, as will be seen, they were to suffer and die alongside their former pupils.

Chapter 9

Masters in Arms

Three Masters from Wilson's Hospital enlisted for the Great War. Considering that the school only had 55 pupils when the war broke out, this is a remarkable figure.However, so far as is known, they did not enlist simultaneously, nor were they all in the same regiment.

We know least about 2nd Lieutenant Henry de Vere. He was the Drill Master at the school before the war. This aspect of the curriculum has long since disappeared but at one time marching, drilling and gymnastic displays were part and parcel of school life.

Such disciplined activities, requiring split second timing, immaculate appearance and uniform patterns of movement were a symbol of the age. Unquestioning acceptance of authority and an insistence on coordinated team activities were the hallmarks of the education system. Such values, instilled into the young, made them ideal recruits for European armies. It may well be that Henry de Vere was a serving soldier before The Great War, perhaps a veteran of the South African campaigns. Many schools employed former Regimental Sergeant Majors at that time to instruct their cadet forces or O.T.C's (Officer Training Corps). At National Schools, they would have been gym instructors.

Most Wilson's boys were destined to serve in the ranks when they enlisted; Henry de Vere may have been a formative influence. This training may have gone hand in hand with the school band, largely Fife (pipes) and Drums, which existed at the time. We know that Henry de Vere was a commissioned officer in The Great War. The original Roll of Honour also listed him as being wounded in action. After the War, it was reported that Lt Henry de Vere "died as a result of war services".

Joseph Laverty was the Science Master at Wilson's when the war broke out. He enlisted in Dublin into the Royal Irish Rifles and served in the ranks. However, by 1917, he was listed as Acting 2nd Lieutenant (Temporary). This almost certainly means that the officers had been so decimated by conflict that men were selected from the ranks to replace them. This may well have been at short or immediate notice and without the normal officer training - hence the designation "acting" or "temporary". In August 1917, the Royal Irish Rifles were in the thick of the conflict in the Ypres Salient. 2nd Lt Laverty's unit was involved in heavy fighting at Hill 35 during the Battle of Langemarck.This was one of the initial engagements in what became known as Third Ypres or Passchendaele.On 16th August 1917, Joseph Laverty was struck by an exploding shell. He died instantly. His body was never recovered for burial. The name of 2nd Lt Joseph Laverty, Royal Irish rifles, is inscribed on the Commonwealth War Memorial at Tyne Cot, Passchendaele, Panel 62, (See also Chapter 13).

**2nd Lt Thomas Farley,
Royal Dublin Fusiliers**

Thomas Farley was born in Navan, Co. Meath in 1894. He became a pupil at Wilson's Hospital School at the age of nine, on October 12th, 1903. He went on to obtain an Assisted Scholarship from the Incorporated Society and completed his secondary education at Sligo Grammar School. On 29th September 1913, Thomas Farley returned to Wilson's Hospital as an Assistant Master. This probably means that, at the age of nineteen, he was recruited as what became known later as the Junior Masters; one without university qualifications, but able to teach and supervise junior pupils. In June, 1916, he enlisted in the Royal Dublin Fusiliers. This was

Tyne Cot Cemetery, Passchendaele

just six weeks after the Easter Rising in Dublin; the timing may help to indicate where loyalties lay at this time in Wilson's Hospital. A year later, he was commissioned into the Royal Irish Rifles.

Thomas Farley was more fortunate than either of his two fellow Masters from Wilson's Hospital. He survived the war, emigrated to India and began work on a Tea Estate in Assam. He did not forget his Alma Mater, making return visits to Multyfarnham in 1925 and 1929. The Warden reported that he was "doing very well."

We should not be surprised that, from such a small school, as many as three Masters should have enlisted for war. In closely knit communities, bonds of friendship are formed very quickly. One advantage of the smaller school is that pupils and staff know each other well. Teachers follow their pupils' careers with interest and concern; that is as true today as it was eighty years

ago. These three Masters would have known about the Wilson's boys who enlisted when War commenced. They were living in the same building as the boys, many of whom could not wait until their turn came; that was the degree of enthusiasm or fever which the War engendered. Henry de Vere, Joseph Laverty and Thomas Farley answered the same call to arms as did their pupils; those whom they had taught amidst the playing fields of Multyfarnham became their colleagues in arms as they fought and died alongside each other on the fields of war.

There are three battles or campaigns in The Great War which will forever be associated with Irish Regiments. The part played by the 10th (Irish) Division at Gallipoli, the 36th (Ulster) Division at The Somme and the 16th (Irish) Division at Ypres are an indelible part of Irish history. Wilson's men fought and died in each of these campaigns. It is to these aspects of our history that attention will now be turned.

Chapter Ten

<u>Gallipoli</u>

At the beginning of 1915, stalemate on the Western Front had set in. Army commanders sought a new initiative which could create a breakthrough and tilt the fortunes of War. In January, 1915, the Russian government sent a telegram to London requesting urgent naval assistance in the war against Turkey. This appeal did not go unheeded. If a passage could be forced through the Dardanelles, and Constantinople captured by the Allies, other benefits might follow; Russian supply lines to the West could be opened; Egypt and the Suez Canal could be secure from attack; Italy and the Balkan States might join the Allied side in the hope of obtaining a favourable settlement at the end of the War; Austria-Hungary would be open to attack from the south-west; the final result might be to bring a swift end to the War.

Such were the calculations. However, the planning and execution of the combined military and naval operation fell far short of what was required. In the event, Allied forces lost 200,000 in killed, wounded and invalided. The Gallipoli campaign was a disastrous failure. It achieved absolutely nothing.

Over the last eighty years, military historians have debated the reasons for the failure. The causes of the disaster can be briefly summarised. First, the Allies attempted the capture of the Dardanelles by naval bombardment alone, without military support on land. Second, endless delays and confusion alerted Turkish defences months in advance as to what was planned. Third, inexperienced and incompetent military commanders, some of whom had no battle experience, failed to make decisive and critical decisions when they were most needed. Lastly, chaotic logistical support with the most basic necessities, food and water, left troops to rot and die unaided.

It is possible to divide the campaign into several stages and follow the fortunes of men from Wilson's Hospital through the information we possess. The first Wilson's man into action at Gallipoli was Able Seaman, Frederick Armstrong. Frederick was 11 years old when he joined Wilson's Hospital on August 14th, 1905. When he left two years later, it was down the well worn path to Clover Hill in County Cavan, where he was taken into service as a gardener. Frederick joined the Royal Navy in 1913 when he was nineteen years old.

On 19th February, 1915, a fleet of British and French battleships began to attack the Turkish forts at the entrance to the Dardanelles Straits. Among these was H.M.S. Majestic, on which Frederick Armstrong was a junior rating. After some initial successes, the fleet suffered severe setbacks; four battleships were sunk by floating mines and two others were damaged. The fleet withdrew to the nearby Island of Lemnos until the mines had been cleared. This was the first, and possibly the most disastrous mistake of the campaign; if the attack had been pressed at this point, with ground support, it is probable that the Turkish defences would have collapsed; the campaign and, arguably, the war might have taken a different turn. As it was, the Turks were well warned. They reinforced and repaired their defences. Turkish Divisions in Gallipoli increased from two to six between January and March 1915. Artillery, machine guns, barbed wire (laid on the beaches and under water) together with a whole series of well dug in and concealed batteries were put in place to resist Allied landings. The element of surprise, which should have been the Allies' greatest asset, had been thrown away. The price was to be paid by the troops who were by now on their way to the Eastern Mediterranean.

The first attempted landings at Gallipoli were made in April by the 29th Division, which included battalions of the Royal Munster Fusiliers, Royal Dublin Fusiliers and the Hampshire Regiment. The latter included many Irishmen, recruited when the regiment was stationed at Mullingar. As far as we know, there were no Wilson's men in this Division.

Devastating casualties were suffered as the 29th Division struggled to get ashore. Many men were shot down in the sea as they waded ashore, others were wounded and drowned. An old collier, The Clyde, was converted into a makeshift troop carrier. As the Fusiliers attempted to disembark, they were cut down by wave after wave of machine gun and small arms fire. Seventy percent of the Dubliners and Munsters on the Clyde were casualties. An officer of the Royal Flying Corps, Air Commodore Samson, flying overhead reported that the calm blue sea was "absolutely red with blood" for a distance of fifty yards from the shore, " An absolutely horrible sight to see". Elsewhere, where the water was crystal clear, could be seen the uniformed bodies of soldiers who had drowned or been hit struggling to get ashore. Each soldier carried 88 pounds of equipment which prevented many of the wounded from reaching safety. In the bitter fighting which followed, a foothold on the peninsula was gained.

As the 29th Division fought to get ashore on the southernmost tip of the Gallipoli peninsular, the Royal Navy lent support. H.M.S. Majestic was one of the battleships brought in to knock out Turkish batteries and give the Division covering fire. In May, however, German submarines began working their way down the coast, attacking warships and supply vessels. A German destroyer sunk the battleship "Goliath" at the beginning of the month. On May 22nd, the "Triumph" was sunk by

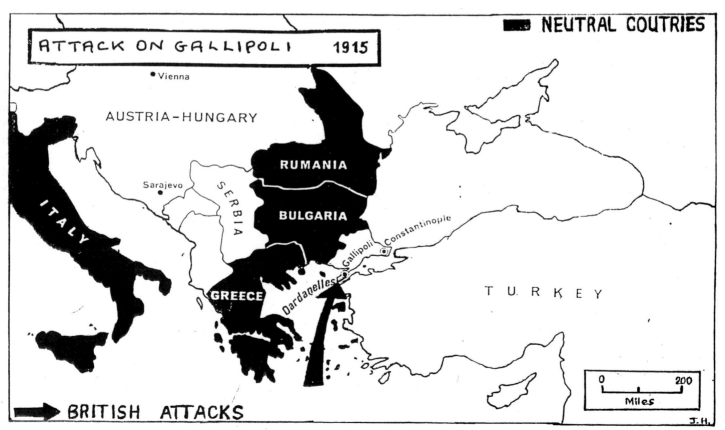

The British Plan at Gallipoli 1915

V Beach at Gallipoli

torpedoes in broad daylight. The following day, Frederick Armstrong's battleship, H.M.S. Majestic, was struck by torpedoes at 6.40am. Along with most of the crew, he was picked up by support vessels and taken back to home waters. H.M.S. Majestic, the oldest battleship in the fleet, sank within 15 minutes. On 31st May, 1916, Frederick Armstrong was in action again, at the Battle of Jutland. We do not know which ship he served on there, but he was ranked First Class Stoker. He visited Wilson's whilst on leave on August 29th 1916 and went on to survive the war.

Involved with 29th Division in the fateful landings on April 25th were the Australian and New Zealand Army Corps, forever known as ANZAC. ANZAC troops were sent further up the western coast of Gallipoli to Gaba Tepe. There, at 04.30 hours, they landed in the murky half-light of dawn. The leading wave of 1,500 were carried by the tide two miles beyond their intended position, but succeeded in making a bridgehead. Intense fighting followed for three weeks, but in spite of Turkish attempts to drive the ANZAC troops back into the sea, they held on. 39,000 ANZAC troops took part in the Gallipoli campaign. Throughout the summer of 1915, alongside British and Irish troops, they fought the elements as well as Turkish defences. In midday, the temperature rose to 110 degrees. There was no shelter on the scorching hillsides except from thorn bushes. Their thirst was inflamed by bully beef and dry biscuits. Water was in scarce supply - such as there was came all the way from Egypt and was heavily chlorinated. Dehydration set in. They were constantly under shell and machine gun fire. In September 1915, seven ANZAC battalions were examined. 78% of the men were suffering from dysentry and 64% had skin sores. ANZAC troops suffered 33,000 casualties at Gallipoli, a figure which includes over 10,000 dead.

As far as is known, there were no Wilsonians among ANZAC troops, although there is evidence of a number having emigrated to Australia. One of these was H.G. White who had been born in Kells and entered Wilson's Hospital in April 1870. Writing to the Warden, he paints a picture of the atmosphere in Australia during the war. The letter is dated April 5th 1915. " At present, Australia is suffering from a severe drought, and unless rain falls soon matters will be serious. Just as much interest is taken in the war as in England. The daily papers publish the latest cablegrams each day; several contingents of soldiers have left for Egypt, many more are in training 12 miles from Melbourne, and altogether the militant feeling is uppermost."

At least five Wilson`s men took part in the third landings at Gallipoli. On August 7th, 1915, 22 Battalions, comprising 20,000 troops landed on the shores of Suvla Bay. Their objectives were low lying hills, two to five miles inland. Kiretch Tepe Sirt, a commanding whaleback ridge, was the foremost of these. From the start, confusion reigned. Excessive secrecy prevented junior commanders knowing their orders, battalions were landed at the wrong position, units became inextricably mixed. Meanwhile, Turkish snipers picked off their targets.

Lieutenant Douglas Figgis, 5th Royal Irish Fusiliers wrote that the planning of the GHQ at Suvla "passes the comprehension". As the sun rose, conditions for the men on the ground worsened. Lips cracked and heads became dizzy in the stifling heat. The unloading of water, guns, ammunition were delayed by confusion. Desperate soldiers were seen puncturing hoses with their bayonets and sucking water through the holes they had made.

6th and 7th Battalions, Royal Munster Fusiliers, led the assault on Kiretch Tepe Sirt, suffering heavy casualties. Shortage of water made the men desperate. The wounded suffered hideously in the heat. Wounds became infected, maggots crawled over them as they lay where they fell. When eventually reached by stretcher bearers, the wounded had to be carried several miles by exhausted men who were themselves desperate for food and drink. Most of the bully beef was thrown away in disgust; in the intense heat of the sun, it turned to a gluey mess on which the flies descended. Diarrhoea and dysentery spread rapidly.

Lt. O.G.E. Mc Williams, 5th Inniskillings, in his book "Suvla and After", wrote that a high proportion of those listed as "missing, believed killed" died alone, of wounds or thirst in the scrub, down deep gullies or ravines. The stench of the putrefying dead was everywhere. One member of the 7th Royal Dublin Fusiliers who died at Suvla on August 8th was Lt. Ernest Lawrence Julian, previously Reid Professor of Law at Trinity College, Dublin. It was losses such as these which so bereft the Irish nation of leadership when the War was over.

Henry Hall was one of those listed as "wounded and missing" at Suvla Bay. He had entered Wilson's Hospital aged 9 in 1904 from his home at Bahallboyne, County Meath. He had gone on to obtain an Assisted Scholarship from the Incorporated Society and completed his education at Ranelagh School, Athlone. He enlisted in the Royal Dublin fusiliers and went to Gallipoli with the 10th (Irish) Division in 1915. An indication of the chaos at Suvla is that, despite the military report which had listed him as " wounded and missing", he did return to Ireland and was in Dublin in 1916. That year, he returned to France with his regiment and was wounded for a second time. He survived the war.

Lieutenant Charles Harvey, 7th Battalion Royal Dublin Fusiliers, was also a Wilson's man. Born at Athboy County Meath, he was 11 years 6 months old when he entered Wilson's in 1891, nominated by the Lord Primate. After leaving school, he worked in the Accountant General's Office, Bank of Ireland from 1891 until he enlisted at the outbreak of war. He survived to bring home the story of the disaster and horrors of the Gallipoli campaign.

James Fry was born at The Gate Lodge of Wilson's Hospital on January 25th 1886. He was baptised in the School Chapel on April 12th the same year. At the age of 7, James was admitted as a pupil of the school. His father, who was employed on the school land, inherited a farm near Ardlogher, Co. Cavan, in 1900. At this point, James left Wilson's Hospital to be with his family and help his father on the farm. He was then 14 years old. Six years later, James Fry enlisted in the Royal Inniskilling

H.M.S. Majestic, sunk by German torpedo

Fusiliers. He was wounded in the advance of the 10th (Irish) Division on Kiretch Tepe Sirt on 7th August 1915. One can imagine, only too well, the conditions in which he suffered. Happily, though, James Fry recovered from his wounds and returned home to Cavan after the war.

George Pakenham from Killucan, County Westmeath, entered Wilson's on January 21st 1902 aged 10 years, 11 months. In August, 1904, when he was 13 years old, George went into service at Dunboden. He was a professional soldier, enlisting with the Leinster Regiment in 1911. He served with the 6th Battalion at Suvla Bay. He, too, was one of the thousands who were wounded in the advance. The reports are that these wounds were very serious and, although he survived the war, there are no further indications that he was on active service with his Battalion again.

The sixth and last Wilsonian to serve with the 10th Division at Gallipoli was Austin Kelly from Clonmellon, County Westmeath. Austin was born in 1886 and entered the school on September 12th 1907, aged 10 years and 10 months. Four years later, he went as a clerk to Laird's Shipping Company in Belfast. When war broke out, Austin Kelly enlisted in the 7th Battalion, Royal Dublin Fusiliers and was posted to "C" company. He sailed with the 10th (Irish) Division from Liverpool in July 1915. On August 8th, he landed with the 7th Battalion at Suvla Bay. His unit established itself despite the chaos on the beaches. For five days, they had to endure appalling conditions. They were exposed to the blazing heat of the sun and shell fire. Swarms of flies settled all over their bodies. Dirty, unshaven and soiled, the Fusiliers had to cope with infected latrines, contaminated food and a dire shortage of water. On August 13th, relief supplies refreshed them. On August 14th, orders were received to take the ridge, Kiretch Tepe Sirt, which was still held by the Turks.

The following morning, August 15th, the attack was preceded by Divine Services. Private Austin Kelly attended Holy Communion which was offered by Canon MacLean in a marquee of a field ambulance station. Nearby, the Chaplain of 7th Royal Dublin Fusiliers, Father Murphy, said Mass and gave absolution in the open air.

The attack began at 1210 hours. 7th Royal Dublins were part of 30th brigade, ordered to advance on the left towards the ridge. One can endeavour to imagine the scene. Above Austin Kelly and his Company, Kiretch Tepe Sirt rose to 750 feet. The advance lay over gradually rising ground, through gullies and thorn scrub. Progress was painful and slow. With 250 yards left to the summit, 6th Munsters and 6th Dublins were ordered to charge. The northern stretch of the ridge was captured by the thrust of the bayonets. On the southern side of the ridge, Austin Kelly and C Company held a line just below the crest. At 2200 hours the Turks counter-attacked against this line. Scores of grenades rained down. As casualties mounted, 7th Dublins made repeated charges to clear the attackers, but to no effect.

As dawn broke on August 16th, the remnants of C Company were ravaged by thirst and hunger. There was no shelter from the scorching sun on the bare and scrubby hillside. As the grenades continued to fall, desperation set in. One member of 7th Dublins, Albert Wilkin, succeeded in catching five grenades and hurled them back; the sixth exploded in his hand. They even threw rocks at the enemy and rolled boulders over the crest. Still no support or reinforcements came. By dusk, nearly all the officers were dead or wounded. The men, now almost leaderless, fought on. The line held. But among these who survived this terrible carnage, the name of Austin Kelly cannot be numbered. He was killed, along with hundreds of his colleagues, on the bloodstained ridge of Kiretch Tepe Sirt that day, August 16th 1915.

That night, the pitiful remnants of the 7th Royal Dublin Fusiliers were ordered to retire to their original starting line. The Division had lost 114 officers and 5,000 men. The campaign ground to a halt amidst muddle and incompetence, disease and death. Yet through it all, shone bravery, heroism and a devotion to duty by the men of the 10th (Irish) Division. The sacrifices which they made on the ground were far beyond that which their military or political commanders had any right to deserve. The tragedy of the Gallipoli campaign lies in its futility. Eight months after the initial landings, the Allied troops withdrew. The whole enterprise was abandoned. The evacuation, on the night of January 6th, 1916 was the one aspect of the campaign which was accomplished without a hitch. 38,000 men who took part in the Gallipoli Campaign lie buried on that peninsula. Absolutely nothing had been gained. As the troops departed, one is reputed have said, as he turned to look back on the graves of his friends, "I hope, I do hope, they won't hear us marching away to the beach."

Among the dead lay Private Austin Kelly. He was just 18 years old, the youngest boy from Wilson's Hospital to be killed in The Great War. The grief which his parents, John and Annie Kelly, must have felt when the news reached them in Clonmellon, does not bear contemplation. Their son's name is carved on the Helles Memorial at the southern tip of the Gallipoli Peninsula, overlooking the Aegean Sea.

" A hundred thousand million mites we go
Wheeling and tacking o'er the eternal plain,
Some black with death - and some are white with woe.
Who sent us forth ? Who takes us home again ?

And there is sound of hymns of praise - to whom ?
And curses - on whom curses ? - snap the air.
And there is hope goes hand in hand with gloom,
And blood and indignation and despair........"

Charles Sorley

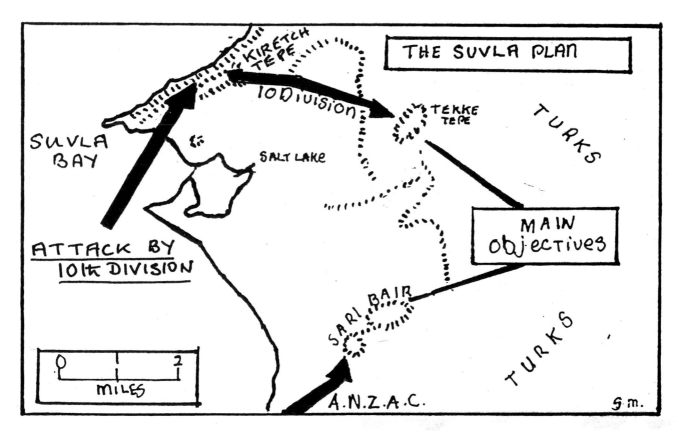

The Suvla Plan

Chapter Eleven

The War in the Trenches: The Somme

By 1915, the main theatres of conflict in The Great War were well established. Fighting had spread to the Middle East, to Africa and to the Atlantic. On the Eastern Front, where Russian troops were badly led and equipped, war eventually gave way to revolution. In 1917, Russia withdrew from the war, conceding vast areas of national territory to Germany.

On the Western Front, Allied and German troops faced each other across a line of trenches which stretched from the Belgian coast to the Swiss frontier. The intervening strip of land between these fortified lines was known as no-man's land. A soldier posted to the front in Northern France found a maze of trenches. The British system was usually made up of four principal trenches; two front lines, support line and reserve trench. They were dug in a zig-zag pattern, intersected by communication trenches which ran at right angles. The only shelters were dug-outs or holes scraped out of trench walls. The trenches were floored with duckboards and protected by sandbag replacements and barbed wire.

A soldier arriving with his battalion at the front could expect to spend anything from four to eight days on duty there, before relief came. Two of the battalion's four companies would be in the front lines, the third in the support trench and the fourth in the reserve trench. Even on the quietest sectors, sporadic artillery fire and sniping were maintained. At night, patrols were sent out to bring back information about the enemy, repairs were made to the barbed wire and supplies brought up from the rear. All the time, sentry duties had to be carried out. Night duty was feared the most; falling asleep was punishable by death.

The daily routine of life in the trenches has been described as 90% boredom, 10% terror. The day began at dawn with "stand-to". All soldiers in the front line manned the fire steps in case there should be an attack. This was frequently accompanied by "morning hate", an exchange of artillery fire. At dusk, this routine was repeated; the whine and roar of "evening hate" searing across the darkening skies. In between, soldiers snatched sleep, carried out maintenance, wrote letters home. At any time, an artillery barrage might open up. Enemy snipers were on constant look-out for the unwary. At no time did the soldiers have any cover other than the niches they scraped out of the trench walls. Dug-outs were usually reserved for officers. Soldiers were exposed to the elements in all weathers. Patrick MacGill, from Glenties in County Donegal, expressed the feelings of the infantryman:

"It's a far, far cry to my own land
A hundred leagues or more...
A candle stuck on the muddy floor
Lights up the dug-out wall,
And I see in its flame the prancing sea
And the mountains straight and tall;
For my heart is more than often back
By the hills of Donegal".

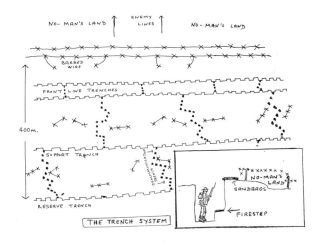

The Trench System

HOW TO PREVENT SORE FEET.

To prevent sore feet cleanliness and strict attention to the fitting of boots and socks are necessary. Before marching the feet should be washed with soap and water and carefully dried. The inside of the socks should be well rubbed with soft or yellow soap. After the march the feet must be again washed and clean dry socks put on. Soaking the feet in salt or alum and water hardens the skin. The nails should be cut straight across and not too close. 'A blister will probably be occasioned by an unevenness or hole in the sock, or an unevenness in the lining of the boot; the cause therefore should be ascertained and removed. The edge of a blister should be pricked with a needle and the fluid drained away by gently pressing the blister; a small pad of cotton wool or soft rag should be applied, and kept in place by a small piece of sticking plaster. Men are cautioned against getting boots too small for them.

Excerpt from the Soldiers' Rule Book

The horrors of the trench were not confined to artillery and sniper fire from the enemy. The men not only lived like rats in the underground dug-outs; they had to live among rats. The sound of rats at night, as they fed on the carnage of war, unnerved many soldiers. To this was added the mud, the slime and the lice. In the worst winters, trenches could be knee-deep in water. The cold was intense. Men on sentry duty found their fingers frozen to their rifles. Clothing became sodden, filthy and lousy. A gruesome pastime for soldiers at the front was hunting for lice, fleas and other parasites in each other's hair and clothing. The powder which soldiers were given to kill the vermin brought their skin out in large red, itchy blotches.

The lice and the rats were not the only health hazard. In winter, soldiers developed "Trench Foot". Standing in mud and slime for days and nights, their feet began to swell and then go "dead". This was followed by a terrible burning sensation. When relief troops were sent up the front line, many of those who suffered could only crawl away or be carried pick-a-back by their comrades. Eventually, a cure for this was found. The men had to rub their feet two or three times a day with oil. Some of the Ulstermen swore by pigs' fat. It has been estimated that there were two to three cases of disease at the front for every wound victim. Typhoid was feared the most. If the first case went undetected, a whole battalion might be put out of action for six months.

The medical system for dealing with casualties was based on a series of First Aid posts near the trenches. Behind these were advanced dressing stations, temporary and base hospitals. The men of the Royal Army Medical Corps went out into no-man's land with stretchers to bring back the wounded. Back inside the aid posts, these cases were treated where they lay. Conditions were cramped and unhygienic. Buckets of sand were available to throw over the blood on the floor. Shock, lockjaw and gangrene were common causes of death. Saws and cutters were used for amputations. "Sealing irons" were applied to stop the bleeding on the stumps. In such conditions and faced with appalling wounds, it was not unknown for doctors and medical orderlies to seek refuge in alcohol; it was their escape from reality. These were the living and fighting conditions for thousands of Irishmen who took part in one of the most cataclysmic battles of the twentieth century.

On July 1st, 1916, the first day of the Battle of the Somme, 20,000 Allied soldiers were killed. That amounted to 60% of the officers and 40% of the men who began the advance towards German lines at 7.30 a.m. that fateful morning. The first Battalion, Royal Irish Rifles, lost 65% of their strength in the first hour alone. It was the worst day in the history of the British Army. The battle raged on until November 1916. At least four men from Wilson's Hospital School were in the thick of this appalling devastation, of whom three lost their lives.

The task of the historian is not to condone what happened, but to explain. The former would be impossible; the latter, while difficult, must be attempted. The name of The Somme is forever associated with the 36th (Ulster) Division but, in truth, the 16th (Irish) Division also played a major part in the later stages of the battle. In addition, the 2nd battalion, Royal Dublin Fusiliers, fighting with the fourth Division, suffered severe losses on July 1st. A similar fate was experienced by The Tyneside Irish Brigade, properly known as the 24th-27th Northumberland Fusiliers, in the 34th Division. The first truth about the battle of the Somme is that men from all four Provinces of Ireland fought and died in this sector. It is characteristic of the nature of Wilson's Hospital that her men were to be found in both the 36th (Ulster) Division and in the 16th (Irish) Division at the Somme.

The cause of the attack by Allied troops at the Somme lies in the deadlock into which the trench warfare had settled. After eighteen months of war, there had been no significant breakthrough. Both the Allies and the Central Powers strove to find a position where a devastating attack might turn the tide in their favour. On 21st February 1916, the German armies launched a massive assault on the fortress of Verdun on the northeast sector of the Western Front. Over 1,000,000 German troops were thrown into this attack. Falkenhayn, the German Chief of Staff calculated that France would defend the symbolic fortress at Verdun to the last man; France was to be bled to death. In five months, 23 million shells were fired by the two sides. The losses were estimated at 300,000 French and 350,000 German dead. German troops advanced no more than four miles into a cratered wasteland half the size of Berlin.

British and French plans for a joint attack by their forces on the Western Front had begun as early as December 1915. The French General, Joffre, proposed a combined assault at the point where British and French forces lay alongside each other; astride the River Somme. The British refused to be rushed into an attack until their preparations were ready; Joffre pressed for an attack as soon as possible to relieve Verdun. By July, the number of French divisions available for an attack on the Somme had fallen from 40 divisions which Joffre had envisaged seven months earlier to 5 divisions. The defence of Verdun by the legendary General Petain- "Ils ne passeront pas" cost France dearly.

The consequence of Verdun was that the brunt of the attack at The Somme was borne by British Divisions. Throughout early months of 1916, both sides prepared for battle. For the Allies, this involved meeting the needs of 400,000 men and 100,000 animals; building 600 miles of light railway to bring up supplies; laying scores of miles of water mains. Behind this fevered activity, the troops carried out training and exercises.

One cause of the terrible casualties on July 1st can be found in the defensive preparations which the German armies made at the Somme. The land they held was on chalk hills. It was higher ground. Here the German armies created an underground system of dug-outs, casualty stations and communications. These were sunk to a depth of 30 to 40 feet; they were bombproof. Above ground, where they overlooked the British trenches, powerful defensive fortresses were constructed, reinforced with concrete, protected by up to 15 rows of barbed wire entanglements. Machine gun posts ensured that an attack from almost any position would come under crossfire. This formidable network was skilfully concealed.

The British attack was based on the premise that a heavy and sustained bombardment by artillery for seven days would destroy German defences. "If the artillery does its work well", said General Rawlinson, "The rest will be easy". One officer told his platoon on June 30th, "Tomorrow you'll just light your pipes and cigarettes, slope arms and walk across. It'll be like a Sunday stroll; there'll be no opposition." In practice, when the attack was launched on July 1st, the German Divisions were well prepared and operationally intact. Irish troops at The Somme walked into a bloodbath.

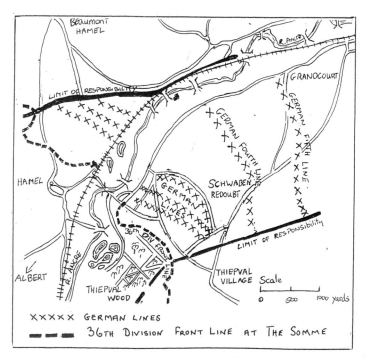

Objectives of 36th Division at The Somme

Royal Irish Rifles, resting in the trenches, July 1st 1916

One such soldier was George William Nelson, born in Edenderry, King's County. He came to Wilson's Hospital School in 1887 aged nine, and enlisted in the army when war broke out at the recruiting office in Boyle. On the morning of July 1st 1916, Private George Nelson was a member of the 36th (Ulster Division) preparing to go into battle.

He and his colleagues in the 9th Battalion, Royal Inniskilling Fusiliers, waited nervously for the regimental bugle to sound the advance. The leading wave moved out across No Man's Land onto a sunken road. As they moved across, an artillery barrage made them dive for cover. No sooner had this lifted than heavy machine gun fire raked them from the German held Thiepval cemetery, causing heavy casualties. Among these was Private George Nelson. His body was never recovered. His name can be found on the Thiepval Memorial. It is a lasting witness to the disaster at The Somme. The majority of those who were killed in the Somme sector have no named graves. The Thiepval Memorial alone commemorates 72,085 such men.

In the 36th (Ulster) Division there were over 5,500 casualties on July 1st. Extraordinary bravery took them through the German front line; they captured a major stronghold, the Schwaben Redoubt. By evening, nearly all officers were wounded, the supplies of ammunition were exhausted, there was no support on their flanks, reinforcements had not arrived: the order was given to retire. The next day, July 2nd, the decimated 36th (Ulster) Division was taken out of the line. In Ulster, mourning was widespread. From that day to this, the name of The Somme has been engraved on the memories of the families who were bereaved and on the political consciousness of Ulster Protestants.

The battle did not end on July 1st. It raged on until 19th November 1916. A succession of engagements, particularly at Guillemont and Ginchy, brought heavy fighting. In the latter, three more Wilson's boys came into the firing line. On September 9th, 1916, the 16th (Irish) Division was ordered to attack the German held fortress at Ginchy. This was a heavily fortified village on a high plain. Beneath it, concealed in lower ground, lay a defensive loop trench full of machine guns, protected by swathes of barbed wire up to 60 yards thick - this was known as the Quadrilateral. Previous assaults on Ginchy had all been bloodily repulsed.

On the night of 8th/9th September, assembly trenches for the attack were dug east of Ginchy by the 1st Battalion, Royal Munster Fusiliers. Included in their ranks was Captain James William White Bell who had entered Wilson's Hospital in August 1891. The trenches were little more than a few feet deep, so little time had been made available. Throughout the following day, the Munsters waited in these shallow positions in full view of German observers. The attack was not to start until 1645 hours that afternoon. For nine hours, Captain Bell and his men were subjected to an almost continuous barrage from German artillery. They had no cover save the pathetic little ditch hastily dug under the cover of darkness in the hours beforehand. To add insult to the hopelessness of their position, British artillery, falling short of its target, landed shells on their trenches. The casualties during this phase, even before the projected attack, included Captain James Bell. The 1st Battalion, Royal Munsters Fusiliers, had lost 169 officers and men in a helplessly exposed position. In the pulverised battlefield, Captain Bell's body was never recovered for burial.

These setbacks notwithstanding, 16th (Irish) Division went on to capture Ginchy. Attacking in successive waves, 48th Brigade advanced steadily through a barrage of artillery and machine gun fire. At 5.25pm Ginchy was taken, but at an appalling price. In the ensuing days, The Irish Guards were brought in for "mopping up" operations on the Ginchy Quadrilateral. Serving with the 2nd Battalion, Irish Guards was Private John Hegarty from Castlekiernan, Camross, Kells, County Meath. He had been a pupil at Wilson's Hospital 25 years previously. In the desperate fighting to take the Quadrilateral, the 2nd Battalion of the Irish Guards was almost completely destroyed. Among these who fell was Private Hegarty. A few days later in Kells, his wife, Ann Kate Hegarty, received the brown buff envelope containing the telegram which all servicemen's wives dreaded to see. John Hegarty, pupil of Wilson's Hospital, was buried on September 15th 1916 in La Neuville Cemetery on The Somme, Grave No. 11.D.64.

The one Wilson's man to survive the battles on the Somme-Guillemont-Ginchy sector in July 1916 was Captain Isaiah Somersett, 7th Battalion, Royal Irish Rifles. He, too, took part in the assault on Ginchy in September 1916. He was wounded in action, but survived. He was fortunate. Between 3rd and 9th September alone, the 16th (Irish) Division lost 224 officers and 4,090 men. The two great Irish Divisions which had fought so heroically and suffered such severe losses in the Somme battlefields were now moved; within a year, they were positioned alongside each other in the Ypres Salient at Messines Ridge, to which our attention will next be turned.

This chapter cannot close, however, without recording the death of poet, scholar and soldier, Lieutenant Tom Kettle. This was a man who, because of his age and poor health, should never have been in the front line at all. Lt. Tom Kettle insisted on leading B company, 9th Battalion Royal Dublin Fusiliers into battle. At 1725 hours on the 9th September 1916, he was killed by a bullet wound to the chest as he led his men on Ginchy. In his last letter to his wife he had written, "It has taken all the folly of England and Ireland to produce the situation in which our unhappy country is now involved..."

Tom Kettle's last poem, written for his daughter for that time in the future when she might ask why father had gone to "dice with death", serves as a fitting epitaph for Irishmen of all traditions who lost their lives "in some corner of a foreign field";

"And Oh! they'll give you rhyme
And reason: some will call the thing sublime,
And some decry it in a knowing tone.
So here, while the mad guns curse overhead,
And tired men sigh with mud for couch and floor,
Know that we fools, now with the foolish dead,
Died not for flag, nor King, nor Emperor,
But for a dream, born in a herdsman's shed,
And for the secret Scripture of the poor."

The Thiepval Memorial

Chapter Twelve

The Ypres Salient - Messines Ridge

At the time of writing, a Memorial to the Irishmen of all political and religious denominations who were killed in the Great War is to be dedicated at Messines Ridge in Belgium. Jointly financed in Northern Ireland and the Republic of Ireland, this will be known as the Island of Ireland War Memorial. This round tower, which will commemorate 50,000 Irishmen, will be so constructed that the rays of the sun will enter it at 11.00 a.m. on November 11th - the time of the Armistice in 1918, "The Eleventh Hour".

Messines Ridge was chosen as the site for the Memorial because it was one place in the Great War where the 36th (Ulster) Division and the 16th (Irish) Division fought side by side. It was, also, one of the few operations in the War which can be described as clearly successful; objectives attained with minimum casualties. At least one Wilsonian took part in the assault on Messines Ridge, 2nd Lt. Philip Eyre Tennant, 6th Battalion of the Connaught Rangers.

An explanation of the attack at Messines Ridge must be preceded by an explanation of the Ypres Salient - or else it has no meaning. In 1914, when German troops invaded Belgium, they were halted at the River Marne and driven back; both sides dug in ; the trenches extended from the Belgian coast to the Swiss frontier. The only part of Belgium held by the Allies between 1915 and 1918 was a small sector on the coast adjoining the frontier with France.

The King of the Belgians, Albert 1, set up his headquarters in the coastal town of La Panne and remained there throughout the War. In the race towards the sea, the front line across Belgium was noteworthy for a bulge or salient round Ypres. This protruded into German held territory and could therefore be attacked from three sides. It would have been tactically more sensible for the British to withdraw from Ypres, straighten the front line, and greatly reduce the dangers of shellfire from three

different directions. Ypres, however, became a symbol of Allied resistance to German aggression. The attack on Belgium had brought Britain and Ireland into the War. Memories of atrocities committed by German troops on the civilian population were fresh in the mind. The superb Cathedral and Cloth Hall in the

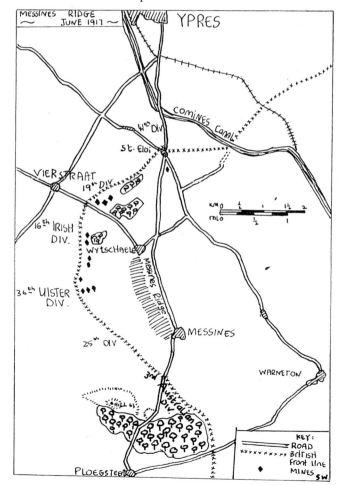

Messines Ridge

2nd Lt Philip Eyre Tennant, Connaught Rangers

The attack on Messines Ridge was an essential prelude to the Allies' attempts to break out of the Ypres Salient. Running East from Ypres, the Ridge dominated the plain below. From this vantage point 200 feet above the Salient, German artillery looked down onto the Allied trenches beneath them. By the Spring of 1917, 25% of all Allied deaths in the war had been suffered in the Ypres Salient. It was a landscape of rubble and tree stumps. Shell craters pitted the ground, filled with mud and fetid water. Overhead, smoke and fog hung like a evil cloud. The stench of poison gas never cleared. The decay and detritus of hundreds of thousands of soldiers, dead and alive, sunk into the putrid soil. It was hell on earth.

The capture of the Messines Ridge was essential if the Allied troops in the Salient were to have any relief from constant bombardment. German defensive measures were thorough in every respect except one; against an Allied attack from underground. The Ridge was considered by the Germans too waterlogged to be mined or tunnelled successfully. Yet this is exactly what happened. For over a year prior to June 1917, British, Canadian and Australian troops laid a series of tunnels 200 to 2000 feet in length. Great care was taken to dispose of the blue clay excavated out of the Ridge so that it could not be detected from the air. Altogether, 24 tunnels were dug and charges were placed in them at depths of 50 to 100 feet under German held positions on the Ridge above.

The attack was preceded by an artillery barrage which lasted for 18 days. Three and a half million shells were fired onto German positions. Assault troops stretched in a line extending for 10 miles beneath the Ridge. In the centre and right of IX Corps, the 36th (Ulster) Division and the 16th (Irish) Division prepared to advance.

At 3.10 a.m. on the morning of June 7th, 1917, nineteen of the mines under the Messines Ridge were exploded. 500 tons of explosive were detonated, creating a series of volcanic eruptions. Four mines were exploded in front of the 36th, four in front of the 16th Division. Enormous columns of earth rose into the sky amidst a deafening roar. The effect was like an earthquake. The thunderous reverberations were heard in

centre of Ypres became synonymous with the cause of the Allies. Battles raged round Ypres in 1914 and 1915, but the salient held in spite of appalling losses.

2nd Lieutenant Philip Eyre Tennant was part of the 16th (Irish) Division brought into the line for the assault on Messines Ridge. He had been born in Parkstown, Thurles, Co. Tipperary in 1879, and entered Wilson's Hospital aged 12 in August 1891. By that time, Philip's father, John Tennant, had died. Philip's place in the school was sponsored by the Bishop of Kilmore. Eight years later, Philip joined the Bank of Ireland in October 1898. He was clearly sympathetic towards the calls to enlist because he joined the Officer Training Corps of the Inns of Court in December 1915. Two years later, in March 1917, aged 38, he was commissioned into the Connaught Rangers. He was sent to France two months later. Philip Tennant found himself thrown into one of the most awesome battles of The Great War within four weeks of his arrival at the front.

London. As tall, rose coloured mushroom clouds rose into the air, earth and stones fell from the sky for several minutes. Before the rumble had died away, an artillery barrage was laid down 700 metres into the German lines from the roar of 2,226 guns and howitzers.

Behind this barrage, 80,000 Allied troops advanced, the two Irish Divisions together in the centre. Lt. Philip Tennant and the 6th Battalion, Connaught Rangers, had been in position since 0100 hours that morning. They were to move forward in the third wave of attackers, behind 6th Royal Irish and 7th Leinsters. Each Battalion had to move forward with two machine guns and two Stokes mortars. It was the Rangers' task to help move these weapons and ammunition forward and to mop up any remaining resistance.

The Royal Irish and the Leinsters reached their destination at Wytschaete Village precisely on time, at zero and 3 hours 40 minutes. Following up, Lt. Tennant and the Connaught Rangers fell on an enemy position outside the village which the first two waves had bypassed. At this point in the battle, Lt. Tennant and the Rangers took 98 prisoners including one officer. As they searched the village, The Rangers uncovered two deep dug-outs with machine guns which they placed on the parapet "for the Munsters to collect." Lt. Tennant and his Company then improved the position of the supporting mortar and machine gun batteries before retiring for the night to the cover of Rossignol Wood.

When the battle of Messines Ridge ended, all the objectives had been captured and nearly 7,500 prisoners taken. The 36th (Ulster) Division and the 16th (Irish) Division, nearly 30,000 Irishmen, had played a major part in the success of the Battle. By the standards of The Great War, casualties on the Allied side were light. The 16th Division lost 748 men, the 36th 700 men. This should be set alongside the German losses for the Battle estimated at 10,000 killed. It was the Duke of Wellington who said "Nothing except a battle lost can be half so melancholy as a battle won." Just outside the village of Wytschaete in the Ypres Salient, there is a simple Celtic Cross. On it are inscribed the words:

"Dochum Glóire Dé agus Onóra na hÉireann"
"To the Glory of God and the Honour of Ireland."

On the night preceding the Battle of Messines Ridge, the Leinster Regiment had held a dinner in the Officers' Mess. One of the guests was Major Willie Redmond from Divisional H.Q., one of the four Nationalist M.P's serving with the 16th (Irish) Division. Redmond spoke at the dinner, making a heartfelt plea that Ireland should discover peace and prosperity. Major Redmond died in battle at Messines. At the age of 54, he had been deemed too old and ordered to remain at Divisional H.Q. At his own insistence, Redmond was permitted to join his Battalion for attack. Stung with anger and deeply hurt by anonymous letters which had accused him of cowardice, Redmond moved forward with his unit. He fell wounded and was carried to a Field Dressing Station by stretcher-bearers from the 36th (Ulster) Division. He was not young or fit enough to withstand the shock and died a few hours later.

The poignancy of Major Willie Redmond's death in these circumstances, tended and cared for in the last moments of life by Ulstermen, was given a further twist after his death. In the resulting by-election in County Clare, the newly elected M.P. was a man of a different hue, Eamonn de Valera.

Messines Ridge after the attack

Chapter Thirteen

Third Ypres - Passchendaele

The successful advance on Messines Ridge had prepared the way for an Allied attack out of the Ypres Salient. This had always been the "obvious" place to turn the tide of the War; one flank would be protected by neutral Holland and, if a breakthrough could be achieved, the German lines could be turned and encircled. Moreover, the capture of the Belgian coastline would rob German U Boats of their best bases ; by 1917, British shipping losses amounted to 25% of all ships which left port.

The single most important factor in the horror of what became known to the world as "Passchendaele" lay in the geography of the terrain. Flanders is a flat and somewhat monotonous area. There are few landmarks. Rivers and canals intersect as they meander towards the sea. There is very little gradient; the rivers flood in heavy rain. Dikes and water-courses are everywhere. The ground itself is a fine grained clay with little topsoil. Rain water which cannot escape forms swamps, the ground remains permanently saturated and water is reached at a depth of eighteen inches. In peacetime, such problems can be kept under control. In time of war, they spell disaster. It is a measure of the single-mindedness, desperation and miscalculation of General Haig that he insisted on advance in this sector. It was to cost Ireland dearly.

Four men from Wilson's Hospital were killed in the Ypres Salient. The first was George Schoales from Clara, King's County, of whom mention has already been made. Fighting with the 2nd Battalion, East Lancashire regiment, Private Schoales was ordered to advance on Auburs Ridge, some 4000 yards behind the German front-line trenches. This was the opening phase in what became known as the 2nd Battle of Ypres, in May 1915. Schoales' Battalion never stood a chance. In the face of machine-gun emplacements positioned every twenty yards in heavily fortified parapets, Private Schoales and his comrades were mown down. George Schoales was killed on 9th May,

The Ypres Salient, June 1917

1915, a few months short of his 25th birthday. Two years later, the same fate was to befall three more soldiers from Wilson's Hospital. With good reason, one historian, Alan Clarke, coined the phrase "lions led by donkeys". It is a metaphor which does ample justice to soldier and commander alike in the Ypres Salient.

On July 31st, the 3rd Battle of Ypres began. The German defenders had made a significant change in tactics. Instead of long, continuous lines of trenches, massive strongpoints had been constructed at regular intervals. These had been built by Russian prisoners and were made of ferro-concrete. Each of these was supported by numerous pill-boxes. All were manned by machine-gunners so that every possible line of attack would be met by a withering cross-fire of bullets. On that first day of the battle, 16th (Irish) Division was in the front line. 2nd Lieutenant Philip Tennant and the 6th Battalion, Connaught Rangers were

Trenches at Ypres

"Many pens have tried to depict the ghastly expanse of mud which covered this waterlogged country, but few have been able to paint a picture sufficiently intense. Imagine a fertile countryside, dotted every few yards with peasant farms and an occasional hamlet; water everywhere, for only an intricate system of small drainage canals relieved the land of the ever present danger of flooding..... Then imagine this same country-side battered, beaten and torn by a torrent of shell and explosive...... such as no land in the world had yet witnessed- the soil shaken and reshaken, fields tossed into new and fantastic shapes, roads blotted out from the landscape, houses and hamlets pounded into dust so thoroughly that no man could point to where they had stood, and the intensive and essential drainage system utterly and irretrievably destroyed. This alone presents a battle-ground of tremendous difficulty. But then came the incessant rain. The broken earth became a fluid clay; the little brooks and tiny canals became formidable obstacles, and every shell-hole was a dismal pond; hills and valleys alike were but waves and troughs of a gigantic sea of mud. Still the guns churned this treacherous slime. Every day conditions grew worse. What had once been difficult now became impossible. The surplus water poured into the trenches as its natural outlet, and they became impassable for troops; nor was it possible to walk over the open field; men staggered warily over duckboard tracks. Wounded men falling headlong into the shell-holes were in danger of drowning. Mules slipped from the tracks and were often drowned in the giant shell-holes alongside. Guns sank till they became useless; rifles caked and would not fire; even food was tainted with the inevitable mud. No battle in history was ever fought under such conditions as that of Passchendaele."

After the opening of the Battle on 31st July, General Haig had told Gough, "The next advance is to be made as soon as possible, but only after adequate bombardment and domination of hostile artillery." On August 16th, the 36th (Ulster) Division was ordered to advance on Langemarck, some 800 yards beyond the Allied front-line, six miles west of Passchendaele. Far from the prior shelling of Langemarck being adequate, the Corps artillery had made no impact whatsoever. Langemarck's massive defences remained virtually intact. What had been created by the artillery, however, was a marshland; shell-holes filled with mud and water as far as the eye could see.

ordered to advance on a German held, fortified position at Shrewsbury Forest. The objective was not taken. Philip Tennant was struck by an explosive bullet and died instantly. His Battalion Commander wrote to his mother.

"He was a gallant officer at all times, and his Company Commander tells me that his gallantry was particularly conspicuous on the day of his death. He is a great loss to us, and we shall miss him very much."

2nd Lieutenant Tennant's body was never recovered. In the slough of despond which the salient had become, like thousands of other soldiers alongside him, Philip Tennant has no known grave. His name can be found on the Menin gate in Ypres, panel 42, which lists all the officers and men of the Connaught Rangers who lost their lives in this desolate wasteland. To understand what fighting at Ypres had become, the description of General Gough, Commander 5th Army is worth quoting :

Machine gun position, Ypres 1917

2nd Lieutenant Joseph Laverty, 13th Battalion, Royal Irish Rifles, was ordered to advance with his Company across this swamp. They were observed by the German defensive positions and subjected to constant bombardment. Machine gun positions raked the lines of the 13th Battalion as they struggled desperately to find cover. Gas shells landed amongst the Irishmen and sent them reeling and choking for air. In this hell on earth, the Science Master at Wilson's Hospital lost his life. Advancing on Hill 35 on the morning of August 16th, he was killed along with many other hapless members of his unit. His body sank beneath the mud and was never recovered. The name of 2nd Lieutenant Joseph Laverty is carved on Panel 62 of the Commonwealth War Memorial at Tyne Cot on the gentle slope leading up to Passchendaele. (See also Chapter 9).

Ernest Victor Woods was born in Castlepollard in June 1895. He entered Wilson's Hospital on August 13th 1906 and was at school there for four years. We do not know for certain what he did when he left in 1910 except that his father "undertook for him". However, as his father was the proprietor of the Central Hotel in Castlepollard, we may assume that he was employed there, learning the trade. Ernest Woods enlisted in 1914 into the 9th Battalion, Royal Dublin Fusiliers which formed part of the 16th (Irish) Division. In August 1917 he, too, was thrust into the jaws of the Ypres Salient. On 16th August, the 9th Battalion was ordered into the assault on Langemarck as part of the 48th Brigade. Casualties had been so severe in the Somme sector that the 8th and 2nd Battalions of the Royal Dublin Fusiliers were amalgamated for the attack. Their combined forces mustered only 20 officers and 378 men.

The attack began at 04:45 hours on August 16th. To reach their objectives, the Battalion would have had to cross nearly a mile of No Man's Land. Machine gunfire devastated their ranks from enemy pill - boxes and strong - points. In spite of this hail of fire, two officers and ten men of the Royal Dublin's reached a vantage point within 100 yards of their objective. Private Ernest Victor Woods was one of these men. The Dubs held their ground all day in the position they had taken. That night, at 2200 hours, they retreated under cover of darkness. Private Ernest Woods was seriously injured. He was evacuated to the Regimental Aid Post behind the cover of the Frezenberg Ridge. From there, he was stretchered back behind the lines. Four days later, on August 20th 1917, Private Ernest Victor Woods died from the wounds received in action. In the Westmeath Examiner, the following death notice was published:

"Private Ernest Victor WOODS, Royal Dublin Fusiliers, eldest and dearly loved son of John Woods, Central Hotel, Castlepollard, who died of wounds received in action August 17th, 1917. 'Until the day break and the shadows flee away.'"

Within that announcement lay another tragedy for John Woods. He had now lost his eldest son as well as his wife. Private Ernest Woods is one of the few men from Wilson's Hospital killed in the War to be buried in a marked grave. In the summer of 1997, this writer and his wife visited the Ypres Salient. Private Woods is buried in the military cemetery at Lijssenthoek, seven miles south of Ypres, grave No XVII.H.20. It is a tranquil and beautiful place, immaculate in every respect. Flowers blossom on each of the graves. The day we were there, a gentle breeze rustled the leaves on the nearby sycamore trees, gardeners murmured in their hut. For the rest, there was silence. The date was August 20th, exactly 80 years to the day since Ernest Woods had been killed at Ypres. We stood for a few moments in silent tribute on behalf of the School and moved quietly away.

The Battle of Passchendaele continued on its grim course until November 20th. The 16th (Irish) and 36th (Ulster) Divisions were involved in almost every portion of this horrendous conflict in the mud. There are two memorials to those who died without any known grave in the Ypres Salient. On the Menin gate are listed 54,896 names. The Tyne cot Memorial at Passchendaele numbers 34,888 names. In addition, there are 11,000 named graves at this place of Remembrance. It has been estimated that in the last desperate advance on the Passchendaele Ridge, 35 men died for every metre of ground which was taken. The work on the Menin gate took so long to complete that when the German armies invaded Ypres in May 1940, stonemasons had still not completed carving the names on the Roll of Honour from the First World War. They were evacuated to safety in Britain, returning in 1945 to complete their work.

A few miles from where Private Ernest Victor Woods lies buried can be found the grave of another young Irishman. In Artillery Wood Cemetery at Boesinghe, Lance Corporal Francis Ledwidge was laid to rest in August 1917. The 26 year old poet from County Meath, veteran of battles in Gallipoli and Salonica, was killed on the first day of the battle for Passchendaele, along with many of his comrades in the Royal Inniskilling Fusiliers. In a poem written shortly before the war he had, perhaps, a preview of his own death:

"And now I'm drinking wine in France,
The helpless child of circumstance.
Tomorrow will be loud with war,
How will I be accounted for?

It is too late now to retrieve
A fallen dream, too late to grieve
A man unmade, but not too late
To thank the gods for what is great;

A keen-edged sword, a soldier's heart,
Is greater than a poet's art.
And greater than a poet's fame
A little grave that has no name."

The grave of Pte Ernest Victor Woods,
Royal Dublin Fusiliers

FOR SALE.
THE SALIENT ESTATE.
COMPLETE IN EVERY DETAIL.

INTENDING PURCHASERS WILL BE SHOWN ROUND ANYTIME DAY OR NIGHT
UNDERGROUND RESIDENCES READY FOR HABITATION.

—o—o—o—o—

Splendid Motoring Estate! Shooting Perfect!!
Fishing Good!!!

—o—o—o—o—

NOW'S THE TIME. HAVE A STAKE IN THE COUNTRY.
NO REASONABLE OFFER REFUSED.

DO FOR HOME FOR INEBRIATES OR OTHER CHARITABLE INSTITUTION.

Delay is dangerous! You might miss it!!

—o—o—o—o—

Apply for particulars, etc., to

Thomas, Atkins, Sapper & Co., Zillebeke
and Hooge.

HOUSEBREAKERS : WOOLEY, BEAR, CRUMP & CO. TELEGRAMS : "ADSUM, WIPERS"

—54—

The Wipers Times was a satirical newsheet whose ironic articles reflected the disillusion of soldiers at Ypres

Chapter Fourteen

<u>At the Eleventh Hour</u>

On November 11th, 1918, the eleventh hour of the eleventh day of the eleventh month, the guns ceased firing. Nine million soldiers and a further five million civilians had been killed. Four Empires had collapsed and at home, in Ireland, a further five years of war lay ahead.

In The Great War, at least 50,000 Irish soldiers lost their lives. Their names are commemorated on the War Memorial at Islandbridge, designed by Sir Edward Lutyens. Yet for the 200,000 Irishmen who survived the war and returned home, there was no heroes' welcome. The living and the dead from The Great War passed into oblivion. The events in Ireland between 1916 and 1923 swept away the men of 1914 as if they had never existed. Ireland's dead from The Great War were airbrushed out of history. The "terrible beauty" of 1916 began an interpretation of history which was at once unbalanced and myopic. The Irish soldiers of The Great War were deemed to have been conscripts, fighting England's wars. Such prejudice has yet to be entirely stilled. A reading of Irish school text books may reveal a brief mention of Irish soldiers in The Great War; followed by several chapters devoted to events in which infinitely less Irishmen were involved. We like to consider ourselves a liberal, pluralist society. The truth is that our history has been dominated for the last 75 years by a narrow minded, vengeful interpretation of events which is an abject betrayal of 250,000 Irishmen, their friends and families alike. To this writer's knowledge there has yet to be one single question about the part played by Irish soldiers in The Great War on any Junior or Senior Leaving Certificate paper. Political correctness extends to Irish historians smothering their own history.

The Island of Ireland Memorial at Messines Ridge marks, let us hope, a more pluralistic attitude to our inheritance. Those who left these shores in 1914 to fight in Europe were Irishmen. They were fighting in Irish regiments. They fought and died, as they believed, in defence of freedom. It is worth remembering Sean Lemass' remarks on this subject in 1966: He spoke of

"Tens of thousands of generous young Irishmen who, responding to the call of their parliamentary leaders, had volunteered enthusiastically to fight, as they believed for the liberty of Belgium." "In later years", Lemass continued, "It was common- and I was also guilty in this respect - to question the motives of these men who joined the new British armies formed at the outbreak of war, but it must, in fairness to their memories, be said that they were motivated by the highest purpose, and died in their tens of thousands in Flanders and Gallipoli, believing that they were giving their lives in the cause of human liberty everywhere, not excluding Ireland."

It is to be hoped that, before the twentieth century closes, Ireland will at last honour the men who honoured the name of Ireland in the Great War, 1914 - 1918. No country can understand

The Roll of Honour 1914 - 1918

itself unless it understands its own history. To be complete and rounded, the latter must be based on thorough research, both at national and local level. In Wilson's Hospital this research has, hopefully, added to our knowledge of an important part of our history. The original Roll of Honour in the Chapel was put in place after The Great War. It was compiled with loving care and is most beautifully presented. On it are the names of 78 former pupils and masters from Wilson's who fought in the War. A simple Cross or the letter W further marks the names of those who paid a greater sacrifice.

The new Roll of Honour for the Great War will list a further 15 names, including 8 who lost their lives. The original list will be amended to add Crosses to three more names, and a W to two more names. The total number of men from Wilson's who took part in the War has been found to be not 78, but 93; the total who lost their lives has risen from 9 to 20. Some explanation is required.

Approximately 250,000 Irishmen took part in the Great War. Of these, 42,000 were professional soldiers before the War began. A further 80,000 enlisted during the course of the War in Irish regiments. The balance can be found in the Royal Navy, the Royal Flying Corps and among those Irishmen who enlisted in English, Scottish or Welsh Regiments - or overseas, in Canada, Australia, New Zealand or the USA.

The overall figures show how difficult it is to be precise or accurate. A school such as Wilson's Hospital sent its sons out all over Ireland and all over the world. Their exodus is a reflection of the Irish Diaspora; their names are scattered round the globe. After the War, it was very hard to assemble a complete list. Apart from those overseas, many men who left Wilson's in the previous twenty-five years had lost all contact with the school. It was only years later, sometimes ten or fifteen years, that information concerning these men filtered back to the school. The School Register contains many a handwritten entry, written long after 1918, providing details of service careers.

In recent years, a complete list of every pupil to have entered the school since the Foundation has been placed on computer disc. This immediately made research much easier; the list of pupils in Wilson's Hospital could be set alongside army records. In these ways, the original Roll of Honour has been carefully amended to include the results of this research. Work on this has now been completed; our understanding of our heritage should be more mature.

Of the 93 men from Wilson's Hospital who served in The Great War, 73 returned home. They went their separate ways, largely back to the employment they had been in before the war. The ways of the countryside and the farms they lived on must have made a surreal contrast to the devastation they had left behind. We need not doubt that, for some, the adjustment to civilian life would not have been easy. Soldiers of the Great War were haunted for the rest of their lives by the images which recurred in the darkness of their minds; the agonised deaths of so many of their friends and colleagues; images of such horror and brutality that many men never fully recovered.

Robert Selvey lived with The War until he died. Robert came from Ballyboy in King`s County and entered Wilson's Hospital in July 1909 aged 11 years. Four years later, he went to service in Clover Hill, County Cavan. When the war broke out, he enlisted in the 5th Lancers. That immediately strikes one of the most ironic chords in the conflict. The 5th Royal Irish Lancers were attached to the 3rd Cavalry Brigade. Before 1914, they had their own H.Q. and two regiments at the Curragh and the third in Marlborough Barracks, Dublin. We can be fairly certain that when Robert Selvey was accepted into the 5th Lancers, it was because he had experience with horses. He was probably employed at Clover Hill in the stables. We can imagine him working out the horses along the lanes and boreens of County Cavan, saddling them up for his employers, the Sanderson family, whenever required.

Many young men joined the cavalry in 1914 with images of galloping through open country, an enemy in retreat, sabres flashing and glinting in the sun. The reality could not have been more different. Robert Selvey was sent to the Ypres Salient in 1917. The horses were employed dragging artillery through the swamps of mud which convulsed the landscape. Men, horses and artillery often sank without trace, sucked down into the glutinous wasteland. Robert Selvey did not die in this way. He died at home. But it was a long, lingering, painful death. Robert Selvey was gassed in the Ypres Salient.

In July 1917, the German armies introduced mustard gas as a weapon of war - tear, chlorine and phosgene had already been used since 1915 by both sides. Unlike the other gasses, mustard gas was used to incapacitate rather than to kill. On the first day of its use, July 12th 1917, the Germans fired 50,000 mustard gas shells at Allied lines. Eighty seven soldiers were killed, more than 2,000 severely affected and invalided home. Robert Selvey was one of these. One of those who tended the wounded at Ypres was Nurse Millard. Afterwards, she described the effects of mustard gas :

"Gas cases are terrible. They cannot breathe lying down or standing up. They just struggle for breath but nothing can be done. Their lungs are gone - literally burnt out. Some have their eyes and faces entirely eaten away by gasses and their bodies covered with first degree burns.........gas cases are invariably beyond endurance and they cannot help crying out. One boy today, screaming to die, the entire top layer of his skin burnt from face and body...........where will it all end ? "

Robert Selvey did not die at Ypres. He died at home in Ireland, his eyes and lungs permanently damaged. For the rest of his life, a dreadful hacking cough racked his frame. For Robert Selvey, The Great War never ended. A few days after Robert Selvey had been gassed at Ypres, two soldiers of The War met at Craiglockart War Hospital outside Edinburgh. The date was July 23rd 1917. Their names were Siegfried Sassoon and Wilfrid Owen. The result of the encouragement which Sassoon gave to his comrade in arms was one of the most powerful poems of the War, Wilford Owen's "Dulce et Decorum Est". This poem is about soldiers such as Private Robert Selvey.

"Bent double, like beggars under sacks,
 Knocked-kneed, coughing like hags, we cursed through sludge,
 Till on the haunting fires we turned our backs
And towards our distant rest began to trudge.
 Men marched asleep. Many had lost their boots
But limped on, blood-shod. All went lame; all blind;
Drunk with fatigue; deaf even to the hoots
 Of gas shells dropping softly behind.

Gas! Gas! Quick, boys! -An ecstasy of fumbling,
Fitting the clumsy helmets just in time,
 And flound'ring like a man in fire or lime...
Dim, through mist panes. and thick green light,
As under a green sea, I saw him drowning.

In all my dreams, before my helpless sight,
He plunges at me, guttering, choking, drowning.

If in some smothering dreams, you too could pace
Behind the wagon that we flung him in,
And watch the white eyes writhing in his face,
His hanging face, like a devil's sick of sin;
If you could hear, at every jolt, the blood
Come gargling from the froth-corrupted lungs,
Obscene as cancer, bitter as the cud,
Of vile, incurable sores on innocent tongues, -
My friend, you would not tell me with such high zest
The old Lie: Dulce et decorum est
Pro patria mori."

Three months before The Great War ended, a young man from Streete, County Westmeath, joined the Royal Air Force. His name was John Abraham. He was 18 years and one month old when he joined. He was the last boy from Wilson's to enlist in the armed forces. His choice of Service, The Royal Air Force (which changed its name from the Royal Flying Corps in 1917) is significant. Like Edward Montserrat, Robert McAllister and Hugh Nummy who joined the Royal Navy in the closing stages of the War, John Abraham did not choose to enlist in an infantry regiment. The reasons for this have already been suggested. What is noteworthy is that it is a precursor of events to come. In the second World War, the majority of boys from Wilson's Hospital who enlisted chose The Royal Air Force. William Butler Yeats' poem "An Irish Airman foresees his death" (written in memory of Lady Gregory's son, Robert) carries strong resonances of the poem which Tom Kettle had written for his daughter (quoted in Chapter 11). It provides us with some evidence of the motivation for preferring the Air Force:

"I know that I shall meet my fate
Somewhere among the clouds above:
Those that I fight I do not hate,
Those that I guard I do not love;
My country is Kiltartan Cross,
My countrymen Kiltartan's poor,
No likely end could bring them loss
Or leave them happier than before.
Nor law, nor duty bade me fight,
Nor public men, nor cheering crowds,
A lonely impulse of delight
Drove me to this tumult in the clouds;
I balanced all, brought all to mind,
The years to come seemed waste of breath,
A waste of breath the years behind
In balance with this life, this death."

The Menin Gate, Ypres

From the closing months of World War 1, John Abraham points an unwitting finger in the direction which boys from Wilson's Hospital would follow in World War Two. For the former, the sacrifices which they had made were not so much forgotten in Ireland, as ignored. One of the main motivations for this research has been that they should be remembered; that their actions should be commemorated as a part of Irish history. The most terrible insult we can hurl at these young men who suffered so terribly is simply to forget who they were and what they did. Shortly after the war, Siegfried Sassoon wrote a poem entitled "Aftermath, March 1919." He expresses his anger at those who forget - not least, perhaps, those who most wanted to forget - the soldiers themselves. It is a message for posterity.

"Have you forgotten yet?
Look down, and swear by the slain of the War that you'll never forget.

Do you remember the dark months when you held the sector at Mametz-
The nights you watched and wired and dug and piled sandbags on parapet;
Do you remember the rats; and the stench
Of corpses rotting in front of the front-line trench-
And dawn coming, dirty-white, and chill with a hopeless rain?
Do you ever stop and ask, "Is it all going to happen again?"

Do you remember that hour of din before the attack -
And the anger, the blind compassion that seized and shook you then
As you peered at the doomed and haggard faces of your men?
Do you remember the stretcher cases lurching back
With dying eyes and lolling heads - those ashen-gray
Masks of the lads who were once keen and kind and gay?

Have you forgotten yet?
Look up, and swear by the green of the spring that you'll never forget."

PART TWO

THE SECOND WORLD WAR

1939 - 1945

Chapter Fifteen

Europe between the Wars

Those who fought and died in the Second World War are entitled to an explanation as to why "The war to end all wars" was followed only twenty years later by an even greater catastrophe. The truth lies in one of the most dreadful ironies of the twentieth century. "The First World War explains the second and, in fact, caused it, in so far as one event causes another," wrote the historian A.J.P. Taylor. "The link between the two wars went deeper. Germany fought specifically in the Second war to reverse the verdict of the First and to destroy the settlement that followed it."

A walk through the cemeteries of the fallen from the First World War in France or Belgium is an intensely moving and unforgettable experience. Their symmetry, beauty and tranquillity are in stark contrast with the killing fields which spawned them. The serried ranks of white headstones, each tended and cared for, cleaned and maintained as if they had only just been laid, cannot fail to shake the emotions of the visitor. They are the gardens of the dead, monuments to the lost generation.

The serene tranquillity of these cemeteries holds the first key to unlocking the question of why another war occurred two decades later. The allies, France in particular, wanted not just justice, or even recompense, but revenge. Ten million Frenchmen had enlisted for the First War, of whom nearly 40% now lay in the graveyards of northern Europe. France had been invaded and defeated by Prussia in 1871; the Provinces of Alsace and Lorraine had been seized and taken into Bismarck's Germany. Victory in 1918 was the opportunity for revenge against German militarism. Versailles was the appointed place.

It is one of the cardinal principles of the judicial system that criminals, no matter how heinous their crime, must receive a fair and a proper hearing. They are entitled to be present at the trial. They are entitled to legal representation. If found guilty, the sentence must be proportionate to the guilt of the accused. If these principles are not observed, a miscarriage of justice takes place. That is what happened at the Treaty of Versailles. It was the dictate of the victors which determined the verdict and the sentence. It was not in any real sense a fair trial; Germany was not even allowed to send representatives to the Peace Conference.

This is not to dispute Germany's guilt for what took place in 1914 and the years which preceded it. It is simply to condemn the manner in which the peace was exploited by the victors; exploited in such a manner that Germany had a legitimate sense of grievance. That grievance provided the seed from which sprang the National Socialist party in Germany and the evil genius of Adolf Hitler.

Hitler at a Nazi Youth Rally, Nuremburg

Polish cavalrymen on manoeuvres 1939

The terms of the Treaty of Versailles which caused such resentment in Germany can be easily summarized. Germany was to be partitioned; Poland was given West Prussia and access to the Baltic, known as the "Polish Corridor". The Saar was placed under international control. The Rhineland was to be demilitarized. Alsace and Lorraine were returned to France. German colonies were confiscated and redistributed amongst the victors. Germany was to be permanently disarmed. The creation of Czechoslovakia out of the remnants of the Austro-Hungarian Empire locked three million German speaking peoples inside the new state. Finally, the imposition of massive reparations was to punish Germany and to compensate the victors. Article 231 of the Treaty, the "War Guilt" clause, was the stamp which the court placed on this mistrial and disproportionate sentence.

There were, of course, other clauses in the Treaty which were important - the ban on German-Austrian unification which was contrary to the principles of self-determination - but the evidence cited here is sufficient to understand why Germany felt that the Treaty was a miscarriage of justice. These feelings were

not confined to Germany. As the dust settled, politicians throughout Europe, particularly in France and Britain, became uneasy about the settlement. They, in their turn, felt guilty. That guilt led them to try to make amends; the policy of "appeasement" was born.

On January, 30th 1933, Adolf Hitler became Chancellor of Germany. His rise to power was based on his determination to overthrow The Treaty of Versailles and all that it stood for. He wanted to reunite the German speaking peoples in a new Reich (Grossdeutschland) and to carve out living-space for the German people in Eastern Europe (Lebensraum). These policies, which he had hawked up and down the hustings in successive elections, touched vital nerves in the German psyche; resentment, the feeling of injustice and demand for revenge. Massive unemployment (it reached 6 million in 1932), the crash of the stock markets, the collapse of the Deutschmark; all these factors made the National Socialist party the largest in Germany. Brandishing the ballot box in one hand and the swastika in the other, Hitler had bribed, bullied and intimidated his way into power.

When Hitler became Chancellor, he set about reversing all the principal clauses in the Treaty of Versailles. This brought him into direct conflict with the principal signatories to the Treaty, Britain and France; the USA had withdrawn into splendid isolation. As Hitler made his demands, he unilaterally tore up clauses in the Treaty. The Allies made concessions; the Rhineland was, after all, part of Germany; reparations were excessive; Germany had to be able to defend herself; why shouldn't Germany and Austria unite if they so wished? Bit by bit, the Treaty was dismantled. Britain and France gave ground, turned a blind eye, did everything to avoid confrontation. That was seen as the route to war. The mood in Paris and London was to avoid war at all costs; the ghosts of the dead hung over the Cabinet rooms.

Hitler treated every concession as the springboard for the next demand. He regarded Chamberlain and Daladier, Prime Ministers of Britain and France, as effete and spineless. He considered democracies to be corrupt, impotent and degenerate.

Only he, Adolf Hitler, advocating policies of racial purity and iron dictatorship, could purge Europe of the scourge of Judaism and communism. The triumph of his will would be imposed.

1938 was to prove a turning point in the inter-war crises. Hitler regarded Czechoslovakia as a non-state. It was composed largely of peoples whom Hitler considered racially inferior. The three million Germans in the western borders, the Sudetenland, had to be reunited with the Fatherland. Otherwise, there would be war. On September 12th 1939, Hitler moved troops to the Czech border and, in the series of inflammatory speeches, he wound up the tension to crisis pitch.

Chamberlain and Daladier were cowed into submission. Even if they had the means, they certainly lacked the will to resist. At a series of meetings that month, every demand which Hitler made was conceded. Munich was to become a by-word for appeasement: the place at which legitimate concession became craven submission. There was only one positive outcome; Chamberlain and Daladier had laid their political lives on the integrity and trustworthiness of Herr Hitler. Returning to London, Chamberlain waved the piece of paper in the air which carried Hitler's signature: Hitler had signed an agreement, and Herr Hitler was, of course, an honourable man. A grateful crowd cheered him to the echo; war had been avoided.

Ten days after placing his signature on the Agreement at Munich, Hitler ordered General Keitel to prepare plans which would lead to the liquidation of the rest of Czechoslovakia. In March 1939, the Wehrmacht marched into Prague; an independent state had been first dismembered, then destroyed. Hitler claimed he had made his "final demands". Britain and France, betrayed and humiliated, now determined to stand firm before the whole of Europe fell under the Nazi jackboot. When Hitler next turned his attention to Poland, Chamberlain made it clear in the British House of Commons that the policy of appeasement had been abandoned.

"In the event of any action which may threaten Polish independence.....H.M Government would feel themselves bound at once to lend the Polish Government all support in their power".

To borrow a phrase from contemporary military conflicts, a line had been drawn in the sand. Britain and France had declared, clearly and unequivocally, that any further aggression by Germany would lead to a declaration of war.

On August 23rd 1939, Germany signed a pact with the Soviet Union; a secret article agreed that Poland was to be destroyed and partitioned. Eight days later, on September 1st 1939, Hitler invaded Poland. This time, Britain and France stood firm. War was declared. Within a year, the name of a small port on the north coast of France was to become engraved on the history books for future generation; its name was Dunkirk. For the second time in twenty-five years, Wilsonians were to find themselves fighting on the Fields of Flanders.

Between the wars, Europe had greatly changed. Ireland, too, had changed. It was partitioned. The Irish Free State had come into existence in 1921. Wilson's Hospital was a school no longer under British jurisdiction. The question arises as to how much the school had changed in twenty-five years; to what extent the political changes in Ireland would affect its response to war in Europe in 1939.

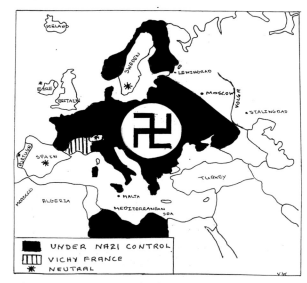

Europe at height of Nazi power

Chapter Sixteen

<u>Wilson's Hospital between the Wars</u>

One of the most important ingredients in a child's education is continuity; disruption brings many attendant dangers. It is therefore greatly to the credit of Wilson's Hospital that all the political changes and upheavals between 1916 and 1923 failed to disrupt the continuity of the education which was available.

The Warden,The Reverend Henry de Vere White continued in office. Indeed, he was to continue serving as Warden until after the Second World War ended in 1945. Dr Trevor Winkworth (Past Pupil and Medical Officer) remembers him well. A strict disciplinarian, " he took no prisoners", and swished his cane with regularity on miscreants. He was a great classical scholar, a Triple Mod from Trinity College and instilled a love of Latin and Greek into many of his pupils. His rolling gait, head held in the air and "little squinty eyes" gave him a distinctive appearance. As the Dean of Clonmacnoise moved down the long corridor in his black frock coat and gaiters, unwary pupils hurtled into him at their peril.

Wilson's Hospital was still a National School. James Gillespie remained as its most important influence until he was taken ill in 1938 and could no longer remain as Headmaster. Generations of Wilsonians remember him with genuine respect and affection. He was more than a Master to them. He was their friend, guide and mentor. Many years after the boys left Wilson's, they kept in touch with him. James Gillespie also gave many past pupils financial help when they ran into difficulties in later years. From all accounts, it was not just the worthy who received his help; the rascals were not turned away either.

The greatest educational change came in 1932 when Wilson's Hospital became a secondary school. Pupils could now take the Inter-Cert examinations. However there was no Leaving Certificate available for a further three decades and the majority who were continuing with their education went

Advertisement in The Wilsonian 1934

on to Mountjoy school in Dublin.

The numbers fluctuated. The decision to open the Secondary Department in 1932 came just in time; there were only 65 pupils in the school.This decision saved the school from closure. As an Endowed School, Wilson's Hospital charged no fees until 1932. In the previous ten years, income from the estate had dwindled. Financial mismanagement by the Trustees had been compounded by the Free State Government's steps to break up large estates and sell off the land.When Ranelagh School closed in 1936, Wilson's was the beneficiary. The numbers jumped to 90 by 1939. However, when one considers how many were to enlist in the armed forces in the Second World War, even this was a very small number.

Glimpses of change begin to appear in the subsequent careers of Wilsonians. In part, this was due to the secondary department opening; pupils had higher career expectations. Compared to their predecessors fifty years earlier, pupils in the 1930's were aiming higher up the ladder of employment. Between the wars, there was a steady stream of boys enlisting in the British Army, many of whom had moved back into civilian life before the war in 1939. Seven such careers are recorded in the school register, including John Matthews from Tyrrellspass and Ernest Matthews from Newtown. Both these men volunteered for service in World War 11 and, although they were placed on the Reserves, they were not called up.

A new feature in the careers' list is those entering the forces of the new Irish Free State. George Sandes from Roscommon was the first boy to enter the Garda Siochana. Six boys enlisted in the Irish Free State Army between the wars, including Edward Bond who joined the Free State Military Police

in 1923. The others were Andrew Gray from Balbriggan, Francis Smith from Skerries, George O'Neill from Castlepollard, Ivor Delaney from Longford and Robert Sproule from Dublin.

Signs of The Troubles are present as well. James Rothwell from Paynestown, County Meath, was murdered in Belfast in October 1923 while performing his duties with the Royal Ulster Constabulary. Closer to home, the murder of a former Wilson's pupil was reported in "The Irish Times" on January 22nd 1921.

"KIDNAPPED AND SHOT"
"An official report states that the dead body of William Chartres who was kidnapped on the 22nd instant from his own home in County Longford, has been found in a lake about two miles from Ballinalee in the same County. He had been taken from his own house, blindfolded and shot."

Drill Display, Wilson's Hospital 1935

Emigration is a continuous feature in the subsequent careers of Wilson's boys. At least twenty are recorded as having left for Canada, Australia, New Zealand and the USA. The latter was to see six Wilson's boys enlisting for the war under the banner of the Stars and Stripes. Work in the colonial forces continued to attract. John Halligan from Laracor in County Meath became a Sergeant in the Indian Police in Calcutta in 1923.

The overall picture is of a school gradually moving outwards and upwards. The horizons and the opportunities are expanding. The pupils are taking advantage of career possibilities both in the former administration and in the new. In that sense, political boundaries were irrelevant. A young man leaving Wilson's went where he felt his talents would be best employed. Neither the search for employment nor the concept of duty recognised any borders.

Two years after the secondary department opened, "The Wilsonian" came out for the first time. A school magazine provides a unique insight into the life of a school. Browsing through the pages of the magazines from the 1930's, one can gain a fair impression of the lives and outlook of Wilsonians. Sport features prominently, as one would expect. The lists of teams carry the names and photographs of many a boy who would later be listed in less gentle pursuits. Mr. K. Hood and James Grier smile wistfully out of the cricket photographs. George Hatton and Noel Kerr appear in the same Junior Cup rugby team in 1934. Richard Stubbs, who became a Squadron Leader and won the D.F.C. in 1941, appears in a photograph of the choir. The Prize Lists feature many servicemen; G.C. Williams winning the Form 11 Maths Prize in 1936. And, interspersed among these reports, the advertisements from T.L. Hutchinson & Son, Mullingar. "The complete school outfit -youths' long trouser suits - overcoats and raincoats -collars and caps" surmounted by the image of the model schoolboy ; jacket and short trousers, long socks and cap, and an ever so slightly insouciant expression.

The foundation of the Wilsonian Club of America in 1935 is recorded; Treasurer, James J. Grier; Secretary, Seward Fetherston. These names will be seen again under different headings. Thomas Dowdall writes essays in Greek - and also appears as 'The Heroine' in "The Ghost Train". K. Hood Esquire is the subject of a school boy ditty:

"He teaches Irish History
And he teaches it with zeal.
He starts the job at nine o' clock
Before he's had a meal."

Light hearted lyrics and limericks were very much the flavour of the day. Noel Kerr, who would later fly with Bomber Command, mused on the indignities of rugby in "Reflection":

"Dreadfully staring
thro' muddy impurity
As when, with daring,
caught by his heels was he
Down did he come;
- Alas, for the rarity
of Christian charity!"

There are signs, too, of political awareness, borne out of a sense of history. Brian Ronaldson was clearly influenced by the naval battle at Jutland in 1916. Was he thinking of Frederick Armstrong, whose name was on the Roll of Honour in the Chapel?

"In Jutland's fight there fought a lad
To his ship and country true;
Fearless he strove at the steaming gun,
the last of her fearless crew."

He also wrote a poem "Superstition" which reflected his own anxieties - Brian Ronaldson later avoided having his photograph taken when he was wearing uniform. Some of the lines in the poem have a poignant ring - Brian was to lose his life in the war -
"If he fears, there's one thing certain - as certain as black's not blue -
The thing he fears will happen; he is his own Hoodoo."

"Police Verso" was the pseudonym for the poet who reflected on "Armistice 1918".:

"About a field of muddy horror strewn
with waste of craftsman's deadly instruments,
And mortal members torn from comely forms, -
Divinely joined in gentle mystery."

And, in a second verse "1936", he pondered
"Is man yet mad, that through that throb once more
The roll of drums our Hallow'd Silence breaks?"

The most overt references to politics and the approach of war in 1939 come with the report in The Wilsonian entitled "Hitler and the Germany of Today." Through the auspices of a parent, Herr Christopher Meyer of Bremen gave a lecture to the pupils on May 26th 1936. In view of the fact that he was addressing boys who were subsequently to enlist in the war to defeat Hitler, the tone in which the report is written is noteworthy.

"Herr Meyer spoke about Germany and the youth of today. Besides indulging in many manly sports, they also go through a vigorous military training. A socialist system is worked in some of Hitler's organisations in connection with the buying of clothes, whereby those who can afford it pay more than the less fortunate."

"When the questioning started, the lecture took on a more political turn. Our visitor's views were in complete agreement with Hitler's on the problem of the Jews. When questioned about the Treaty of Versailles, Herr Meyer asked us - candidly enough - how we imagined any country could hope to exist under the terms laid down by it. He, like Hitler, had no use for the League of Nations as at present constituted; but, as regards war, Herr Meyer was most emphatic in declaring that Germany wanted no more of it. He begged us all to realise the folly of war and to work for world peace."

"To the disappointment of some, our lecturer would not discuss Hitler's, Germany's or his own attitude towards England, beyond assuring us they wished to be friendly."

"Herr Meyer was greatly struck by the amount of land there is to each man in Ireland; he thought that it should be better distributed. The leisurely habits of the people appalled him..."

The implicit distaste for Herr Meyer's views are clear in the tone of the writing (by R.J. Perry, Form V). Three years before the war broke out, Wilsonians had heard for themselves the opinions and attitudes of a Nazi. Before the war ended, over one hundred Wilsonians were to enlist for a war to defeat the man whom Herr Meyer had been at such pains to praise. How they and Ireland responded to the outbreak of war in 1939 will now be examined.

Chapter 17

The Call To Arms : 1939

During the years of The Great War 1914~1918, the whole of Ireland was under British Rule. The elected leaders of the country supported the call to arms in 1914 when Britain declared war on Germany in defence of Belgian neutrality. Both Carson for the Unionists and Redmond for the Home Rule Party pledged their support for the war effort. Both believed that their reward would come at the end of the war. As a result of their efforts, no less than three Divisions left Irish shores during the war to fight, in John Redmond's words, "as far as the firing line extends". Those wishing to enlist, could do so easily. Recruiting offices opened up in almost every County town in Ireland. Different regiments vied with each other to secure the services of Ireland's youth. The enthusiasm for the war was widespread - certainly for the first three years. Ireland sent 250,000 of her sons to fight in the Fields of Flanders. One small country school in the Irish Midlands, Wilson's Hospital, whose enrolment numbered between 35 and 65 pupils in these years, sent no less than 93 former pupils and Masters to the war. The figures are astonishing, both at national and school level. The question to be answered first is, in what ways had the political changes in Ireland in the intervening 20 years affected the likelihood of recruitment for a second war in Europe in such a short span of time ?

Eire declared itself a neutral country in 1939. It was independent and sovereign, beyond British jurisdiction. The 1921 "Treaty Ports" had been returned to Irish jurisdiction in 1938. An Taoiseach, Eamonn De Valera, had set a course which was to lead to a Republic being officially declared in 1949. The will of the government in Dail Eireann was to keep out of the war. There were, of course, no recruiting stations in The Free State during the war. To enlist, a man would have had to travel to Northern Ireland or to Britain. The journey to the latter was more difficult than to-day; no frequent planes to hop onto at Dublin Airport; the journey had to be made by sea. Careful security checks were maintained at all sea ports. After the war

Giving the Fuhrer a spanking.

Propaganda Poster 1939 (U.K.)

started, the reasons for travel outside the country had to be stated before permits were granted.

All these factors were potential deterrents to recruits in 1939. Yet, over 80,000 Irishmen enlisted of their own free-will and initiative by travelling to the North or to Britain. Of these, over 100 came from Wilson's Hospital; a school which had only 65 pupils in 1935; 90 in 1939. What was their motivation ? Why did so many leave Ireland to fight in Europe only twenty years after the last war had ended ?

The 1914 concept of adventure and excitement may have prevailed in some minds. But the casualty figures for The Great War had taken most of the gloss off that motivation. Tales of Gallipoli, The Somme and Passchendaele had become

Wilson's Hospital School

synonymous in Ireland with senseless slaughter. There had to be a stronger motivation than adventure this time around.

A weekly wage, bed and board were motivations in 1914. This may have affected some recruits in 1939. The collapse of the Wall Street stock exchange in 1929 had triggered a worldwide recession. The 'Economic War' between Britain and the Free State 1932-1938 had caused severe hardship in the farming community. "That bloody man, de Valera. He's ruining the country !", the Warden of Wilson's Hospital was heard to exclaim as he patrolled the long corridor before the war. However, to enlist for a war, a young man needed a stronger motive than the King's shilling; that was now too small an incentive to persuade recruits to enlist in large numbers.

The motivation is probably threefold. First, there was still a strong tradition of soldiering in Ireland. This cut right across the political and religious divide. It was a way of life handed down from father to son. When the first Fire Brigades went up to Belfast from Dublin in 1942 to help in the Blitz, many of the firemen were said to be astounded at the number of Dublin accents they heard among the soldiers in the North.

Second, whatever doubts historians might now have about the justice of fighting a war in 1914, very few doubted the concept of the just war in 1939. The Irish Free State might have

been neutral, for pragmatic as much as political considerations, but the cause of freedom and democracy in Europe was not to be denied. Hitler's blatant, naked aggression against Austria, Czechoslovakia and Poland before 1939; his violation of Belgian and Dutch neutrality; his invasion of Denmark, Norway and France; all these factors led to one conclusion. Freedom and democracy were in dire peril. Hitler's racism, his treatment of the Jews, the disappearance of thousands of liberals and trade unionists, the pictures of the Nazi rallies; all these images flickered across the cinema screens in Ireland. If ever there were a just war, this appeared to be it.

Lastly, there was the response to a call to duty which went beyond the boundaries of the State. Most of those who enlisted would have been brought up by parents born under British rule; there was undoubtedly that element, which retained a loyalty towards Britain, not least amongst Church of Ireland families. But it went deeper than that. It was a concept of citizenship which acknowledged a community wider than that of the Free State. It was the motivation which felt a common humanity with those whose liberty had been destroyed. The Free State had joined the League of Nations; it was to become a strong advocate of the United Nations and the European Community. The Republic was to send many of its sons to fight in future years under the flag of the U.N. It was this same concept of a wider belonging, a greater loyalty than that to immediate family or state, which drew so many young Irishmen to enlist in 1939. Further proof of this, if it were needed, can be found in the years 1936-1939. Wilsonians were among those who enlisted in The International Brigade to fight General Franco, the fascist dictator, in the Spanish Civil War. This is recorded in the annals of the Past Pupils Association but not, unfortunately, the names of those who fought.

The question remains, certainly as far as Wilson's Hospital is concerned, why did so many enlist in the Royal Air Force ? The statistics are very clear. Out of the total enrolment, just 49%, 53 altogether, enrolled in the RAF. This compares to 27% in the army and 6% in the Royal Navy. The answer to this must lie in The Great War. The boys who enlisted would all have sat under the Roll of Honour in the School Chapel. The list of those killed and wounded would have been there for all to see.

On Armistice Day, the Service in the Chapel would have brought a reading of the Fallen. Those who returned from the war would have brought home stories of the realities of war. The thought of a repetition of the horrors of the trenches must have directed many towards the Royal Air Force. There is the added factor of the Easter Rising in Dublin and the executions which followed; not to mention the reputation the Black and Tans had earned during the War of Independence. These factors must have been influential in steering so many in the direction of the R.A.F. It was, perhaps, Yeats' concept of "A lonely impulse of delight drove to this tumult in the clouds" which provided the last, romantic motivation for so many recruits.

In both wars, very few men from Wilson's Hospital enlisted in the Royal Navy; only a handful in each case. At first sight, this seems surprising. Ireland is an island nation. The Navy has a reputation untarnished by conflict in Ireland. The reasons why so few Wilsonians joined the navy may be twofold. First, it was not an inherited tradition, an important factor in a small school. Second, very few boys, living largely in the Midlands, would have been to sea before either war. Indeed, many might never have seen the sea. The navy had neither the tradition of the army nor the novelty and romance of the air force.

In The Great War, there was a marked majority from the counties of Westmeath, Meath and Cavan among the places of birth of recruits. The breakdown for the Second World War makes an interesting comparison. The number of Counties represented has gone up from 15 to 22. Westmeath still has the largest number of recruits; 34 in 1914, 29 in 1939. If one takes the four counties from which the school draws its greatest numbers in these years - Westmeath, Meath, Cavan and Longford, the figures are; 68 in 1914 and 61 in 1939. The pattern and strength of recruitment has changed very little between the wars. Similarly, three Masters served in each war.

In the Second World War, a breakdown of the years in which all the men enlisted has not been possible. However, it has been possible to work out how old the men were in 1939 - or on the date they enlisted, where this is known. Again, a comparison with 1914 is interesting. In World War II, the average age of those on active service has gone down from 22. 4 to 20.7 years. However, in the Second World War, there is no evidence of 'boy soldiers' or anyone under the age of 18 being allowed to enlist. In the First War, the oldest was William Little, aged 46 when he saw active service. In the Second World War, the two oldest were John James Grier who served with the United States Merchant Marine Service aged 39, and Edward Montserrat, veteran of World War 1.

The connections with The Great War do not end with Edward Montserrat. Hugh Nummy, also a boy soldier in the closing months of 1918, served with the Royal Navy in the Second World War. There are three cases of fathers and sons serving successively in the two wars. George Pakenham, who was wounded in 1915 saw his son, Charles, enlist in the R.A.F. in 1939. William Martin, who died in a prisoner of war camp in Germany in 1942, had seen his father return home from the war in 1918. Robert Morrow, from Longford, returned home safely from the war in 1918. His son, also Robert, was killed fighting with the Royal Inniskilling Fusiliers near Cleves on 23rd March 1945.

The single greatest difference in the recruiting figures for the Second World War lies in the choice of Service. The Royal Air Force emerged as the preferred option; it had by far the largest number of recruits. Before this is assessed, however, the initial impact on Wilson's Hospital came, as it did in 1914, with the news from France.

Chapter 18

<u>Dunkirk</u>

The name Dunkirk stands out among the battles and campaigns of World War 11 as something of a paradox; a victory snatched from the jaws of defeat. But it was a victory only in the sense that the Allies survived to fight another day. The evacuation of the British Expeditionary Force from Dunkirk between May 27th and June 4th 1940 ranks as one of the most remarkable escape stories in military history. At least six former pupils from Wilson's Hospital were involved in this evacuation; they fought by land, sea and air. One was to lose his life.

At dawn on September 1st 1939, Poland was subjected to a Blitzkrieg attack by Nazi Germany. German panzer divisions, aided by Stuka bombers in the air, savaged Poland in a lighting war. Men on horses fell pitifully before the advance of tanks. From the East, Poland was attacked by the Soviet Union. On September 29th, Poland was partitioned by Hitler and Stalin, the result of the cynical pact they had signed together in Moscow only one month earlier.

At 11:15 a.m. on September 3rd 1939, the British Prime Minister, Neville Chamberlain, gave a broadcast which was heard throughout Britain and Ireland. "This morning, the British Ambassador in Berlin handed the German Government a final note, stating that unless the British Government heard by 11 o'clock that they were prepared to remove their troops from Poland, a state of war would exist between us." The dry, thin voice of the Prime Minister crackled over the air waves. It was a quiet, still Sunday morning. Hundreds of thousands sat in sombre silence as the implications became clear.

"I have to tell you now", Chamberlain continued, "That no such undertaking has been received, and that consequently this country is at war with Germany...."

There was no cheering, no shouting, no mass hysteria as there had been twenty five years before. War was not regarded with enthusiasm anywhere in Britain or Ireland. The experience of The Great War had left a scar on peoples' memories. War would bring death and destruction. It was faced with grim sorrow.

In the East, Stalin continued his advance across Latvia, Lithuania and Estonia. Finland was next on his list, but fierce resistance inflicted severe casualties on Soviet troops. A Treaty was signed in March 1940 conceding key areas of Finland to Stalin. Ironically, the inability of the Soviet armies to crush Finland quickly, led Hitler to believe that the Soviets would fall easy victims to German armies. This miscalculation led Hitler to invade the Soviet Union in June 1914; it was to prove a fatal mistake.

In the West, the immediate threat by Hitler was seen to be against France. By December 1939, the British Expeditionary Force had landed in France. It consisted of five Infantry Divisions. These were supplemented by eight further Divisions, all Territorials: former part-time, "Saturday night soldiers" as

The beaches at Dunkirk

they were known. The 1st Armoured Tank Division was not yet ready for battle formation. The BEF took up its position on the Franco-Belgian border. The aim was to prepare for the threat of a German attack in the west following the collapse of Poland.

Among the troops already in France were two Wilsonians. Ernest Montserrat from Tullamore, County Offaly, was the older of the two. He had joined Wilson's in August 1917 when he was 11 years old. His elder brother, Edward, was in the Royal Navy in both Wars. Ernest Montserrat left school in July 1922 and joined the motor trade in County Offaly. He enlisted in the Royal Field Artillery in 1925 and became a professional soldier. The second was William Hunt from Navan in County Meath. He had joined the school in 1921 when he was 11 years old. Four years later, he left school to work for Kennan and Sons. He joined the Royal Tank Corps in 1928, subsequently transferring to the Royal Field Artillery. Both these men were in France in the autumn of 1939 with the British Expeditionary Force. It was a wet, cold and soggy end to the year. A young platoon commander later described the type of conditions for the troops:

"They lived in barns and stables and slept on straw which was never more than two inches thick.... the buildings were full of holes and were swept by icy drafts.... they had to wash in water drawn the night before... on which there was an inch, sometimes two inches of ice in the morning..."

As French and British troops prepared for the expected attack on France, Hitler ordered his forces North. In April and May, both Denmark and Norway fell to the Nazis. Hitler now felt secure from attack from behind while he concentrated on his next victims; Belgium, Holland and France. In the same month, Winston Churchill became Prime Minister in Britain. In the House of Commons, he warned parliament that "I have nothing to offer but blood, toil, tears and sweat."

At 4.30 am on the morning of May 10th, 1940, German paratroops invaded Holland. Holland was a neutral country. It had not taken part in The Great War 1914-1918; it wanted to keep out of the Second World War as well. The Nazi attack was as brutal as it was unprovoked. Caught by surprise, half the tiny Dutch airforce of 125 planes was destroyed on the ground. The Luftwaffe landed the whole of the 22nd Airborne Division in Holland. Three days later, Rotterdam was flattened; Dutch resistance collapsed. There then began the Nazi occupation of Holland which was ruthless, savage and without mercy. An innocent, neutral country had been raped.

Simultaneously on May 10th, German troops invaded Belgium, also a neutral country. The assault was launched at dawn by Junkers Ju52 towing a fleet of gliders. Each glider carried up to 10 specially trained assault troops. The key Belgian defences at the Eban Emael Fort and bridges critical to the advance of the German 6th Army were captured. Sensing that this was a repeat of 1914, the BEF and French troops advanced to occupy positions from Moerdikk in the north to Sedan in the south.

As the British Expeditionary Force began its advance through Belgium, names known to the world twenty years earlier met their eyes. Ernest Montserrat was at Wilson's during the terrible battles of 1917 at Ypres. The name of Passchendaele would have been familiar to him. He and William Hunt would have learnt about Mons. They would have sat beneath the Roll of Honour in the School Chapel which listed the names of all those who had fought and died on the Fields of Flanders. The American War Correspondent, Drew Middleton, wrote, "It was almost as if they were retracing steps taken in a dream. They saw again faces of those long dead and heard the half-remembered names of towns and villages." They must have wondered if they were advancing into the same dreadful place of slaughter as their predecessors had done two decades earlier."

The third Wilsonian in action at this time was Robert Wright who had been in the school from 1932 to 1935. He joined the RAF on April 19th 1939 and trained

Robert Wright, Royal Air Force

Railway Pass, Southampton to Newtownforbes, Robert Wright

as a Wireless Operator. He was sent to France in 1940 and was based on the maginot line. His duties were to transmit messages from RAF spotter planes operating over Nazi lines back to RAF Fighter Command H.Q. He remained in France until its defeat, thereafter being based in Northern Ireland.

The Allied troops were in the wrong place at the wrong time. The German attack in 1940 on the Low Countries was a feint. As the British and French advanced through Flanders, the real Nazi attack came through the Ardennes - where it was least expected. Seven Panzer Divisions and 1,800 tanks smashed their way through feeble defences and stormed their way across France towards the Channel ports. British and French troops were cut off, surrounded on all sides. The German attack, Sichelschnitt ("Cut of the Sickle") was more successful than even Hitler had anticipated.

At this stage of the campaign, a fourth Wilsonian saw action. Richard Parker had entered Wilson's Hospital in May 1924. He was from Killeshandra in County Cavan. Like his elder brother, Robert, his ambition was to be a professional soldier. While Robert had made his way out to India, Richard enlisted

with the 1st Battalion Royal Tank Corps in 1931, three years after he had left school.

On May 21st, as German troops raced towards the Atlantic ports, two tank and two infantry battalions struck hard at the 7th Panzer and S.S. Totenkopf (Death's Head`) Divisions near Arras, 60 miles south-east of Calais. Dick Parker and the 1st Royal Tank Corps caught the German advance by surprise; it was over-extended and over-confident. The Matilda tanks' heavy armour caused initial panic in the German advance. However, when Rommel called up Stukas, the German fighter-bombers, into action, the British were forced to retreat.

The 1st Royal Tank Corps, though now in retreat, had achieved one important result; it had bought time. The German advance had been impeded. Hitler hesitated; further time was gained for Allied troops to seek refuge in the port which was still open to them - Dunkirk. Judiciously, while urging his commanders to counter-attack, Churchill had also required the Admiralty to "assemble a large number of small vessels in readiness to proceed to ports and inlets on the French coast".

At 7.57p.m. on May 26th, Vice Admiral Bertram Ramsay, received a signal from the Admiralty at his Headquarters in Dover; "Operation Dynamo is to commence". This was his order to marshal a fleet of rescue boats to proceed to Dunkirk to bring out the BEF and as many French troops as possible. Every boat that the Admiralty could requisition set out for Dunkirk. Paddle steamers, passenger ferries - anything that could float and was over 30 feet in length was taken. Cabin boats, fishing boats and barges set

Queuing for rescue, Dunkirk

**Arnold Boumphrey,
Royal Air Force**

out for France in what was to become the greatest rescue act in history.

Among these was Godfrey Lockhart from St. Bartholomew's, Dublin. He had joined the school for three years in 1926. He joined the Royal Navy and served on board H.M.S. Kelt. In the operation to rescue the BEF from Dunkirk, Lockhart was on one of the Royal Naval vessels endeavouring to protect and assist the fleet of small boats swarming towards Dunkirk.

As the BEF retreated onto the beaches, Stukas harried them from the air. Heavy artillery pounded the soldiers as they sought desperately for shelter. Long, thin lines of men queued patiently for a craft to get them off. One Wilsonian who knew the men who were there desperately seeking an escape route, described it afterwards as "the horrors of Dunkirk". (Herbert Sharman).

The Royal Air Force sent every Squadron of Fighter Command to Dunkirk, except three kept in reserve in Scotland. Bomber Command tried to smash the German supply convoys as they attacked Dunkirk. Among these was Arnold Boumphrey from St. George's, Dublin. He was in Wilson's from 1927 to 1933. He joined the Royal Air Force in 1939, and the following year was flying Lancasters in support of the BEF as they retreated towards Dunkirk.

In the six days following May 27th 1940, 338,000 troops (224,000 British, 95,000 French - the remainder Dutch, Belgian and Polish) were successfully evacuated from Dunkirk. Among these, Ernest Montserrat and William Hunt lived to tell the tale. Dick Parker was wounded most dreadfully as the Tank Corps fought desperately to hold up the German advance and give the others a chance to be rescued. Herbert Sharman later wrote "Dick's subsequent sufferings beggar description and only an iron will pulled him through."

Looking back on Dunkirk

Godfrey Lockhart survived Dunkirk, but not the war. He went down with his ship, H.M.S. Kelt, on 5th December 1942. He had served for three years as part of the Royal Naval Patrol Service. His name is engraved on the War Memorial in Lowestoft, Panel 9, Column 1. Arnold Boumphrey fought on over the skies of Northern France, bombing and harrying the German advance. He was a member of 73 Squadron. On June 17th 1940, his Lancaster was shot down over France. His body was never recovered for burial. His name is on the RAF memorial at Runnymede, Panel 24.

Churchill warned the British parliament that wars were not won by evacuations. Dunkirk, however, will be remembered as a crushing military defeat which had been turned into a psychological victory. The cost of survival, however, was severe. For one Wilsonian, Arnold Boumphrey, there was no homecoming. Another, Dick Parker, had suffered appalling wounds when his tank was hit by shell fire. As news of the greatest evacuation in history reached the shores of Ireland, relief was joined with sorrow for those who had paid a terrible price.

The evacuation of the B.E.F. and the fall of France in 1940 were the prelude to the Battle of Britain, July to October that year. Hitler's failure to invade Britain in this Battle led to his plans to bomb it into submission. The war in the air began in earnest. The part played by Wilsonians in the Royal Air Force will now be considered.

Chapter 19

Bomber Command

R.A.F. Bomber Command was at the heart of the Allied war effort to defeat Nazi Germany. Over 50 former pupils from Wilson's Hospital served in Bomber Command during the war. Before assessing their individual contributions, the overall strategy of Bomber Command will be analysed. The fundamental aim was to wreak havoc on German industries, communications, military installations and other resources vital to the Nazi war machine. This policy began in an atmosphere of suicidal folly; daylight raids over Germany without fighter escort. On December 18th 1939, 24 Wellington Bombers of No 3 Group, RAF Bomber Command, took off from airfields in East Anglia at 9.30 am. The skies were clear as the fleet climbed to 14,000 feet. Thirty miles off the German coast, they were picked up on radar; the sighting was disregarded. The German defence forces refused to believe that the RAF would attack in daylight under clear skies. Of the 24 Wellingtons which attacked the German naval base at Wilhelmshaven that December morning, only 10 returned to base; the rest had been destroyed by hastily scrambled Messerschmitt Me109's and twin-engined Me110's.

Crew Conference

In the spring of 1940, Bomber Command switched tactics. Night-time operations became the norm. There followed a series of raids on German oil plants and blast furnaces at Duisburg in the Ruhr, Germany's industrial heartland. In the autumn of 1940, ports on the French, Belgian and Dutch coasts which could be used as bases for an invasion of Britain were attacked. In August 1940, Berlin was bombed for the first time.

However, assessments of the success of these operations were not optimistic. The indications were that the targets were not being hit accurately, the majority of bombs not reaching their aiming point. The Air Ministry concluded that night attacks on single targets were then beyond the capability of both aircraft and crews. Moreover, losses were heavy. German radar, searchlights, anti-aircraft batteries and fighter defences took a severe toll among attacking bombers. In February 1942, it was estimated that Bomber Command had lost, in the previous four months, the equivalent of its entire original strength when the war started in 1939.

New and aggressive leadership was needed if the war in the air was not to be lost and, with it, any hopes of defeating Nazi Germany. On February 22nd 1942, Air Marshal Arthur Harris was appointed Commander in Chief of Bomber Command. Harris' policy was to select strategic targets and destroy them from the air, causing massive destruction of the German war effort. This meant sending large fleets of bombers to large targets, often whole cities.

Since World War II ended, Arthur Harris, known as "Butch" within the RAF, became known as "Bomber Harris" to the outside world. He was given the reputation of being responsible for what the Nazis called "Terror bombing", when the German civilian casualties were very high. Politicians were quick to disassociate themselves from policies which they themselves had supported in the War. Within the RAF and the Air

Lancaster bomber returning home

Ministry, Harris was subsequently attacked by rivals who were interested in personal vendettas and political in-fighting. Consequently, Harris' reputation has suffered and with it, by implication, that of the officers and men of Bomber Command who served under him.

Recent evidence, however, has come to a more balanced evaluation of Harris' strategy. Foremost among this has been the availability of the Nazis' own assessment of the work of the RAF. This shows that as a result of Bomber Command's operations under Harris, German production of tanks fell by 35%, aircraft by 31% and army lorries by 42%. By 1944, German industrial production needed to switch 33% of its capacity to anti-aircraft guns to defend itself from attack. Moreover, the destruction of German cities such as Dresden and Hamburg have obscured the consequences; the Luftwaffe was unable to reinforce the Eastern Front where Germany was engaged in a war to the death with the Soviet Union. The necessity for the Luftwaffe to defend Nazi Germany from Bomber Command in the West was a major factor in the defeat of Germany in the East. This defeat was the beginning of the end for Hitler and the Nazi war machine. A final comment on Bomber Command's part in the ultimate victory should not be forgotten. Arthur Harris took over command at a time when morale was low in the RAF and in Britain; within 18 months, he had given the Allied war effort some spectacular and much needed successes.

From the start, Harris made it clear to the War Cabinet that he required priority for Bomber Command and for his men. This meant not just more aircraft, but more sophisticated instruments; these would not only bring success to operations, but ensure the safe return of as many crews as possible. Bomber Command was the most international of all the Allied forces. Nearly 70% were British, but the balance were volunteers from far flung parts of the world who wanted to play their part in the war effort. Recruits came from Canada, Australia, New Zealand, the USA (before that country entered the war), Rhodesia, South Africa; as well as from countries already defeated by Nazi Germany, France, Poland, Norway and Czechoslovakia. Among this international force was a large number of volunteers from neutral Eire. These numbers included no less than 53 former pupils of Wilson's Hospital.

An assessment of the role these men played in the Royal Air Force can be followed by looking at the duties of key members of the crew of a typical aircraft in Bomber Command. We know that Wilson's men flew in Blenheims, Albermarles, Lancasters, and Wellingtons. Before any recruit was allowed near a plane, however, there were intensive periods of training. The initial work which all recruits would have undertaken was groundwork; the theory of navigation, meteorology, airmanship. This would have lasted ten weeks and ended with examinations. Next would follow a period of 15 weeks in Grading School; recruits were assessed as to where their talents best lay. A recruit who was graded as a Bomb Aimer would spend his time studying theory of bombing and gunnery. Successful recruits would at this stage move into Advanced Flying Units and, finally, Officer Training Units (O.T.U.'s)

It was at O.T.U.'s that the crews got together. A complete crew would require pilot, navigator, wireless operator, bomb aimer and air gunner. The crews were usually left to pick themselves ; a procedure which seems strange, but which was intended to foster team-work and loyalty towards each other; virtues which were essential in a difficult operation. The crews now practised flying techniques, known in the RAF as circuits and bumps, in which the theory was put into operation. A final period at a Finishing School preceded a posting to a squadron. All the weeks of work were now to be put to the test.

The day before a bombing raid, it was usual for a battle order to be pinned up in the Sergeants' Mess. Several hours before take-off, the pilot, navigator and bomb aimer would attend a pre-briefing which lasted an hour before the main briefing took place for the complete crews. The Squadron Commander would detail the target by the use of large maps on the walls. Red ribbons attached to pins marked the route. Heavily defended areas of enemy territory were marked by red circles with stripes across. The Squadron Commander would emphasize the reasons why the target had been chosen for attack. Finally, the meteorologist would provide a weather report for the night.

Many crews then spent a few minutes together, while the Captain checked over the details with each member of the crew. He would emphasise the route and target details to make certain each man understood his role. When the briefing was over, the crews collected their gear, assisted by the WAAF's (Women's Auxiliary Air Force) who looked after the kit and packed the parachutes. The flying suits were thickly padded, making movement in the plane cumbersome and unwieldy. They were necessary because temperatures at flying altitude were so low. Meanwhile, ground crew would have serviced and prepared the engines. Armourers would have checked the guns and checked the ammunition on board. This included the bomb loads, known to the crews as "cookies". A Lancaster could carry up to 14,000 lbs bombs on a single operation. Finally, the petrol load was topped up; a Lancaster could carry up to 2,154 gallons.

Such were the preparations before a bombing operation. For many of the crews in Bomber Command, there was no return from their mission. They were, in RAF jargon, "one-way tickets". For one young Navigator in September 1942, this was to be the case. Brian Sidney Ronaldson had entered Wilson's Hospital in September 5th 1933 aged 12 years 6 months. When he left five years later, he had passed Inter Cert with Honours. He volunteered for the RAF when war broke out and was allocated to 150 Squadron in Bomber Command.

Pilot Officer Brian Ronaldson

Brian Ronaldson was a fine young man who had acquitted himself well at school. A photograph of him accepting a prize at the 1938 School Prizegiving still hangs on the wall above the courtyard. That was a far cry from the night of 3rd September 1942, when Sergeant Ronaldson climbed aboard his Wellington. A squadron of 11 aircraft had been detailed to attack Emden, a seaport in North East Germany close to the Ems estuary. At home in Milltown Pass, County Westmeath, Brian's parents, Sidney and Olive Ronaldson, would have waited night after night, month after month, thinking about their son. The next day, they were to receive the telegram they so dreaded. Two Wellingtons were lost on the raid over Emden that night. Sergeant Brian Ronaldson, Navigator, was among those who never returned. He has no grave. Sergeant Ronaldson's name is engraved on Panel 92 of the R.A.F. Memorial at Runnymede. One of the postcards which Brian Ronaldson had sent home while he was on active service contained the words of the hymn dedicated to the R.A.F. by Patience Strong:

"Immortal is the name they bear
And high the honour that they share.
Until a thousand years have rolled
Their deeds of valour shall be told."

Of all the tasks aboard a bomber aircraft in the World War 11, perhaps the loneliest was that of Rear Air Gunner. His was an unenviable position, right at the back of the plane in the rear turret. He was entirely cut off from the rest of the crew, except by intercom. These air-gunners were known as the "Tail-end Charlies". Rear gunners were in an exposed position and subjected to freezing temperatures. Frost-bite was common where the oxygen masks fitted and around their fingers and toes. Two Air Gunners from Wilson's in the RAF were Charles Thorpe and Albert Riggs. Charles Thorpe was the elder of the two. He was born in Mullingar and entered Wilson's in June 1925 when he was eleven years old. He won an Assisted Scholarship to complete his education at Ranelagh School three years later. After enlisting in the RAF, he joined 115 Squadron Bomber Command. On the night of 27th April 1943, a massive air raid took place on Duisburg. The Ruhr was at the centre of Germany's industrial network, essential to the Nazi war plans. A fleet of 561 bombers took part in the raid. 115 Squadron was part of 3 Group Bomber Command, based at Mildenhall and East Wretham. Of the fleet of 561 bomber aircraft, 17 were lost on the raid. Charles Thorpe was among those killed. His plane was shot down by anti-aircraft fire on the Dutch-German border. Charles Thorpe is buried in the Reichwald War Cemetery, near the town of Cleves, Grave no. 9.D.13. He was 29 years of age.

Albert Riggs also became an Air Gunner in Bomber Command. He joined Wilson's Hospital School in September 1928 aged 11 and stayed for three years. His parents were Thomas and Anne Riggs of Tullamore, County Offaly. On the night of 23rd September 1942, 83 Lancasters were sent to attack the Dornier factory at Wismar, on the northern coast of Germany. Sergeant Riggs was a member of 9 Squadron, attached to No. 5 Group, based at Waddington and Boardney. The attack that night on the Dornier factory was successful. However, for one Wilsonian there was no homecoming. Four Lancasters were lost in the operation, among them the aircraft on which Sergeant Riggs was Air Gunner. His Lancaster was brought down during the operation and crashed in Mecklenberg. Albert Riggs is buried in the War Cemetery in Berlin, Grave No 9J. 23.26.

Between March and July 1943, the war in the air reached its greatest intensity to date for Bomber Command. On the night of March 5th, Air Marshal Harris launched the start of what was to become known as the Battle of The Ruhr. It lasted for four months and was to claim the lives of two more young Pilot Officers who had been pupils at Wilson's Hospital. The primary targets were Essen and the Krupps industrial complex. This was where the German heavy armaments were manufactured. Its destruction would strike a severe blow at Nazi Germany at a time when the war was approaching a climax. Attacks were preceded by pathfinder Mosquitoes which dropped yellow flares along the approach to Essen. The key target of Krupps was marked with glowing red indicators. Behind the pathfinders came the fleet of Bomber Command, loaded with high explosive and incendiary bombs. On the initial raid, 1070 tonnes of bombs were dropped in 38 minutes. In the battle which stretched ahead until July, a further 4000 tonnes of bombs were dropped on the target area. Krupps was badly damaged. A major blow had been struck by Bomber Command.

The cost of the Battle was severe to the Royal Air Force. A total of 18,506 sorties were flown in this onslaught on the Ruhr. The five month battle involved 1,552 aircraft of Bomber Command. Of these, 872 failed to return to base. Among these losses were nearly half the aircraft of 617 Squadron led by Wing Commander Leonard Cheshire. This was the renowned "Dambuster" operation in April 1943, the most spectacular raid of the Battle of The Ruhr.

Pilot Officer Daniel Anthony Traill was among the young Captains of Bomber Command who were in the thick of this battle. Born in Kells, County Meath in April 1920, he joined Wilson's Hospital in February 1935. After completing the Inter Cert exams, he left in 1937 to go into business in Belfast. This was where he enlisted for the Royal Air Force when war broke out. By this time, Daniel's parents, Alexander and Margaret Traill, had moved to Newburgh in Fife, Scotland. In the final stages of his training, when he was in the Officer Training Unit, Daniel Traill crewed up with several of his friends. They selected each other - that was the system. They were Australian volunteers. When the crews were allocated to squadrons, Pilot officer Daniel Traill served with the Royal Australian Air Force attached to 466 squadron. On the night of 13th May, 1943, Daniel and his crew came under heavy anti - aircraft fire. Pilot Officer

Traill was severely wounded. Although his plane was able to make it back to base in Yorkshire, Daniel Traill died from his wounds. He is buried in Driffield Cemetery in Yorkshire, Grave No. 6218. The raid he had been sent on that night was also to Duisburg. Like Charles Thorpe one month earlier, Daniel Traill had paid the supreme sacrifice.

The third Wilsonian to lose his life in the battle of the Ruhr was Stanley O'Connor Tate from Ardbraccan, County Meath. Stanley came from a family which has enjoyed a close association with Wilson's Hospital before and since. He entered Wilson's on January 31st 1925 when he was 14 years and 5 months old. Stanley left the school two years later and entered the grocery business in Dublin. He joined the Royal Air Force when war broke out along with so many of his contemporaries from Wilson's. After the successful completion of his course in the Officer Training Unit, Pilot Officer Stanley Tate was attached to 467 squadron, Bomber Command. At home in Ardbraccan, his parents William and Marie-Louise must have been very proud of him. When Stanley enlisted, he took with him not only the thoughts and prayers of the family into which he had been born, but those of his young wife, Alice Catherine from Dunmore, County Waterford. On the night of July 13th 1943, 467 squadron was detailed to a bombing raid on Duisburg. Pilot Officer Stanley Tate and his crew never returned to base from their mission. His name is recorded on Panel 133 of the Royal Air Force Memorial at Runnymede, overlooking the banks of the River Thames.

Two brothers who served together in the Royal Air Force were Thomas and Frederick Calvert from St. Ann's in Dublin. Thomas was the younger but entered the school one month ahead of his brother, in February 1928 when he was eight years old. Frederick joined the school in March when he was ten years old. The school magazines of the early thirties carry many details about Frederick's career in the school. He was Captain of rugby in 1934 and 1935. His essays feature in The Wilsonian. Most notable is that written in the 1936 edition, entitled "The plough, the pen and the pupil." Frederick Calvert concluded the essay with these words: "There is little in history to make men wise, but much to make them sad." Frederick Calvert was fatally injured in a plane crash in 1941 whilst serving with the R.A.F.

Tom Calvert, RAF   Pilot Officer Stanley Tate

By the end of the Second World War, the price paid by Bomber Command for its part in victory over Nazi Germany had been great. Bomber Command lost 50,000 men killed in operations against the enemy; a figure that is higher than the number of British Army Officers killed during World War One. Fourteen of the 53 young men from Wilson's who enlisted in the Royal Air Force lost their lives. The supreme sacrifice which they paid was one which had to be borne with heavy sorrow for years to come by their families and friends.

A tribute to these men was paid by the distinguished historian, John Keegan. In his major work "The Second World War", he emphasised how great a debt of gratitude was owed by civilisation to the young men who had paid such a heavy price in defence of freedom: "Bomber Command justifiably prided itself on having for three years (1939 to 1942) been the only instrument of force the Western Powers had brought directly to bear against the territory of the Reich." In assessing the operations over the German Reich, Keegan continued : "R.A.F. bombers carried out their missions with an effectiveness which not only supported the army very efficiently, but went far towards determining the Germans' defeat."

It has been stated by the historian James Hampton, in "Selected for Aircrew" that Bomber Command's success was such that it sank half of all the heavy German warships destroyed by the allies; it destroyed 80 German U boats; its mines, laid in the sea ports, sank 1,000 other ships; it delayed the use of Hitler's secret weapon, the V rocket, by 6 Months; and it carried out much of the preparatory work for the invasion of Normandy. The work of the Bomber Command was carried out at great cost to the lives of the young men throughout the Free World who volunteered to fight to defeat evil fascist regimes. Some 44.5% of Bomber Command paid the supreme sacrifice.

On 11th December 1941, an American pilot in the Royal Canadian Air Force was killed in action. His name was John Magee. He was 19 years of age. Before his death, he wrote a poem which is dedicated to the airmen of all nations who died in World War 11.
"High Flight"
"Oh I have slipped the surly binds of Earth

And danced the skies on laughter - silvered wings;
Sunward I've climbed, and joined the tumbling mirth
Of sun - split clouds - and done a hundred things
You have not dreamed of - wheeled and soared and swung
High in the sunlit silence. Hovering there,
I've chased the shouting wind along, and flung
My eager craft through footless halls of air.
Up, up the long, delirious, burning blue
I've topped the windswept heights with easy grace
Where never lark, nor even eagle flew.
And, while with silent, lifting mind I've trod
The high, untrespassed sanctity of space,
Put out my hands and touched the face of God.

Successive chapters will now be devoted to individual members of the Royal Air Force who had one thing in common; they had all begun their education at Wilson's Hospital School.

The Krupps factories, Essen, after a raid

Chapter 20

<u>Squadron Leader George Hatton</u>

George Albert Hatton was born in August 1918 in Baylin, Mount Temple, Athlone. He entered Wilson's Hospital on October 2nd 1929, aged 11 years and two months. Photographs survive showing him in the Junior Rugby XV of 1934. Close by him sits Noel Kerr, who was to lose his life in the war. When George left school in 1936, he went to work in a factory in Dublin. In 1941, he volunteered for service with the Royal Air Force in Belfast.

In April 1942, George and twenty other young volunteers from Eire crossed over to London where they were accommodated in what had been luxury flats in Viceroy Court. Their uniforms were issued a few days later in the centre of Lord's Cricket Ground. For the next two years, George Hatton underwent the rigorous training necessary before he was qualified to join an operational squadron. In June 1943, he sailed on the liner Aquitania for New York en route to Canada where he trained with the Royal Canadian Air Force. George Hatton was then a Leading Aircraftman, receiving the princely sum of three shillings and sixpence (17.5p) per day.

On March 9th 1944, George Hatton spent what he describes as a "memorable evening" sewing on his stripes. Having passed all his exams in air and ground work, he had been promoted to Sergeant. His proud moment was, however, summarily interrupted. He was summoned to the Station Commander's office to be told that he was improperly dressed. His Sergeant's stripes were removed. A white armband replaced them. He was told to report to the Òfficers' Mess. George Hatton had been awarded the King's Commission and promoted to the rank of Pilot Officer. After ten days' leave in Toronto and New York, George Hatton returned to England on board the P & O Liner, Empress of Scotland. By December 1944, George Hatton was part of a Lancaster heavy bomber crew and was posted to 153 Squadron at RAF Scampton in Lincolnshire.

Pilot Officer George Hatton

Pilot Officer George Hatton served throughout the remainder of the war with 153 Squadron. When the war ended, the most able officers were offered permanent commissions. George Hatton was one of these. He went on to a lengthy and distinguished career in the RAF, attaining the rank of Squadron Leader. George Hatton served in operations in Malaya and Korea, training on Tiger Moths before completing a conversion

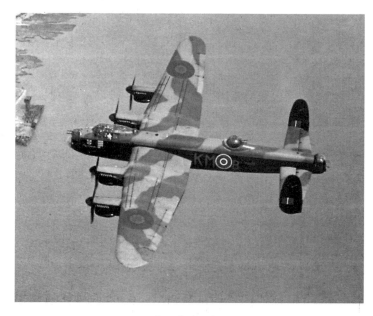

Avro Lancaster

course to Sunderland Flying Boats. George Hatton retired in 1983 after 41 years' service.

In two assessments of the war, George Hatton recalls two very different operations for 153 Squadron, Bomber Command. Although they both took place at the end of the war, they provide a good insight into the varying roles of the Royal Air Force.

A ONE THOUSAND BOMBER RAID

Friday 2nd March 1945 found my Squadron No. 153 on operations against Germany. It was a daylight raid. We were called at 03.30 hours, had breakfast and went for navigation briefing at 05.00. It was a really lovely morning, clear skies with bright sunshine and not the sort of day to be flying over enemy territory, to be attacked by enemy fighter aircraft and to be fired on by the ground anti-aircraft guns.

On entering the briefing room, one look at the huge wall map showed the target to be in the Ruhr valley. It was to be the city of Cologne. The Allied ground forces were advancing towards the Rhine. Bridges over the river as well as the German ground defences had to be destroyed. Main briefing, when all the crew members were present, was at 05.30 hours. It was then we were told that this was going to be the final raid on this target and that one thousand bombers would be taking part. H-hour, the time the bombing of Cologne was to commence was 10.00 hours. At briefing, we were given our heights to fly, how the target would be marked by our Pathfinders, who would be far below us, what anti-aircraft fire to expect and where to expect to encounter the first German fighter aircraft.

After briefing, we all departed to our locker rooms where we donned our flying clothing, flying boots and thick socks, flying helmet. Then we collected our parachutes and various other pieces of equipment. We proceeded to the bus which took us out to our aircraft, Lancaster 'W' for whisky. My task on arrival at the aircraft dispersal was to check the bomb load and ensure that all the safety pins in the bomb fuses were properly connected. Our bomb load on this occasion was one 4,000lb, twelve 500lb and four 250lb. I was the Radar Navigator/ Bomb Aimer. My next pre-flight check was the bomb sight and computer in the nose of the aircraft. All other members of the crew, the pilot, engineer, navigator plotter, radio operator, mid-upper gunner and tail gunner were also busy checking their equipment.

At 06.45 a green Very was fired from the control tower, which meant that the operation was 'ON' and it was time to start the engines. The bomb doors were closed and all the aircraft dispersals came to life with the roar of one hundred Merlin engines starting up. Our complete squadron of twenty five Lancasters were taking part. We taxied out to the runway. We were third to take off and, at exactly 07.00, we were airborne and climbing to twenty one thousand feet which was to be our bombing height. Once airborne, there were more checks to do as we set course for Reading which was the rendezvous for all the bombers. Arriving over Reading, we altered course for our next turning point on the Dutch coast and then south-east towards Cologne. Everywhere one looked, there were aircraft - above, below, to port and to starboard - Lancasters, Halifaxes and even some Wellington medium bombers.

On crossing the Kent coast, the gunners would fire a short burst on their machine guns to ensure they were operating correctly. I would leave my seat by the navigation table, descend into the nose of the aircraft and start setting up the bombsight computer. I had to enter the TV (Terminal Velocity) of the bombs, the order in which each one would drop when the bomb release button was pressed, the forecast wind speed and direction over the target and, finally, select the bomb fuse switch. I would then return to my seat by the navigator/plotter and resume operating the radar and obtaining pin-points. On approaching the Dutch coast, puffs of brown smoke could be seen just below the aircraft ahead. These were the anti-aircraft shells bursting. As we advanced towards Cologne, the anti-craft fire (FLAK) became more intense. The moment when it eased off for a brief period was when the German fighter aircraft would attack. About thirty miles from Cologne, I returned to the nose position and could see the bridges over the Rhine in the distance. Surprisingly, there was not a lot of opposition near or over the target area, probably because there were so many aircraft that the ground defences could not cope with them. The sky was full of aircraft, some in a long stream heading towards the target and others having already bombed, turning for home.

Instructions came over the radio from the Master Bomber, flying in the vicinity of the target area several thousand feet below, that we were now to aim our bombs at the newly laid green marker, which we later learned was the site of the marshalling yards. Some slight heading corrections to the pilot brought the green markers into line of the bombsight, the bomb door opened and at 10.06 hours I pressed the bomb release button and watched the lights on the selector panel go out in rapid succession. A quick visual check into the Bomb Bay confirmed that all bombs had gone. The pilot then had to maintain a steady course for about a minute while photographs of the bombs bursting on the target were obtained on the aircraft camera. It was then "Bomb doors closed - let's get out of here and go home for another breakfast." As we returned home, I caught a glimpse of the twin towers of Cologne Cathedral still standing majestically among the smoke and fires caused by the bombing. We encountered occasional bursts of FLAK until we reached the Dutch coast. It was still a clear sunny morning as we crossed the English coast and commenced descent to our base at Scampton just four miles north of Lincoln. We landed at 12.35 hours. Back in dispersal, we completed our after flight checks and then went for de-briefing by the Intelligence Officers.

It was not until some days later that reconnaissance aircraft were able to obtain clear pictures of Cologne, as it was still being obscured by smoke. When clear pictures were eventually taken, they showed the damage to be very great. Apart from broken windows, the Gothic Cathedral was undamaged. Hundreds of factory buildings were destroyed or seriously damaged. Cologne appeared to be a dead city.

A MISSION OF MERCY

Apart from the bombing raids on Germany, the following entries appear in my Flying Log Book for the month of April 1945:-

8th Low level cross-country
17th Low level cross-country
20th Practice container drop over the airfield.
21st Low level cross-country at a height of 500ft., map reading and photographing pinpoints such as bridges, buildings etc.
27th Low level cross-country.

It looked very much as if a low level bombing raid on some specific target in Germany was being planned. Daylight bombing raids were not popular among the aircrews. Our Lancaster and Halifax bomber aircraft could easily be targeted by the German fighter aircraft and flying at low-level would be even worse as we then came under the intense fire of the German ground defences.

Saturday evening April 28th, the Order of Battle was pinned on the notice boards. We were on "Ops" the next day. Navigation briefing at 08:30hrs and main briefing at 09:30hrs. Was this going to be that low level bombing raid? Next day,

"No plane will fly over the Reich territory" - Goering

Sunday, was a bright, clear sunny morning. On entering the briefing room shortly after 8 o'clock that morning we looked at the huge map of Europe on the wall and, to our surprise, we saw that the white track which indicated our track to the target started at our base (RAF Scampton, 4 miles north of Lincoln) across the North Sea to The Hague in Holland. Above the board showing the aircraft letter and crew allocation was the word 'MANNA'.

Operation MANNA - Bread from Heaven. This was a low level operation but, instead of bombs, the bomb bays were loaded with tons of food for the starving Dutch.

At this time, the Allied armies were advancing towards Germany and although the greater part of Holland was in Allied hands, a large pocket in the west of the country, including Amsterdam, Rotterdam and The Hague, was still occupied by the Germans. Food stocks were exhausted and the civilian population, especially the old, the sick and small children were dying from starvation. My Squadron, No. 153 (Bomber)

equipped with Lancaster aircraft was one of the many taking part in this operation. Each Lancaster carried four panniers, each of which contained seventy-one sacks making a total of 284 sacks. The total weight of 5,016 lb. consisted of items such as sugar, flour, tea, coffee, dried egg powder, salt, margarine, cheese, tinned meat, dried milk, cereals etc.

A limited truce had been agreed with the German authorities occupying Holland for food drops to begin. We were airborne from Scampton at 11.25 hours heading for the Lincolnshire coast and then flying at 500 feet across the North Sea to The Hague. I think many of us were somewhat apprehensive over the realization that we would be flying in broad daylight at very low level in full view of the German anti-aircraft defences. However, as we arrived over the dropping zone just outside the city and the sacks of food started dropping from the bomb bays of the aircraft, the reception by the beleaguered Dutch people who flooded out onto the roof tops, the streets and the open spaces, waving anything that came to hand, calmed all our fears. Many of the crews had attached their flying rations of chocolate and sweets to handkerchiefs and parachuted them to the children below. Having dropped our consignment of food we headed back to our base flying at 500 feet (or below !).It was a very happy, carefree operation which was to be repeated every day until 8 May when the war came to an end. Supplies were also dropped on the racecourse outside Rotterdam.

153 (Bomber) Squadron carried out one hundred and eleven sorties and dropped 271 tons of life saving provisions. In total, the Royal Airforce dropped 7,030 tons of food over the ten day period. The Dutch hailed the bomber crews as their 'Liberators'. They still do to this day. I remember thinking, as we flew back to our base after the first operation MANNA, how wonderful it would be if, after the war, the only items carried in the bomb bays of military aircraft would be food for the starving people of the world. Alas, it was not to be. Less than five years later, I was involved in the Korean war.

Chapter 21

Pilot Officer Thomas Noble Forster

Pilot Offer Tom Forster

There are some young men who served and died in time of war about whom we know little. All that is left to us is a name, address and Service number. Others, however, are more accessible. Thomas Noble Forster is one of these. A remarkable record has been kept by his family from his earliest days in school to the last moments of his life. Through these documents, a complete story can be told.

Tom Forster joined Wilson's Hospital on September 5th 1933, four weeks before his twelfth birthday. He was the son of Thomas Elliot and Frances Maria Forster of Ballinalee, County Longford. The Forsters have a long association with Wilson's Hospital, one which has been maintained to this day

In June 1934, James Gillespie who was then in his thirtieth year of teaching in the school, reported on Tom's progress. "He has worked well", Mr. Gillespie wrote at the end of Tom's first year, but "Still weak in grammar and composition." This, indeed, was Tom's weakest subject at the time. Arithmetic 95%, Algebra 100% and Irish 100% brought his average up to 72%, placing him second in the class. Tom's parents must have been pleased with this start in school, duly noting the Warden's printed stricture to all parents at the bottom of the report: "All boys must return punctually on 4th September bringing with them their Certificates of Health, signed by their parents."

By the end of the Easter term 1935, Tom had made rapid strides in English composition. "80% Very good - has literary ability." Six months later, December 1935, Tom was described as having "Great ability" in English composition. Algebra, Geometry and Trigonometry are shown as his best subjects; "100% Excellent. Has shown great interest." The Warden concluded the report by stating that Tom's religious knowledge was "Very good."

WILSON'S HOSPITAL, MULTYFARNHAM

Report for Term ending....*December*....................193*5*

NAME....*Thomas N. Forster*....................................

FORM........*II*....................

	Marks Obtained	Maximum	Place in Form	Number in Form	REMARKS
Irish	57	150	10	17	*Could do much better.*
English Composition	20	50	} 10.	17	*Fairly Good. Has great ability. wats*
English Literature	55	100			*could do better*
History and Geography	40	100	13.	17.	*quite Good.*
Latin	43.	100	6.	16.	*Shows good progress.*
French	56.	100	4.	17	*Excellent. Has shown*
Arithmetic	100	100	1	17	*great interest in*
Algebra	92	100	1	17	*these subjects.* AC.
Geometry	85	100	2	17	
Trigonometry					
...... Year Science					
Drawing					
Geography	33.	100	13.	17	*should work harder*
All Subjects	581	1000	2	17	

Religious Knowledge

Conduct ....*V. Good*

Boys must return punctually on *Monday 13th January 1936.*

Headmaster....................

From the school magazines of the era, we catch glimpses of Tom Forster in other aspects of school life. He was a member of the Junior Cup Team for the rugby season 1936/37 and in the following school year, Tom was made a Prefect. One legacy remains of Tom Forster's time in Wilson's Hospital. When he was in 3rd Form, he carved his name on the inside of one of the shutters in his form room. It is still there. Like generations of schoolboys before and since, Tom had left his mark.

In July 1938, Tom went on to Mountjoy School to complete his education. He had obtained the Inter Cert with Honours. At that time Wilson's did not offer schooling beyond that level; Mountjoy was a well trodden path for those who wanted higher qualifications.

When war broke out in 1939, Tom would have been eighteen years old. Sensibly, he completed his schooling at Mountjoy before joining the Royal Air Force in 1942. Tom Forster undertook his initial training in Canada and at the end of this course he was awarded his Wings. He returned to England in the autumn of 1942 and began to assemble his crew. During his training, Tom sent letters home regularly to his family. They provide a picture of a young man who loved his family and kept in touch with all of them. The letters also show us a few glimpses of life in the Royal Air Force for a young man as a Pilot Officer.

Officers Mess,
RAF Honey Bourne
Worcs.
13/10/42.

My Dear Willie,
You appear to be having a lively time in Belfast, though the papers here don't say much about it. Did Uncle Mac's tomatoes get ripe yet? They should be good ones by now......
I remain,
Your loving brother,
Tom.

Officers' Mess,
RAF Honey Bourne,
Worcs.
14/10/42.

My Dear Mother and Father,
Received your welcome letter a few days ago...... I got the Longford Leader O.K. You were asking what sort of billets I am in. Well, it's just the plain RAF huts. The food we get in the Mess is very good. We've had chicken a few times, or so-called

chicken anyway. We get eggs about twice a week and I've had four or five oranges since I came here...... I saw "Gone With The Wind" last night. It wasn't as good as I thought it would be. It lasted nearly four hours.

Must close now,

I remain,

Your loving son,

Tom.

Officers' Mess,

RAF Station,

Long Marston,

Warwick.

3/11/42.

My Dear Mother and Father,

I hope you are quite well, I am fine. As you see by the address, I have been changed to another place, but it is only a few miles away. We are still at the same O.T.U (1) with the same instructor and planes. We arrived here Sunday and it teemed rain all that day without stop. This is really only called a............(2)................ The Mess is much smaller than...........(2)..........

I had a couple of days off last week and went to Bletchley. Freddie was home on leave. All well there but apparently Auntie Rema hadn't been too well before that. Auntie Danie has rooms in another house across the street now. Freddie has completely finished his training now and is being sent somewhere else but don't know where yet.

We only started burning fires in the Mess officially from the first of this month. Actually, we had wood fires for a couple of hours each night for some time before that. Even now it is mostly wood that is burned but it is very scarce. I got a letter from you last Saturday and it............(2)........................... two days to come. That is the quickest so far. It hadn't been....(2).................. I got to Longford...(2)........................

We still have not got a navigator so we will be late finishing the course. With luck it may finish just at Christmas. Of course the winter weather may delay it more. We had snow here a few days ago.

For the last couple of weeks at the last station it was a bat woman (3) we had instead a of a batman. I think that is about all the news I have at present.

I remain, your loving son,

Tom

(1) Officer Training Unit

(2) The dotted lines indicate places where the Censor had cut out pieces of information from the letters which it was feared might result in breaches of security if the information fell into the hands of enemy agents. This was a practice which had started in The Great War when soldiers at the front could only send information home on official postcards. Tom Forster's letters would have been submitted to a censor before they were allowed to be posted.

(3) A batman or batwoman was a servant who waited on officers in the armed forces, tidying up their rooms, cleaning and looking after their kit. The batman/woman would have held the rank equivalent to Private in the army, where the same system applied.

Officers Mess,

R.A.F. Station,

Long Marston.

Warwick.

15/11/42

My Dear Mother and Father,

I am afraid I'm late writing again. I received the pullover from Auntie Martha. It was a very good fit and warm. In your last letter you were asking how the crews got together. Well, we just pick ourselves out. We have a certain amount of ground instruction before we do any flying. I have got my complete crew now. You also wanted to know who could be a Pilot Officer. Well, anybody can, even if you have never seen an aeroplane. It is just a rank, the same as 2nd Lieutenant in the army. Bomb aimers and navigators have the same kind of wings. It is just one wing with 0 at the root, and the air gunner has the same, with A.G. at the root.

The weather here has not been too good lately but I suppose it will be like this for the rest of the winter. This is about all the news I have at present.
I remain,
Your loving son,
Tom.

Tom Forster is being characteristically modest. "Anyone" could become a Pilot Officer in the R.A.F.; provided, of course, he passed all the preliminary tests and elimination exercises. There then followed at least 14 weeks of specialised training; a Pilot Officer had to be successful at the end of the course in order to qualify. The average age of an R.A.F. crew in Bomber Command was 21 years.

"Officers Mess,
Long Marston,
Nr Stratford-on-Avon.
 23/11/42

My Dear Mother and Father,
    I hope you are quite well. I am fine. You needn't expect me for another couple of weeks yet. It will be about the 10th of December that I will be finished here I think. We are beginning to do longer cross- countries now. The other night I was up for over 7 hours. I have been over a good many places. I've been over the Isle of Man, Liverpool, Bristol, Plymouth, Isle of Wight, London and all up the East Coast.

    The weather is getting colder here now. We've had hard frost a couple of nights now. It's nice going to bed with a nice log fire but it is very cold getting up.

    25/11 received your welcome letter today. The only question I can think of at present is, How far can a rabbit run into the wood? My new number is 125685

I remain your loving son,
Tom.

Answer to that question, Half Way. After that, he is coming out again."

Tom Forster's little question at the end of the letter may strike us today as quaint. It is, however, very characteristic of the jokes and puzzles which featured in the school magazine at Wilson's Hospital. One example from the 1940 magazine:

SERGEANT: " Well, Private Smyth, when did you blow in ?"

RECRUIT: " Last draft, Sir."

Tom Forster lived in an age which, for all the horror of the War in which Europe was engaged, seems very innocent compared to contemporary society. His letters reflect what William Wordsworth called "Simple Virtues." Tom Forster went on to complete his training. He and his crew joined Bomber Command and were attached to 78 squadron. They flew Halifax Mark 2 on their operations. This was a four engined heavy bomber with a crew of seven. Its maximum bomb load was 13,000lb. It cruised at 225m.p.h. at a maximum height of 22,000 feet.

Tom Forster also carried on a regular correspondence with a good friend of his, David Howard, who was a fighter pilot. One of these letters provides an interesting insight on the life in an RAF fighter squadron during the war years:

"Sgt D.N. Howard,
Sergeants' Mess,
R.A.F. Dyce,
Aberdeenshire,
Scotland.
March 3rd 1943

Dear Tom,

    So you're finally on "ops" eh ? No, I haven't got there yet, but barring accidents it shouldn't be long now. Here we fly Spitfires and so far I've got about six hours on them. Boy, they're swell kites. They're by far the loveliest thing I've ever handled, and by far the most powerful. The other day I did my first bit of acrobatics in the easiest way.

Pilot Officer Tom Forster is awarded his Wings

Our most important job here, though, is cross-countries. Most of our time is spent doing these.... These Spits are fitted with fuel tanks in the wings and in the fuselage. They have an endurance of about six hours.... You can guess how binding the trips are, just sat in a cramped cockpit, unable to stretch, with the dinghy as a seat (and that's darned uncomfortable)....

This is a really swell station. The Sergeants' Mess is really super. They turn out some swell meals. We're always asking for "seconds", and believe me that's something new compared to all the previous places....

I think that's all the news,
Cheerio for now,
David."

By February 1943, Pilot Officer Tom Forster had assembled a full crew of 6 members in addition to himself.

These were:

Pilot Officer T.N. Forster	-Captain
Sergeant G.E. Sendall	-Navigator
Pilot Officer H. Jamieson	-Bomb Aimer
Sergeant E. Drury	-Wireless Operator
Sergeant W.F. Hodgson	-Flight Engineer
Sergeant C. Wayte	-Air Gunner
Sergeant D. Baxter	-Air Gunner

With the occasional change of personnel, this formed the basis of the crew that was to fly on 16 bombing raids over Nazi occupied Europe. Each crew would have expected to complete 25 operations - this was later increased to 30 - before being permitted to stand down, on leave. At no time were their odds of survival rated better than even: in 1942 Bomber Command lost three crews out of every ten before their tour of operations had been completed. The operations involved differing strengths of attack, varying from half a dozen aircraft up to as many as 300.

The aircraft which Pilot Officer Tom Forster and his crew flew was a Halifax Mark 2. The operations on which Pilot Officer Tom Forster was involved were all night flights, takeoff at 1830 hours or later. A former member of bomber command, John Shelton, has written about the last few hours before an operation. Each operation was preceded by a traditional "breakfast", bacon and eggs, followed by briefings for all the crews. Here they would learn their target. The atmosphere was tense. Nervous jokes and laughter punctuated the details of the briefing. The last hour before take-off was the worst. Secret hopes grew that at the final moment there might be a cancellation. As the seconds ticked by, the feeling of apprehension gripped the crew.

Crews were despatched to the locker- rooms before take-off to leave behind their personal possessions. Parachutes, flying kit and even "illegal" mascots- momentos from girlfriends- were collected. Airwomen drivers took the crew to their planes. At last, they climbed aboard. The fear, the dry mouth had to be choked down with all the courage that could be summoned. The moment of truth had arrived. For Tom Forster and his crew, that would have been the routine before every flight. Once airborne, with work to be done, the mind was able to focus on the details of the operation. However many operations bomber crews went on, none of them ever really got used to that nerve racking last hour; it was always the worst part of the night.

At 1848 hours on February 5th 1943, Pilot Officer Tom Forster and his crew took off on a bombing mission. The aircraft was Halifax Mark 2, HR 569. The target was Lorient in France. Two hours later, the Halifax was over the target at 10,000 feet. It was identified by the contours at the south end of the town. Pilot Officer Jamieson, the bomb aimer, reported the target in the bomb sight, but the bomb had not been seen to explode. Other bombs were seen in the vicinity of the target. One large explosion was seen to the north of the town. The visibility was very good, but the town was partly obscured by haze and smoke.

The bomb load delivered, Pilot Officer Tom Forster headed for home. At precisely 0120 hours the following morning, HR 659 landed safely at Linton-on-Ouse. The operation had taken 6 hours 32 minutes to complete.

Each operation was followed by a de-briefing. An Intelligence Officer would question the crew painstakingly. What was the flak like? How many enemy fighters were in the air? How many bombers went down ? Any information which could shed light on the operation and prepare the way for the next was carefully sought.

On February 8th 1943, Halifax Mark 2, DT 771, took off at 1840 hours, Pilot Officer T.N. Forster, Captain. The duty was Gardening. The target was Langeoog. Gardening was the code name for the laying of mines by parachute in important sea lanes and harbours. Langeoog is one of the Frisian Islands off the coast of Germany. It was not far from the very important German U Boat bases at Wilhelmshaven. The operation report states that the vegetables were planted as ordered at 2040 hours from a height of 500 feet. The position had been located at pinpoint on Langeoog. Both parachutes were seen to open. There was a clear sky. The operation took 5 hours 51 minutes. Halifax DT 771 returned to base at Linton-on-Ouse at 2331 hours for de-briefing.

On the night of February 19th, 1943, Tom Forster and his crew took part in their first bombing mission over Germany. The primary target was Wilhelmshaven, one of the most important of the German seaports after Hamburg. At 1734 hours, Halifax W 7937 took off from Linton-on-Ouse. This was an R.A.F. station used by bomber command, situated in the North of England, ten miles north-west of the historic city of York. The fleet of bombers on the operation was preceded by Pathfinder Squadrons. Their duty was to fly into the target area of the bombers and light up the target with Parametta flares. These were like enormous Roman Candles which burned for periods up to half an hour.

At 2001 hours, the fleet was over Wilhelmshaven at height of 15,500 feet. The target was identified by the Parametta flares which were in the bomb sight when Pilot Officer Jamieson called "Steady, steady, left-left, steady, bombs gone, bomb doors closed!" The operational report states that the glow of fires could be seen below the cloud on leaving. Several bomb bursts were recorded. The attack was considered to be concentrated in the target area and successful. Halifax W7937 returned safely to the base at 2318 hours.

On February 25th, Tom Forster took part in an operation which had to be abandoned. This was by no means unknown to bomber crews; there might be an engine or a systems failure; there might be problems on take-off; the bomb doors might jam or fail to open. On this occasion, however, it was severe weather conditions. The target for the operation was in Nuremburg, south-west Germany. Take-off went smoothly at 1832 hours, but the target area was never reached. The mission was abandoned when severe icings on the wings and tail plane left no alternative. The bombs were jettisoned at latitude 5414 North 00.04 West at 21.00 hours from a height of 3000 feet. Leaving the bombload to sink beneath the waves of the North Sea, Halifax W7937 returned safely to base at 2237 hours.

On March 29th 1943, the target was Berlin. Bomber Command crews came to fear the strength of Berlin's defences. One pilot later recalled : "From afar, Berlin was peaceful, silent and harmless, with moonbeams shimmering on its many lakes, then it would suddenly erupt into a volcano of gun flashes and shrapnel."

Halifax mark 2, DT780 took off for Berlin at 2143 hours on the night of March 29th. Pilot Officer T.N. Forster had two changes in his crew for the operation. Flight Sergeant Cooper stood in for Sergeant Wayte as Air Gunner. There was an additional crew member, Sergeant Landon, on board. The target was reached and attacked from a height of 19,000 feet at 0104 hours. Ground markers had been laid down by Pathfinder Squadrons ahead of the bomber fleet. The markers were in the bomb sights at the time of bombing, but the report states that the bursts from FT780's bombload were not seen. Many large fires were concentrated in the target area, the glow being visible 100 miles distant. The raid was believed to be successful. Photographs taken showed the fire tracks of the bombs. The weather was reported clear over the target at the time. The aircraft returned safely to base at 0543 hours. Operational flying time had been exactly seven hours.

At the receiving end in Berlin, Gauleiter Goebbels, Governor of the city, wrote "The air is filled with smoke and the smell of fires. The Wilhelmplatz and the Wilhehelmstrasse present a gruesome picture.... there is no heat, no light, no water. One can neither wash nor shave". For the man who had been at the core of Hitler's plans for a war of aggression and the extermination of the Jewish race, retribution was beginning to be felt in full measure.

Pilot Officer Tom Forster's last operation took place on the night of April 3rd 1943. Halifax Mark 2, No W7937 took off at 1945 hours. Its target was Essen. The plane never returned. The last hours of this fateful operation can now be told. Sergeant N.V. Thornton had replaced Sergeant Baxter as Air Gunner. Sergeant Wayte had returned to the crew. The bleak report in the squadron's records provides minimal details; "This aircraft was airborne from Linton-on- Ouse at 1945 hours. Since that time, no further news has been heard of either aircraft or crew. It is therefore presumed missing." The wider picture of Bomber Command's operations between March and July 1943 reveals a grim statistic. Out of 18, 506 operations, involving 43 major attacks, 872 bombers failed to return. The price of war was grievous.

The next day, April 4th, Squadron leader R.J. Neal, commanding No 78 Squadron Royal Air Force, wrote to Tom's Father, Mr. T.E. Forster in Ballinalee, County Longford:

No 78 Squadron,
Royal Air Force,
Linton-on-Ouse,
Yorks.
4th April 1943

Dear Mr. Forster,

It is with the very deepest feelings of sorrow that I have to confirm my telegram informing you that your son, Pilot Officer Forster, failed to return from last night's raid on Essen. I am afraid that there is absolutely no information that I can give you as no signal was received from the aircraft after it took off, and none of the other crews operating that night had anything to report.

It is quite possible, of course, that he and the other members of the crew landed safely on enemy territory and are now prisoners of war, which we sincerely hope is the case, but nothing definite is known at the moment. You may be assured that I will let you know at once should any news come through. If you hear anything before we do, as sometimes happens, we should be very grateful if you would let us know immediately.

Your son's going has left a sad gap, not only in the work of the squadron, where his enthusiasm for his work made him one of the most able captains of aircraft; but also in the officers' mess, where his very charming personality had gained him many true friends. We all realise that nothing we say can do anything to relieve the grief and anxiety this news must cause you, but we should like you to know that we share these feelings. I trust that you will accept this letter as a sincere expression of the sympathy we all feel for you in your loss.

If there is anything I can do to help, I trust that you will let me know without hesitation. I feel that you might like to know the names of those who were with your son on the night in question, and enclose a list giving their names and the next of kin.

Yours sincerely,
R.J. Neal
Squadron Leader, Commanding
No 78 Squadron, R.A.F.

Mr. T.E. Forster,
Ballinalee,
Edgeworthstown,
Co. Longford,
Eire.

In the days that followed, Mr. and Mrs. Forster, in the family home at The Mill just outside the village of Ballinalee, must have endured dreadful pain as they awaited further news. Two weeks later, a second letter arrived:

No. 78 Squadron,
Royal Air Force
Linton-on Ouse,
Yorks.
29th April 1943.

Dear Mr. Forster,

When I wrote on the 4th April, I said I would let you know immediately we had any news of any member of the crew.

We have no word of your son, but today we received a letter from Mr. Drury, the father of the Wireless Operator, who states that it has been brought to his attention that his son's name had been given over the German radio, as being a Prisoner of War.

At the moment, no confirmation has been received, and this information must, of course, be treated with reserve.

It is sincerely hoped that confirmation may be forthcoming from the Air Ministry, that not only Sgt. Drury, but also the rest of the crew are safe.

Yours sincerely,

G.B. Warner
Wing Commander, Commanding
No. 78 Squadron R.A.F.

(German radio regularly broadcast propaganda during the war. The intention was to demoralise those countries which were fighting Nazi Germany and undermine their will to resist. William Joyce, nicknamed Lord Haw Haw because of his sneering voice, 'Jairmany calling, Jairmany calling' was one of the principal broadcasters. One of the techniques of propaganda was to read out lists of Allied Soldiers who had been taken Prisoner of War.)

In the months and weeks which followed, the Forster family spared no effort in its endeavour to obtain definite news about Tom. They knew the addresses of the next of kin of all his crew. In addition, they could hope that the Red Cross might be able to obtain an official list of Prisoners of War taken by the Germans on the night of April 3rd. The Red Cross were kind and solicitous in their response to this crisis. They carried out extensive enquiries. By July 1943, it was clear that Tom had been lost. The rest of the crew had been able to bail out successfully and had been taken Prisoners of War. Three of the crew subsequently wrote to Tom's mother from captivity in Germany, in reply to her letters.

KRIEGSGEFANGENENLAGER
Datum:2/7/43
Dear Mrs. Forster,

I have read your letter to Fred (Hodgson) asking him for news of Tom. All I know is that I was the last to leave him. I had handed him his chute and he had perfect control. He should have had ample time to get away, but who knows! I can guess your

Kriegsgefangenenlager   Datum: 21 - 7 - 43

My Dear Mrs. Forster, I'm afraid I can't let you know anything definite about Tom. With Tom being the captain of the aircraft he was the last man to leave the plane. You see with the aircraft being on fire anything may have happened after we bailed out. That is all I can tell you. Yours sincerely L. Wayte

Letter from Prisoner of War, Sergeant Wayte.

feelings and I am very sorry I cannot give good news. We were proud of Tom and whatever happens, I know you must be.

Yours sincerely,
Eric Drury.

Frederick Hodgson, the Flight Engineer, wrote next. The envelope is faded after the passage of over 50 years, but is in itself noteworthy. The letter was inspected and stamped by three Censors. First, in the German Prisoner of War Camp: "KRIEGSGEFANGENENPOST - GEPRUFT 71" (Prisoner of War post - passed 71). The letter must then have been posted on to England. There is a Crown stamped onto the envelope "Passed P.W.4512". From there, the letter reached the Eire censors in Dublin. "SAORTAASAN SCRUDOIR - RELEASED BY THE CENSOR" is stamped on the envelope. Wartime secrecy, the fear of sensitive intelligence information falling into the wrong hands,

caused the censors of three countries to inspect the contents of this letter before Mrs. Forster was allowed to read it for herself in County Longford.

An: Mrs. F.N. Forster,
Empfangsort: Mill Park,
Strasse: Ballinalee
Kreis: Edgeworthstown
Land: Eire
2nd July 1943.

Dear Mrs. Forster,

Very many thanks for your letter of the 24th. I am afraid that I can hold out very little hope for our skipper. I will relate the story of what happened to us and hope that the censors will be decent enough to spare the blue pencil. We took off on the 3rd of April and did our job. As we were returning, the port inner engine cut out and we were losing height. Our port outer was very weak and hardly pulled at all. We were caught in the searchlights and lost more height before we dodged them. Coming over the Dutch coastline, our starboard engine exploded and caught fire. We were then down to 9000 feet. Tommy gave us the order to bail out, but when I told him I couldn't get the fire under control, he was very calm and showed exceptional courage. All the boys jumped except Tommy. I have made extensive enquiries for him but without success. I believe our kite blew up in mid air and, if so, Tom would know nothing about it, as death would be instantaneous. That is the only consolation there is. The rest of the crew and myself wish you to know how sorry we are. I extend our heartfelt sympathies to all of you. He was a gentleman and a very courageous pilot and was liked and respected by all who knew him.

I must close now but will write again later if you will permit me to help you in any way I can. I will let you know immediately if I hear any news. Good luck and be brave.

I remain,
Yours very sincerely,
W Frederick Hodgson.
Flight Engineer
1016 Stalag-Luft 3
Germany.

Tom Forster's mother also wrote to Sergeant Wayte and received a reply on 21st July 1943.

"My Dear Mrs Forster, I'm afraid I can't let you know anything definite about Tom. With Tom being the captain of the aircraft, he was the last man to leave the plane. You see, with the aircraft being on fire, anything may have happened after we bailed out. That is all I can tell you. Your sincerely, C. Wayte"

There is one other fragment of a letter from another member of the crew which has survived. It confirms Frederick Hodgson's belief that it was Tom Forster's dedication to duty, courage and self sacrifice which saved the lives of the rest of the crew:

"..........Seemed to realize he would be killed, but kept the kite flying so that we could get out. It was through his courage that we were able to get out as we were on fire and losing height rapidly. He smiled at me just before I went back to jump. It gave me confidence. He was a skipper to be proud of and did more than his duty to save the rest of his crew. I hope that his folks......... "

That night in April 1943 when Pilot Officer Tom Forster and his crew had departed on their last operation together, a total of 348 aircraft had taken part in the raid on Essen. Of these, 23 failed to return to base on the morning on the 4th of April. Tom Forster has no known grave. His name can be found engraved on the R.A.F. Memorial at Runnymede, on panel No 124.

Chapter 22

Teddy Whittle

Edward Gordon Whittle entered Wilson's Hospital on September 12th 1927 aged nine years five months. He was clearly a popular boy at school. His photograph appears frequently in rugby groups and amongst past pupils of his generation.

On the 23rd of March 1946, Wireless Operator E.G.Whittle stepped back into civilian life after five years service with the Royal Air Force (Voluntary Reserve). He had taken part in some of the great events of the Second World War. He had been operational in many other less well known aspects of the conflicts, but ones which were an essential part of the defeat of Nazi Germany. Fifty years after the end of the war, he recorded his own story.

"I left Wilson's in 1934 and worked in Dublin until 1940, when I went up to Belfast to join the R.A.F. I passed my medical and on March 3rd of the following year, I was called up to RAF Blackpool where I began my initial air wireless training. After attending Signals School, I passed out in September 1941. I was then sent to a ground station at RAF Wilmslow, where I met my future wife on my first day. Further training followed in ground signalling and gunnery until I was finally qualified as Wireless Operator/Air Gunner."

"I was the sent to RAF Bicester where I joined a crew to fly Blenheims. There were three men to each crew and ours were all Irish. The pilot came from Offaly, the navigator was from Enniskillen and I was from Dublin. We continued there until the Blenheim was made obsolete after a very bad operation in Northern Africa in which two squadrons were lost, the Commanding Officer gaining the Victoria Cross for his bravery."

"The Navigator and I were posted to RAF Ashbourne to join another crew. We were to fly Albermarles, which required a five man crew; pilot, navigator, bomb aimer, wireless operator

Sgt E.G. Whittle

and a rear gunner. Billy Eames, the bomb aimer was also just 19. Vic Houlgate was the pilot, he was just 19. The air gunner, Harry Meech, whom we called "China" was a bit older. We trained together for a couple of months. Our first solo flight without an instructor made us all pretty tense. Coming in to land, we were all very nervous. Suddenly, over the intercom came China's voice singing "Coming in on a wing and a prayer". That relaxed every body and Vic made a perfect landing."

"Some days later, when we came in to land, the starboard throttle jammed and we slewed off the runway at right angles. We were heading for a hanger full of petrol tankers when we hit the

**The Crew: Vic Houlgate, Bill Hudson, Billy Eames,
Teddy Whittle, Harry Meech (L-R)**

concrete apron which was about a foot higher than the grass. It snapped off and the plane tipped over on to its side. We got out of the aircraft immediately through the top hatch and jumped to the ground. We were taken to the Sick Quarters and given a glass of rum - then off we went again - that's all the counselling that was on offer there !"

"In the Autumn of 1943, five crews were sent to R.A.F Herne to join 570 Squadron. This was attached to 38 Group which was a supplier of aircraft to the airborne forces. Its operational duties involved towing gliders and releasing them over occupied territory ; dropping paratroops behind enemy lines; providing ammunition and supplies to the Resistance groups in France, Denmark, Holland and Norway."

(The Glider Pilot Regiment had been formed after an order by Winston Churchill in June 1940 to form an Airborne Division of glider and parachute troops. All were to be army volunteers with the rank of sergeant or above. They were taught to fly with the R.A.F. and were trained to fight on landing by the army. On arrival over the Dropping Zone, the glider would be released so that it could land)

"We did these operations in between training the airborne troops. Then in March 1944, 570 and 295 Squadrons were transferred to R.A.F. Harwell where we prepared for D - Day. It was near Salisbury Plain and all the airborne troops were close by. They didn't have to go any distance to get abroad the aircraft or gliders."

(D - Day is the codename for the combined Allied Landings on the beaches of Normandy on June 6th 1944. It was the start of the defeat of German forces in occupied Europe.)

"Our camp was sealed on the night of June 3rd. You could get in - but not out ! Our operation on D Day was to tow a glider and release the troops over Normandy. Pilot Officer Vic Houlgate took off at 0145 hours on the morning of June 6th, RAF Albermarle, V1626. The designation was Operation "Tongay". We were all very tense as we thought that it might be a one - way ticket. The French coast was very heavily fortified. As soon as we saw France, there was a terrific amount of flak. We thought we'd never get through. There were a lot of aircraft in the sky that night. There was a Halifax just behind us, about 50 feet above, also towing a glider. The risk of collision was very great. Fortunately, we all managed to get through, release our gliders and return to base. My log book records the night flying time for this Operation as 3 hours 15 minutes, there and back."

(The British and American airborne Divisions began landing in Normandy at 0100 hours on June 6th. A combined attack by land, sea and air succeeded in establishing a toehold in Normandy - the British on one beach, the Americans on two - and had penetrated inland for a distance of two to three miles within 12 hours. The liberation of Europe had begun).

"We then continued to fly on Special Operations (SOE's) to the Resistance Groups until the next airborne operations came along. These were groups in German occupied countries who were determined to resist the invaders and harass them as much as possible. Our job was to arm and equip them so that they could sabotage the German army."

W/O and Mrs Teddy Whittle

"In the meantime, I was supposed to be getting married. We had to postpone the wedding twice. In the end, we decided on September 16th (1944) and I asked the Commanding Officer if it was alright. He said "Yes, but if anything occurs, I'll recall you." I thought "Fair enough!" We got married on Saturday in Stockport. The crew were to come up to the wedding, but they sent a telegram, saying they couldn't make it due to Special Operations. I guessed what was on. So I was just given the week-end off. On the Sunday morning after the wedding, we travelled back. The WVS had got us accommodation for a night, but the next morning I had to report to camp. I'd been told by a chap who'd been flying from Harwell what to expect."

(The next phase of the Allied Landings in Europe was code-named MARKET-GARDEN. MARKET was to be a daylight assault by the 1st Allied Airborne Corps on river and canal crossings in German occupied Holland. GARDEN was to be a ground attack across those bridges by Corps of the British Second Army which were massed along the German-Dutch border. The bridges at Arnhem, Grave and Nijmegen were critical to the success of the attack. The 1st Airborne Division was to seize the town of Arnhem and the bridges over the river there).

"When I got back to the camp at 9 o'clock, of course, I was locked in. The camp was sealed. We took off for Arnhem that afternoon, 1207 hours on Monday, 18th September 1944. We met up with 295 Squadron and the others which comprised 38 group. The Americans were with us as we approached the Dutch coast. They were detailed to make their drops over Nijmegen and went in there. We were taking the British Airborne Division and the British Empire Forces on to Arnhem. We could see little puffs of cloud ahead. It was flak and it was quite heavy as we approached Arnhem. However, we managed to drop our glider and get back to base. It was alright for us that day."

"Two days later we flew again - Operation MARKET 111. We had 15 containers and 4 packages to drop. As we turned round over the dropping zone to come away, two Sterlings got hit behind us. We only saw two parachutes come out, so eight of those crews "bought it". That shook us all up. Normally, we never wore our parachutes because they were awkward to move about in, but we decided after that to wear ours."

"Their petrol tanks must have been hit as they exploded. I told the fellows I was going out of camp to see the wife. So, about 11.30 pm I got going. I put a dummy in my bed off I went. There was a lot of Military traffic on the road, but I got to the cottage alright, stayed a few hours and got back to the camp at around half past three in the morning. My room-mate told me that every thing was alright."

"Next day, we were off to Arnhem again. We had a very heavy fighter escort around us to stop Jerry coming in and shooting us down. We had containers to drop and a couple of army chaps to push out some carriers they had. Approaching Arnhem, the anti-aircraft fire got very severe. One of our fighters came down in front of us. He had dived to try and knock out a battery of guns. We dropped the containers and turned around, but as we did so, the aircraft was hit three times; once in the nose and twice in the body. Suddenly, we tilted and started to go down. Having seen what happened the previous day, I was ready to jump and shouted at the two army chaps "Quick - get your chutes on and out! We're going down!". They couldn't care less - they were so air sick that they didn't bother. So I put my helmet on and just at that moment, Vic said, " Hold on ! I've got her !" The plane pulled out of the dive - we were very close to the ground, just over the tree - tops. We could see our troops among the trees, we were so close. We then started to pick ourselves up and see what damage there was."

"I went up to the nose. Billy was hit twice, in the wrist and thigh. He was bleeding badly. We got the 1st aid kit out and gave him some morphine. Then I put a tourniquet on his arm to try and stop the blood. We had thought of landing at Antwerp which had just been captured - but, the day before, someone had landed there and couldn't get out of the aircraft because Jerry was still in the perimeter. Billy wanted us to get back to England because his girlfriend was there. He was taken off the plane on a stretcher. Billy made a good recovery eventually, but he had lost a lot of blood."

"We got into trouble for coming back in a damaged aircraft to RAF Harwell. The C.O. said that if we had crashed on the runway, we'd have put the station out of action for the next day. He said anyone who got hit in future would have to go to RAF Woodbridge which did not have any squadrons. It catered for damaged aircraft coming in from the North Sea."

"The C.O. was a bit concerned about us all. He had a mess bar opened up. He joined us and we all had a few drinks. We thought we might be going back to Arnhem the next day. It was then we heard that Arnhem was being evacuated (by the Allies) because the Germans had commandeered the Dropping Zones. Apparently, the previous day, our supplies had fallen into the hands of German Troops."

"We continued to carry out the S.O.E. operations. One of these was on the night of April 7th 1944. We were detailed to carry French S.A.S. troops to Holland and drop them behind the enemy lines. The French Troops arrived about ten minutes before take -off in a covered wagon. There were 30 of them, all French Resistance- very experienced fighters, but they had never been dropped by parachute before- so they were nervous. Other aircraft were involved. The plan was to spread out the drops to deceive Jerry into thinking that it was a large-scale operation."

"The French S.A.S were very heavily armed. They had bands of grenades which they carried with them and many guns. None of them could speak English. During the flight, they consumed a large amount of brandy- and left the empty bottles behind in the plane! We had taken off at 20.30 hours and by the time we got to the Dropping Zone over Holland, they were quite squiffy. As they jumped out of the plane, all we could hear was squealing and shouting, heads banging together. Next day, we heard that the operation was successful. The Germans had been deceived into believing that a widespread invasion of Holland was about to take place."

Stirling Bomber

Date	Hour	Aircraft Type and No.	Pilot	Duty	Remarks (including results of bombing, gunnery, exercises, etc.)	Day	Night
3: 9: 44	1045	STIRLING IX LK126	P/O HOULGATE	W/OP	AIR TEST	1·0	
10: 9: 44	2125	LK126	P/O HOULGATE	W/OP	OPERATION :- ACTOR 20 W. FRANCE SUCCESSFUL . LOAD DROPPED		5·45
12: 9: 44	1440	LJ622	P/O HOULGATE	W/OP	LOCAL TOW 10,000' RELEASE	·45	
18: 9: 44	1207	LK126	P/O HOULGATE	W/OP	OPERATION :- MARKET I HEAVY HORSA TOW . HOLLAND) DZ "X" SUCCESSFUL . FLAK.	4·35	
19: 9: 44	1304	LK126	P/O HOULGATE	W/OP	OPERATION :- MARKET II 15 CONTAINERS + 4 PACKAGES DROPPED SUCCESFUL HVY FLAK AT RV & DZ AIR BOMBER WOUNDED BY FLAK. SEVERAL HITS	4·20	
23: 9: 44	1440	LK140	P/O HOULGATE	W/OP	OPERATION :- MARKET RE-SUPPLY 23 CONTAINERS + 4 PACKAGES DROPPED SUCCESSFULLY. INTENSE FLAK AT DZ. SEVERAL HITS	4·45	
						264·40	107·45
		R.F.W. Clixm	S/LDR		SUMMARY FOR SEPTEMBER AIRCRAFT STERLING 570 SQUADRON "A" FLIGHT	15·05	5·45
		O/C 570 SQUADRON "A" FLIGHT			DATE 1:10:44 SIGNED EWLittle		
					TOTAL TIME ...	264·40	107·45

RAF Logbook September 1944

"Our next assignment was to join other squadrons on a bombing raid on Germany. There were two marshalling yards the other side of the Rhine and Field Marshal Montgomery wanted these obliterated. 500 aircraft were to be sent to each of these areas. We took off with 24 x 500 lb bombs. Our altitude was far higher than we would have sought for glider operations. Over the target, there was considerable flack, but it didn't seem to be aimed at us. It was a relatively easy operation compared to others I had been on, and was completed successful. The date for this bombing was February 7th 1945."

(The Rhine was the last natural barrier between the Allied advance and the heart of Nazi Germany. Over 500m wide in places, 825 miles in length and fast flowing, it presented a very formidable obstacle. Those operations began in February/March 1945, under Montgomery's Code-names - "Veritable" and "Grenade".)

"Our next objective was the Rhine crossing. Our squadron took part in this operation together with 295. That morning, we were up at 0400 for preparation and briefing. We took off at 0700 hours on the morning of March 24th, 1945. As we took off, we could see the Ground Staff waving to us at the end of the runway. The people from the surrounding villages had come out to line the roads. They were waving too, as we went off with the gliders for the airborne assault on the Rhine."

Certificate of Service and Release 1946

"Then we all turned in the air and got into line, three abreast as we approached the coast of France and headed for our Dropping Zone. There was no anti-aircraft fire and there were no German fighters to impede our advance. We managed to release our glider on target successfully and made our way home. There were some casualties in other squadrons, but ours got away scot-free."

(The huge armada of aircraft arrived over the Rhine at 09.45 hours to coincide with the crossing of the Rhine on pontoon bridges by tank and infantry troops. By March 28th, 1945, the Allied troops had advanced 28 miles across the Rhine on a front which was 25 miles wide. The entire West bank of the Rhine from Switzerland to the North Sea was now in Allied hands. Victory was clearly in sight.)

"The Rhine crossing was our last big operation before the surrender of Germany. We did a few S.O.E's to Norway in the meantime, but without success. There were also ideas about landing gliders onto prison camps to release our P.O.W's because it was feared that Jerry might send them off to Eastern Germany or Poland as hostages."

"In May 1945, the War in Europe ended. Our job was to transport troops to Norway for the reoccupation. We were also involved in repatriating British and German P.O.W's to their own countries. There were other jobs at that time, taking football teams from Britain to Germany, and one or two trips to North Africa and Cairo."

"We were relieved to avoid one task. There were plans for our squadron to be involved in flying troops to Japan, as the war in the Far East was still continuing. We didn't like that idea, as it sounded like a one-way ticket. Then the atom bomb was dropped, Japan surrendered - the war was finally over and we were all very happy."

"Six months later, we were demobilised. We had a great crew. It was like a family of brothers. We looked after one another and stood by each other. We went our separate ways after the War. I settled in Stockport where my wife and I raised our family. Vic stayed in the R.A.F. until 1957 when he emigrated to Canada. Billy became Air Traffic Controller at Aldergrove Airport, Belfast. Bill, the navigator, went back into the family business, then became Welfare Officer for the British Legion in Northern Ireland. Harry and China are both dead now. China, poor lad, suffered from nerves at the end of the War. He was so bad, he was unable even to cross a road due to his nerves. The three of us who are left are hoping to meet up for a reunion later this year (1998). We'll have a great chin-wag about the old days and our time together in 570 Squadron."

Chapter 23

<u>Pilot Officer Noel James Kerr</u>

Pilot Officer Noel Kerr

When Noel Kerr entered Wilson's Hospital on April 11th 1931, he was 11 years and 1 month old. He was the son of John and Marie Kerr of Athboy, County Meath. From the start, Noel entered into the life of his new school with vigour and enthusiasm. School magazines and photographs on the walls provide evidence of an extrovert and athletic boy who lived life to the full. In 1934, Noel appears in a photograph of the Junior Cup rugby team, along with George Hatton who was also to join the R.A.F. A year later, aged 15, Noel was in the 1st XV. This photograph includes James Grier and George Calvert. Both these

boys were to enlist in the Royal Air Force; Calvert was to lose his life.

In 1936, Noel Kerr was Hon. Secretary of the Rugby Club and also a Monitor. The school magazine included pen portraits of some of the leading players in the 1936 XV. Noel Kerr was described in words which have a poignant ring to them, in view of how he was to lose his life some five years later: "He leads the forwards with vigour. A hard worker, but one who is inclined to disregard the offside rule." Noel did indeed work hard at all aspects of school life. He obtained Intercert with Honours in 1936 and went straight into Mssrs Armstrong Siddely, the engineering works in Coventry. It was only three years before the war broke out. Noel Kerr was among the first to join the R.A.F. Voluntary Reserve and started his training almost immediately.

A small collection of Noel's letters survive, written to his sister Dolly who was a Nursing Sister in England during the War years. They bring us glimpses of life in wartime Britain and in neutral Eire. But above all, perhaps, they convey the image of an outward going young man, full of life, and one who was decidedly popular with the young nurses.

Bexhill-on-sea
Sunday

Dear Dolly,

Many thank for your letter, sorry to be so late in replying but we don't have much time for writing down here. Mother said in a letter that you had a chance of getting a job at Fleetwood as a Sister, that would be very nice, I hope you get it.

This is a very quiet place, frightfully snobbish, but the girls are pretty good looking. We should have gone to our aerodromes yesterday but everything has been postponed for a bit. We had a nice rag on Friday night as we thought we were going on Saturday, and we certainly livened things up a bit.

I was up in town for a weekend but I'm afraid I did not have time to see your friends at Redwood, perhaps I will some of these days.

The aerodrome I'm going to isn't very near so I don't think I'll see you until after Christmas at any rate. Well, give my kind regards to all the girls in Sheffield. Bill sends his love.
    Your loving brother,
        Noel."

Unfortunately this letter was not dated. However, the implication is that it was written in the autumn, probably October 1940. After submitting his name at the enlistment office, Noel would have returned to work until being summoned for a medical. His training would have begun in the spring of 1940. The next letters are more specific.

"Hemswell.
10.X1.40

Dear Dolly,
    Glad to receive a letter from you and photograph. I'm sorry I won't be able to take it over for a long time as I've just come back from leave.

It was grand being home with no black-out and large juicy steaks! At every meal if you feel like it.

How do you like your new place apart from the bombing? I'm sure it would be a nice place in peacetime, but being near London nowadays has lost many of its attractions.

I may be getting a 48 hour pass this month so I might possibly be able to see you if I could be flown down near you. Still, that is a long way off and we'll see what turns up first.

Well, I have very little to say at the moment, so so-long for the present.
    Your loving brother,
    Noel
P.S. They are all well at home and we're hoping you'd be OK in your new job."

"Hemswell,
19.X1.40

Dear Dolly,

Many thanks for your letter. I'm enclosing you £2 to buy a present for yourself as I haven't been able to get into town for the last ten days to be able to buy anything for you.

Hemswell
10:XI:40.

Dear Dolly,
    Glad to recieve a letter from you and photograph. I'm sorry I won't be able to take it over for a long time, as I've just come back from leave.
    It was grand being home with no black out and large juicy steaks! at every meal if you feel like it.
    How do you like your new place apart from the bombing. I'm sure it would be a nice place, in

Letter from Noel to his sister, November 1940

- 101 -

Noel Kerr in a school group (standing centre)

How are things with you nowadays ? I suppose you are working like blazes, with all the extra sick folk knocking around these days. By the way, remember me to all the girls in Sheffield. I hope they are all OK.

Well, this is only a note to let you know that I have a change of address and I haven't got very much to say. So so-long for the present, hoping you are well,

Your Loving brother.
Noel.'

Pilot Officer Noel Kerr's last known letter is not dated. However, It must have been written in the spring of 1941, probably March. The lack of specific factual information about the war or R.A.F operations in these letters does not need much explanation; any such details would have been eliminated by the censors. This letter is written on headed notepaper from the Officers' Mess.

Well, cheerio for the present, hoping you enjoy yourself.
Your loving brother,
Noel"

Early in the New Year of 1941, Noel Kerr was transferred to R.A.F. Cottesmore, near Oakham, in England's smallest County, Rutland.

"Cottesmore,
Tuesday.

Dear Dolly,
Just a line to let you know I'm still alive and kicking. Well, I've moved from Little Rissington as you can see from the address. I'm a bit nearer you now than I was, but I'm afraid the chances of getting some leave to go and see you are nil.

I was commissioned last Saturday and I'm a Pilot Officer, so now I've got a very nice uniform and no money. Well, I suppose it is a lot better in many ways !

"COTTESMORE 241
ROYAL AIR FORCE STATION,
COTTESMORE,
OAKHAM,RUTLAND.

Dear Dolly,

I hear you were expecting a letter from me, so I thought I'd better write even though it's your turn.

Well, I should be moving to a station near Doncaster pretty soon, so I should be able to go and see you if you get any time off.
By the way, have you had any bombs dropped yet? They seem to be attempting to do a lot of damage in this country but without much success.

I hope to get some leave and get over to Ireland pretty soon. It would be very nice to spend some time in the caravan and just sleep. I don't suppose you will have a chance of any leave just then?

POST OFFICE
TELEGRAM

Charges to pay
s.   d.

RECEIVED
Central Telegraph
Office, E.C.I.

No.
OFFICE STAMP

Prefix. Time handed in. Office of Origin and Service Instructions. Words.

39

139   10.40 AM ATHBOY   14

KERR RUSH GREEN EMERGENCY HOSPITAL ROMFORD ESSEX =

RECEIVED WIRE TODAY NOEL MISSING WRITING = KERR +

NOEL MISSING WRITING +

For free repetition of doubtful words telephone " TELEGRAMS ENQUIRY " or call, with this form at office of delivery. Other enquiries should be accompanied by this form and, if possible, the envelope.

Telegram informing that Noel was missing in action

By the way, the last time I had a letter from Bill Garrioch he wished to be reminded to you. He's been moved to a different station since then and I've lost touch with him.

Well, I've very little to say this week so I'd better stop rambling, so cheerio for the present.
Love to all the girls,

Noel
P.S. I'm enclosing a photograph. Please excuse the stuffed cow expression."

After writing that short letter to Dolly, Pilot Officer Noel Kerr was allowed a short period of leave. He took advantage of this to visit his parents and friends in Athboy. All parents of servicemen must have approached the moment of their sons' return to active service with dread. The casualty rates in Bomber Command were very high. They must have known that Noel's chances of returning to Ireland were not strong.

Noel returned to his squadron at the end of the first week in April 1941. He was on service with 144 Squadron of Bomber Command. On the night of April 10th, Pilot Officer Kerr took off with his crew on a bombing operation over enemy territory in occupied Belgium. Their plane was shot down by anti-aircraft fire. Two days later, his sister, Dolly, received the following telegram at the Rush Emergency Hospital in Romford, Essex. It came from her father in Athboy:

"RECEIVED WIRE TODAY NOEL MISSING WRITING - KERR".

The following week, The Meath Chronicle carried the news item which expressed the anxieties of Noel's family and friends:

"POPULAR ATHBOY MAN MISSING".

"Pilot Officer Noel J. Kerr, R.A.F., Athboy is reported missing. He failed to return last Thursday from a bombing raid. The sad news was received by his parents on Saturday. Only twenty-one years of age, this popular Athboy lad was home on holidays a week prior to his eventful journey. Keen, intelligent and daring, he made rapid progress after joining the R.A.F. He had many friends in the Athboy district where his cheery disposition and attractive personality made him a warm favourite with all who knew him. His parents have received many messages of condolence since the news became known and their many friends will friends will pray that Noel is not dead, but a prisoner of war."

Such, unfortunately, did not prove to be the case. Noel's body was recovered for burial. He was laid to rest in the Adegem Canadian War Cemetery, Belgium, in Grave No 111.AA.5. There is a sad irony in Noel Kerr's place of burial. It lies midway between Bruges and Ghent, only a few miles from the Ypres Salient on the Western Front of 1914-1918 where so many Wilson's boys had fought and died only twenty years before.

Chapter 24

The Tottenham Brothers

In its heyday, Tudenham Park was one of the most prestigious of the Anglo-Irish houses in County Westmeath. It stands on a magnificent site overlooking the shores of Lough Ennell. Designed by Richard Cassels, the house was built in 1742 by George Rochford, brother of the 1st Earl of Belvedere. When the families quarrelled, the Earl had a Gothic ruin built, since called The Jealous Wall, between Tudenham and Belvedere House. This magnificent and outrageous Folly had, as its sole purpose, the Earl's desire to obscure the view of his brother's house for ever. In 1836, the house passed to Sir Francis Hopkins, the 2nd Baronet of Athboy. He left it in his Will to Anne Maria, sister of Nicholas Loftus Tottenham.

From this illustrious background, nearly one hundred years later, three brothers came to Wilson's Hospital. It seems, at first sight, an unlikely school for such a family to have chosen for the education of their sons. In the reasons for the choice, lies evidence of the circumstances into which many of the great Anglo-Irish families had fallen. The estate was no longer producing the income required to meet the demands of expensive fee-paying schools. It was, indeed, an increasingly impossible task to run and maintain Tudenham Park. Wilson's Hospital was only a few miles distant and, by the time the eldest boy arrived in 1932, the school was offering education up to Intermediate Certificate.

Nicholas, Anthony and Peter Tottenham were educated at Wilson's Hospital. They all served in the armed forces, though Peter, the youngest by some distance, was in the RAF well after the war had ended. Soldiering had enjoyed a long tradition in the Tottenham family. When the war broke out in 1939, no less than six members of the family were volunteers. The boys' father, Major H.W.L. Tottenham, who had served in the Rifle Brigade and the R.A.F. in The Great War, served in the Royal Norfolk regiment. His wife and both his daughters served in the Womens' Auxiliary Air Force. And, as will be seen, the Major, Nicholas

Pilot Officer Anthony Tottenham D.F.C.

and Anthony were all to suffer grievous experiences in defence of freedom.

Anthony Tottenham was the second son of Major and Mrs Tottenham. He entered Wilson's Hospital in 1933. Six years later, he and his elder brother, Nicholas, emigrated to Australia. They sailed in April 1939 on H.M.S. Jervis Bay. This ship was later sunk in the South Atlantic defending a convoy of Allied ships. Her Commander, Captain Fogarty Fegan, who was Irish, was subsequently awarded the V.C. In Australia, the boys joined a great uncle who had a large holding. The purpose of their journey was to gain experience as farm apprentices, "jackerooing" the sheep.

MULLINGAR MAN'S D.F.C.

Major and Mrs. H. W. L. Tottenham, of Mullingar, with their daughter, Barbara, after receiving their son's D.F.C., which was posthumously awarded to him at Buckingham Palace recently.— (UP.)

Major and Mrs HWL Tottenham at Buckingham Palace

When war broke out, both boys enlisted as soon as they reached the age of 18. Anthony enlisted in the Royal Australian Air Force in 1942. He was accepted while still under age but was required to complete his education - he had left Wilson's when he was only fifteen. Anthony trained on several airfields in Australia and Canada before being posted to England. Here he completed his training on twin and four engined aircraft before being awarded his Wings. Pilot Officer Anthony Tottenham and his crew served with 467 and 463 Squadrons. They completed 34 missions successfully over France and Germany in 1943 and 1944. Such a record merited the right to stand down and take well deserved leave. The crew declined this option and volunteered for photographic missions. This entailed circling a

target area for prolonged periods, taking photographs from different angles. This exposed the aircraft and crew to considerable danger from enemy fighters and anti-aircraft guns.

On September 26th 1944, Pilot Officer Anthony Tottenham and his crew took off in their Lancaster on their seventh and last photographic mission. It was his mother's birthday. A total of 722 aircraft were involved in attacking targets in Northern France. Two Lancasters were lost, one of which Pilot Officer Tottenham captained. The bodies of the crew were recovered and buried in Wissant Cemetery near Calais. Anthony's grave, number 3, was visited forty years later by his brother, Nicholas, on an overseas trip with his wife.

The story does not end there. Anthony Tottenham was subsequently awarded the Distinguished Flying Cross (D.F.C.). The citation records the bravery and courage he had shown on a previous mission, bringing his badly damaged Lancaster and wounded crew safely back to base. One of the Lancasters which he had captained on 9 missions, "S for Sugar", now has pride of place in the museum of the Royal Air Force at Hendon in Berkshire. Those who visit the museum will find the name Pilot Officer A.B.L. Tottenham D.F.C. painted on the outer port engine nacelle.

Anthony's elder brother, Nicholas, who had emigrated with him to Australia in 1939, enlisted in the Australian 2/2 Pioneer Battalion. This was a combined engineer and infantry

S for Sugar, wartime operations

unit. Nick Tottenham recalls what he describes as "interesting training"; route marches of up to 150 miles, including one of 26 miles in one day in 90 degrees of heat, carrying a pack of 90 lbs. In April 1941, his unit sailed aboard the Queen Mary from Australia to the Middle East. They landed in Palestine a month later. At this time, neighbouring Syria was controlled by French troops loyal to the Vichy Regime. In June 1941, the Vice-Premier of Vichy, Admiral Darlan, agreed to let Hitler send German troops to Iraq via Syria. Nicholas' battalion was ordered to advance into Syria and construct rough tracks for artillery vehicles. At Fort Merdjayoun, they were pinned down and finally surrounded by two heavy tanks. His unit had no alternative but to surrender and become prisoners of the Vichy French, whose units included some of the French Foreign Legion. Nick's battalion lost 48 killed in two hours of fighting before the surrender.

A month later, in June 1941, the Vichy French capitulated in Syria and the Australian troops were released. They spent the next seven months building roads and fortifications "against an imagined German attack". As winter approached, the Australian troops experienced their first taste of snow. Nick Tottenham now takes up the story in his words.

"In February 1942, we sailed from Port Tewfik on board the S.S. Orcades, bound for Burma. We landed on Java followed, unfortunately, by the Japanese. The flag of the Rising Sun went up everywhere. The Dutch were the ruling colonial power on Java. They were very poor colonisers and consequently hated. They weren't much use as fighting men either. Our unit had to defend a bridge over a river at Llewilliang. Company A was sent to attack a Japanese force which had crossed this river further up stream. We met a much superior enemy force, got cut off and tried to withdraw. We reached the Port of Tilitchep, only to find that the HMAS naval ships, Houston and Perth, had both been sunk. We had to surrender.

We spent a year in four different Prisoner of War camps on Java, bereft of decent food, bedding or clothing. When we were shipped off to Singapore, disease was beginning to set in and spread among us. The sea voyage took 21½ days on a very

The Cockpit of Lancaster R5868, in which Pilot Officer Anthony Tottenham won the D.F.C.

overcrowded ship before we landed at Barrak Changi. We were paraded next morning for inspection by our Japanese captors. I looked into the next compound, which was full of British prisoners. To my astonishment, there was my father, Major H.W.L. Tottenham. To be reunited with him in such a place and in such circumstances was deeply moving. Everyone stood in respectful silence as we embraced each other and then cheered wildly. I had known that he was in Malaya and had received reports from the Battalion which preceded us that his Company had been cut off by the enemy. But that was all I knew. We had both feared the worst for each other. You can imagine our joy and relief, in spite of the conditions in which we were reunited, after being apart for three years.

My dad had been to Malaya twice before, once before World War One and afterwards in the rubber business. So he knew the languages well. In the war, he was Adjutant to the Sultan of Jahore, but had been enlisted back into the army as Deputy Director of Army Labour. In the prison camp, I was seconded to him. We lived in a self-made tented hut. It was quite

RAAF Recruiting Poster

As I got over the worst of my complaints, I joined the "Dromies". These were prisoners employed in manual labour for the Japanese. This was where I got a beating for telling some Jap to do it himself. We were unloading railway skips of heavy clay at the time, building the foundations of what is now Changi airport. I had had it. I told the Japanese guard, an utter b*****, where to go. This routine, imprisonment and hard labour, continued until the night of August 14th 1945. Our group were all camped in a large room at the bottom of the Changi gaol. Mysteriously, we were all awake at the time, whispering to each other, smoking dried fruit leaves. We knew how close Allied forces were to Japan and that two atomic bombs had been dropped. The next morning, the Commanding Officer told us to remain very quiet. There was to be no rejoicing, although we knew the end was very near. There were rumours circulating that the Japs were going to herd us all into caves and exterminate us. Some believed it. However, a small group of R.A.P.W.I. troops (Recovery of Allied Prisoners and War Internees) were parachuted in by the Allies. Although they were only armed with revolvers, they ensured that we had some safety.

When we were released, my dad's first cousin, Major General Freddy Loftus Tottenham, saw us briefly. He offered to promote me to Lieutenant so that, as an officer, I could sail home to see my family. However, my C.O., who was Brigadier Black Gallagher, refused permission. At this time, we were inspected by Lord Louis Mountbatten. He gave us a talk and explained how he had reached us. His wife, Lady Mountbatten, was standing by the table. He turned to her and said, "Come up here, Mum, it's your turn". We thought she was lovely, and not just because she was the first white lady we had seen for five years. Most of us admired her and could have fallen in love with her.

I was very lucky to be on one of the first planes home to Australia. As our train crossed the border into Victoria, the reception we received was just wonderful. We had tears of joy....and tears of sorrow for those who had not made it back. It was such a warm welcome home from the ordinary people of Australia, that none of us will ever forget it....it is etched on my mind forever. Those who had survived were overwhelmed by conflicting emotions. August 15th 1945 is more than just the day

comfortable, but food was scarce. The few vegetables we were able to grow were not sufficient as we shared them around. Some of us were beaten by the Japanese; I was, once. We were forced to bow to our Japanese guards every time we passed them. We called them "Darwin's missing link."

Later in 1943, we were moved to Changi gaol and the huts surrounding it. It was from there that prisoners were picked out and sent to work on the notorious Burma Railway. Fortunately for me, I had contracted dysentery, dermatitis and berri berri, so I was not selected. My father had been put into the officers' quarters, so I joined my own Battalion. I used to visit him often. He could give me news of the war which the officers had learned from illegal radios. We knew something of how the war was progressing and how, at long last, the tide was beginning to turn.

Pte N.C.L. Tottenham (first behind Corporal) on parade in Melbourne 1940

the war ended; it is the day those of us who returned, celebrated with our families and rejoiced in our long lost freedom."

After the war, Nick Tottenham worked on his farm in Victoria. This was what was known as a Soldier Settlement. In 1945, as part of the rehabilitation programme, the Australian Government made large blocks of land available to former servicemen. Nick Tottenham was allocated 1,400 acres at £3 an acre. The money could be repaid at 2% interest over 50 years. It was very rough land, rabbit infested. When he left nearly thirty years later, he had 2,000 head of sheep on it. In 1973, Nick Tottenham retired to Port Lonsdale in Victoria. His zest for living has been enhanced rather than diminished by his terrible experiences in Changi gaol. "I like living" he writes. "In Changi, I was determined to be the first out of the gate, or right behind whoever was."

Since 1946, Nick has been a member of the R.S.L. (Returned Servicemens' League) which undertakes similar work to the British Legion. In 1995, he was awarded the League's highest award, The Meritorious Medal, for almost half a century of service on behalf of former soldiers and their families. At the age of 76, he still has work looking after the interests of 23 widows, each of whom he visits two or three times a year.

Sixty years after Nicholas and Anthony Tottenham emigrated to Australia, their family home in Westmeath lies empty and derelict. After the war, the finances of the estate continued to decline. Major Tottenham moved out to the Garden House; a small, compact residence which was much more easily managed. Tudenham Park was left empty, hired out occasionally to the Golf Club or for the Hunt Ball. In 1957, it was sold to a builder who promptly took the roof off, stripped the house of its assets and abandoned it to nature. It is now, as Mark Bence-Jones has described, "A glorious shell". Its once imperious facade is festooned with ivy. Elder bushes have taken root in the hall. Above the doric columned doorcase, rooks fly in and out.

"When wasteful war shall statues overturn,
And broils root out the work of masonry...."

Shakespeare's words seem appropriate to a once great house. Bereft of its men in time of war, it was left to decline and fall. War had its price, far beyond the shores on which the great battles and campaigns were fought. Within the shell of Tudenham, only the memories and dreams of a gentler, bygone age are left. Used as a hospital for the troops in the First World War, the house was again occupied by the military of the Irish Free State in the Second World War. It was a house whose fortunes were inextricably bound to war. Amidst the rolling countryside and loughs of County Westmeath, Tudenham stands; a gaunt and haunting reminder of the family which gave so much to defend the freedom which we enjoy today.

Nicholas Tottenham (right), Anzac Day Service 1996

Chapter 25

The World at War

Twenty-nine former Wilson's Hospital pupils enlisted in the Army during World War 11, representing almost exactly one quarter of the total enlistment. They saw service in all the major theatres of war, from France and Germany in the west, through Italy, Malta and Egypt to India, Burma and Hong Kong. Two of these men (7%) lost their lives ; a figure which is dramatically less than that for The Great War. The majority of those who serve in time of war do so calmly and unostentatiously, fulfilling their duty as required of them. Typical of such soldiers was George Seaman who was at Wilson's hospital from 1936 to 1938. George was staying with his father, who was the stationmaster in Carrick-on-Shannon, while on holiday in 1940. From there, he travelled to Sligo and then to Omagh where he enlisted in the Royal Artillery. Lance Bombardier George Seaman served in Britain and Germany during the closing years of the war, returning home safely after demobilization in 1949.

Pte George Seaman, R.A.S.C.

March, he returned to active service with the 3rd Battalion Irish Guards in North West Germany until VE Day 1945. 2nd Lieutenant Harvey Kelly was awarded the Belgian decorations Chevalier of Order Leopold 11 avec Palme and Criox de Guerre 1940 avec Palme. After the war, he continued as a professional soldier, retiring in 1969 with the rank of Colonel. In 1998, William Harvey-Kelly was awarded the MBE in the New Year's Honours List for welfare work with the ex-service community in the Republic of Ireland.

Colonel William Harvey-Kelly,
Irish Guards

Another Wilsonian who served in Northern Europe in the last two years of the war was William Harvey-Kelly from Clonhugh. William attended the National School at Wilson's Hospital from 1932 to 1933 when he was eight years old. He enlisted in 1943 and was commissioned into the Irish Guards in September that year. Following the D Day invasion in June 1944, 2nd Lt Harvey-Kelly was a platoon commander with the 3rd Battalion Irish Guards in Normandy, Belgium and Holland. He was wounded in October 1944. The following

Victory in World War 11 relied not only on those who fought in the armed forces, but on those who served behind the scenes. One of those who worked in the security services was W.J.C. (Bill) Beacom from Aughnacloy in County Tyrone. Bill was at Wilson's for a year from 1935 to 1936 before his father retired and moved to Belfast, when he went to Methodist College. Bill had been a radio enthusiast since early teenage days and went to the Marconi Wireless College in Belfast. This was a training school for wireless operators, many of whom went on to join the Merchant Navy. Towards the end of his course, Bill Beacom was invited by the Diplomatic Wireless Service for interview in London. He was further trained to receive morse code at a very high speed, then enlisted into the Royal Signals attached to the Radio Security Service. This organisation employed 8,000 people stationed in secret establishments. Their task was to intercept more than 10,000 radio messages per day sent to Bletchley Park, the British code-breaking centre. The messages came in by a whole variety of means; despatch riders, tele-printers and even pigeons.

Bletchley Park was the centre of this security operation. Messages were intercepted from every German U boat, warship, Luftwaffe base and Wehrmacht Division. At Bletchley, the German code was broken. As a result, the Allies had advance notice of German plans. The speed with which these plans were decoded was such that it would have been quicker for Goering to have telephoned Bletchley Park to obtain the Fuhrer's orders rather than wait for them to be decoded at the German end! Bletchley Park did not win the war for the Allies, but it certainly brought it to an end much earlier than might otherwise have been the case. The Battle of the Atlantic would probably have been lost but for the work of Bletchley; Rommel would have been successful in North Africa; D Day would have been postponed until 1946. To this day Bill Beacom remains very proud to have been associated with this vital work which saved an incalculable number of lives.

Major A. E. Matthews was another soldier who served behind the scenes during the war. Arthur Matthews came from

Major A.E. Matthews MBE being presented to H.M. The Queen Mother

Tyrrellspass, County Westmeath, and entered the school in 1919. Between the wars, he served with the Royal Ulster Rifles in India. When war broke out in 1939, Major Matthews volunteered again for active service. He was placed on the reserves and, when two more soldiers were required, his was one of the three names which went into the hat. The two men who went on active service never returned. Major Matthews served in the North during the war, training soldiers for the front. After the war, he was awarded the M.B.E. and was later presented to Her Majesty, the Queen Mother.

The story of Malta "The island that refused to die" is one which has caught the world's imagination. At least one Wilsonian was stationed there during the war. Malta held a strategic place in the Mediterranean. It was a British colony with three airfields and a great naval dockyard at Valetta. Situated only 55 miles south of Sicily, it was an ideal base and launching pad for Allied forces to attack German and Italian forces by land, sea and air in North Africa and Italy.

For these reasons, the Axis powers (Germany and Italy) set out to bomb Malta into surrender. The first bombing raid on Malta began on June 11th 1940 when ten Savoia-Marchetti SM79 three-engined bombers attacked Valetta and the airfields. During the course of the war, Malta had to withstand 3,340 such attacks. The civilian population suffered grievously. They built sandstone shelters as refuges for the women and children. By February 1942, as many as 300 German and Italian bombers were taking part in a single raid. Whole streets were reduced to rubble. Towns and villages were pounded; Rommel wanted Malta and its citizens obliterated. The supplies of food dwindled as convoy after convoy failed to get through. Malta was being starved and bombed into surrender.

But surrender was one option Malta never chose. By August 1942, food supplies were all but exhausted. Military and civilians alike were down to the most meagre rations; there was barely enough food to last two weeks. On August 2nd 1942, the biggest convoy ever sent to Malta left Britain. A convoy of 14 merchant ships, carrying food and supplies, was supported by two battleships, two aircraft carriers, two cruisers and 14

Major Percy Butler heps to serve the troops

On Malta, during those grim months of siege, was Percival George Butler from Streete, County Westmeath. Percy had come to Wilson's in September 1928 aged 10. After he left school in 1931, Percy became a professional soldier. The story is taken up by his widow, Mrs Barbara Butler, writing to her nieces, Julie and Elaine Butler in Wilson's Hospital.

"Percy left Streete in 1936 and joined the Army. He was a keen horseman so he joined a cavalry regiment, and was sent out to Palestine. He used to say it was the best way to see a country, from the back of a horse. Before the war started, tanks were replacing horses. They had to leave the horses behind in Palestine and return to Britain. Percy was transferred to the Dorset Regiment. When war was declared, he was posted to Malta where lack of food, soldiering under siege conditions and constant bombardment took a severe toll on him. He was eventually flown out with pneumonia, very, very thin and sickly. He was sent back to Ireland to convalesce. His mother was a great nurse, and as there was no rationing in Ireland, she fed him on the good things produced in Streete. Six eggs a day, milk, cream, honey, butter - which he had not seen for a very long time. Eventually, he was fit enough to go back to his regiment where he served in various parts of the UK. He came out of the army in 1957 with the rank of Major."

William Eldon was the third Wilsonian from Streete, County Westmeath, to serve in the war. He enlisted in the R.A.F. on September 3rd 1939. His contingent was sent to Southern Rhodesia, where they trained at the Kumalo Airbase. William Eldon has never forgotten being feted by the Bulawayo Irish Association - nor the attentions of a young lady, a Miss Carroll, who even gave him her car for the duration of his stay. A year later, at Youngsfield airbase near Capetown, he met fellow Wilsonian Eric Beale from Athboy, also serving in the R.A.F. Attracted by the "brilliant light, warm weather" and prospects, William Eldon settled in South Africa after the war, as did hundreds of other RAF personnel.

Percy Butler was not the only Wilsonian in the Mediterranean during the war years. Gerald Chaloner from Waterford served with the Royal Engineers as the Allies drove

destroyers. After Gibraltar, 4 more cruisers and 11 more destroyers joined in.

On August 11th, the convoy was detected by German U Boats 50 miles south of Ibiza. A furious and relentless battle followed as the convoy was attacked by sea and from the air. The aircraft-carrier Eagle was sunk, along with nine merchant ships and the heavy cruiser, Manchester. Between August 14th and 15th, four merchant ships finally limped into Valetta harbour. The cargo ship Ohio, repeatedly struck by dive bombers, was cheered home by a people close to starvation. The convoy brought with it over 40,000 tonnes of food and supplies; Malta lived to fight on.

Dragoon Guardsman Leslie Ogden

The Allied route to the Far East lay through Egypt, the Suez Canal and India. This was the supply line for convoys of men and munitions to the major theatres of conflict in South East Asia. Almost a quarter of Wilsonians serving in the army in the war were stationed in both Egypt and India. Mussolini regarded the capture of Egypt as vital to Italian supply routes to his prized possession, Ethiopia. "The loss of Egypt will be the Coup de Grace for Great Britain", Il Duce wrote to his Commander in North Africa, Marshal Rodolfo Graziani. On June 29th 1942, Mussolini mounted a white charger and rode through the streets of Derna in Libya. It was intended as a dress rehearsal for his triumphant entry into Cairo. Like so many of Il Duce's dreams, they sank to nothing in the lone and desert sands.

The place of grief for Mussolini was called El Alamein, 150 miles west of Cairo. Here the Eighth Army took its stand between the sea and the desolate wasteland of soft sand known as the Qattara Depression. In the month of July 1942, the Eighth Army under General Sir Claude Auchinlek ("The Auk" as he was known), brought Rommel's advance towards Cairo to a halt. In October, General Bernard Montgomery took over from Auchinlek and, in a ten day battle, broke Rommel's lines. The Afrika Korps was chased across North Africa and, by May the following year, over 250,000 Italian and German soldiers had

the Axis Powers back across North Africa and up into Italy. William Hewitt, from Kildallon in County Cavan served with the Pioneer Corps in the Allied advance into Northern Italy. From July 1943 to April 1945, bitter fighting took place: through Naples, Monte Cassino and Rome. In the same month that Hitler committed suicide, Mussolini was hanged by Italian partisans; Italy surrendered. On May 8th 1945, VE DAY (Victory in Europe) was declared. For the soldiers, however, the war was not entirely over. Italy was an occupied country. Sporadic outbreaks of conflict occurred as pockets of resistance were still encountered and as partisans took brutal revenge on those who had collaborated with the Nazis. Five months after VE Day, six months after Italy had surrendered, William Hewitt was killed in Northern Italy near Padua. He was 25 years of age and was the last Wilsonian to be killed in the Second World War.

Aircraftsman Jack Thompson (seated, 2nd left), No 4 T.T. Wing Rugby Team, Cosford, November, 1943

been taken prisoner. Egypt and the Suez Canal were saved; the route was open for the Allied advance into Sicily and Italy.

Leslie Ogden from Cork, 1st Battalion Dragoon Guards, served in Egypt during this campaign as did George Thompson from Ferbane in County Offaly. George Thompson entered Wilson's in 1931 when he was 10 and after he left school six years later, he went to work in Watson & Sons, Dublin. He enlisted in the Irish Guards in 1941 and was subsequently commissioned into the Royal Irish Fusiliers. He saw service in Egypt, India and Gibraltar. George's younger brother,Jack Thompson, served in the Royal Air Force during the war. Jack's memories of Wilson's in the 1930's are colourful: "I can remember only two things about my schooldays; hunger and bullies." Nevertheless, to this day, Jack Thompson keeps two photographs of his days in Wilson's on the walls of his flat.

On a return visit to the school in May 1998, the first time for 60 years that he had crossed the threshold of Wilson's Hospital, Jack Thompson reflected on his schooldays and the war years. He remains modest about his own service days; maintaining Mosquitos and Beaufighter Intruder aircraft in the south of England. His mother had stopped him joining the Merchant Navy - "Far too dangerous". Both his younger brother, Hugh, and his sister served in the war as well. Jack attributes enlistment to unemployment. "We cared little for politics and knew even less about such matters; it was a job, and jobs were scarce." After the war, Jack worked for the British Legion. "Soldiers came back from the war broken men; their minds had been shattered by the effects of war. We gave them vouchers which they could exchange for food. Money would have been spent on drink." Jack Thompson was awarded the Gold Medal by the British Legion for his work among ex-servicemen.

Jack Thompson also recalls the circumstances in which his brother, George, left school. "Take the boy away", the Warden told their mother, "He'll do no good." Eight years later, George Thompson was a Major in the Royal Irish Fusiliers. He went on to graduate from the University of Guelph in Ontario and became Director of Indian Affairs for the North West Territories. He was an acknowledged expert in the Inuit language and led the

Major George Thompson, Royal Irish Fusiliers

welcoming party to Prime Minister Pierre Trudeau when he visited Inuvik in July 1968. Jack smiles wryly, "Not bad for someone who would do no good."

India had the largest army of all the countries in the British Empire. By 1945, it numbered 2,000,000 men. In 1941, Iraqi troops, sympathetic to the Nazi cause, attacked British air bases at Habbaniyah which were vital to the air route to India. British, Indian and Australian troops were involved in the fighting to secure Iraq, Syria, Lebanon and Iran during the course of the war. But it was Japan's entry into the war which made India so important to the Allied cause.

Japan had been at war since July 1937. After occupying Manchuria in 1931, Japanese troops launched a full-scale invasion of China in August 1937. Just as Hitler began his war of conquest in Europe, so the Japanese Empire carried on a war of aggression in the Far East. French Indo-China, Malaya, the Dutch East Indies and even Australia were threatened. The attack

The Far East 1942, extent of Japanese Empire

Artillery in 1924 and became a professional soldier. Some years later, he went out to India and became a tea planter. When war broke out in 1939, he joined the Tea Planters' Brigade. This was drawn from among those who owned and worked on the great estates in India. Its purpose was to prepare to defend India from attack - after the fall of Singapore to the Japanese, this was a very real threat. By 1945, Robert Parker had reached the rank of Lieutenant Colonel.

The fall of Singapore to Japanese troops marks one of the most humiliating defeats ever suffered by the British army. It was caused by complacency, incompetence and indecisiveness by the General Officer Commanding Malaya in 1941, Arthur Ernest Percival. At 4.15 a.m. on Monday, December 8th, the first bombs exploded on Singapore. Japanese pilots found the city brightly lit and undefended. Simultaneously, the Japanese landed at three points on the Gulf of Thailand to the north. The aim, the capture of Singapore, was critical to their ambition to conquer the whole of south-east Asia. The Japanese had 50,000 men attacking a defending force of 88,000. Dithering incompetence by Percival led to the humiliation of tens of thousands of troops. 1,600 servicemen escaped to India, but when Percival (nick-named "The Rabbit", by his troops), surrendered on February 15th 1942, the rest were taken prisoner. They were marched off to the Changi jail in Singapore.

Among those who were captured by the Japanese on that February morning was Benjamin Hick from Killashea, County Longford. He had joined Wilson's Hospital on February 24th 1923 aged 8 years and 2 months. Seven years later, after passing the Intermediate Certificate, he went on to Mountjoy School. Benjamin worked in the North of Ireland from 1934 to 1939. When war broke out, he enlisted in the Royal Field Artillery. By 1941, he was in Malaya with British forces defending Singapore and the Malay peninsula. When Bombardier Benjamin Hick became a prisoner of war in February 1942, nothing could have prepared him for the barbarity of the treatment he was to suffer in Japanese hands for the next three years.

The Geneva Convention of 1929 laid down regulations for the treatment of prisoners in time of war. They were to be

on Pearl Harbour at 6.45 a.m. on December 1941 brought the U.S.A. into the conflict and ensured that the war was truly worldwide.

India was now a vital base for Allied troops on land, sea and in the air. At least five Wilsonians were on active service in India during the war. William Wilson from Kilkenny and Walter Scargill from County Kerry both served with the Royal Air Force in India. Norman Kells from Killeshandra in County Cavan entered Wilson's in 1930 aged ten. After school, he joined his father who was already in India. He served with 54 Ordnance Field Depot, India Command.

George Morgan from County Monaghan served in the Manpower Planning Directorate, G.H.Q. India Command - he was on general service, released by the Dragoon Guards where he had been a bandsman. Robert Parker from Killeshandra, County Cavan was the elder brother of Dick Parker, so grievously wounded at Dunkirk. Robert entered Wilson's in 1917 when he was 10 and left 5 years later. He enlisted in the Royal Field

adequately clothed, given food and accommodation as good as their guards, permitted medical treatment and exercise, be allowed their own belongings and receive letters and gifts of food. Corporal punishment was forbidden and the maximum punishment, even for trying to escape, was 30 days' solitary confinement. The Japanese did not accept the Geneva Convention and treated many of their prisoners with abject cruelty.

Benjamin Hick spent two periods in Changi Jail and neighbouring compounds, along with 50,000 other POW's. He was also interned on Formosa Island. The South African, Laurens van der Post, has recorded some of the scenes he witnessed:

He was "made to watch Japanese soldiers having bayonet practice on live prisoners of war tied between bamboo posts. He witnessed numerous executions, for offences as trivial as "not bowing with sufficient alacrity in the direction of the rising sun.... I would never have thought there could have been so many different ways of killing people - from cutting off their heads with swords, bayoneting them... to strangling them and burying them alive."

Benjamin Hick suffered terribly. In the heat of the midday sun, without food or water, he was put to forced labour, struck with daggers and swords when pausing to rest. A friend of his was thrown down a well, dragged out hours later and executed by sword in front of the prisoners. The starvation led to dysentry, beriberi (dropsy with paralytical weakness of the limbs) and other debilitating diseases. When Benjamin Hick was captured, he was a strong, healthy, powerfully built man weighing 14 stone. When he was liberated after three years' imprisonment, he weighed seven stone. Of the men taken into captivity in his camp, only one third came out alive.

Benjamin Hick came home on a troopship. He needed prolonged medical care and attention when he reached home. Gradually he regained his health and returned to work in the Bank of Ireland. Herbert Sharman (Past Pupil and historian of the school) wrote in 1948, "Terrible experiences for three years on Formosa Island at the hands of the Japanese have not dimmed his good humour nor disimproved his cricketing ability". Benjamin Hick went on to enjoy twenty-five years of life after the war, with good health and happiness. He and his wife, Edith, brought up two sons and a daughter. In 1975, his health deteriorated and he died in 1980 at the age of sixty-five.

One other Wilsonian was in the Far East at the end of the war. James Coleman from Bailieborough, County Cavan, came to Wilson's Hospital in 1932 aged 13. After obtaining Junior Cert Honours, he went on to Mountjoy. During the war, he had a commission in the L.D.F. (Local Defence Force) but resigned to join the Merchant Navy as a Chief Radio Officer. He was sent to join a troopship and was in the Far East when Japan surrendered. James Coleman was on the first troopship into Java (Jakarta) to rescue Allied Prisoners of War in 1945.

While the world was at war between 1939 and 1945, Ireland did not escape unscathed. In terms of aerial warfare, Northern Ireland was only a few minutes' flying time away from Multyfarnham. It is appropriate that this study should include the moment when the war was at its closest to home.

Bombardier Ben Hick, Royal Artillery

Chapter 26

<u>The Belfast Blitz</u>

On the night of April 15th/16th 1941 the Luftwaffe launched a massive air raid on the City of Belfast. In the dirt, dust and debris of the devastation that occurred, 950 people lost their lives. Among these were two former pupils of Wilson's Hospital. When war was declared in September 1939, Northern Ireland, as an integral part of the United Kingdom, was at war with Germany. Yet, unlike Britain, the defences for its citizens and industrial and military installations were totally inadequate. "Ulster is ready", Prime Minister Lord Craigavon declared in 1938. The truth was far different. Historians concede that Belfast was probably the worst defended City in the United Kingdom.

Long before 1939, defence experts had warned that Belfast was a probable target for the Luftwaffe. Easily identifiable landmarks, lighthouses, its situation at the end of a Lough, all made Belfast easy to locate. In spite of this, in 1939 Belfast had no balloon barrages, no fighter squadrons, very few searchlights and only twenty anti-aircraft guns. Its system of civil defence, firemen, wardens and rescue staff, were all badly equipped. The number of air-raid shelters was negligible.

The reasons for this lack of preparation can be found in complacency and incompetence. Lord Craigavon declared that Northern Ireland would "hardly be possible to find" - a phrase which has a chilling echo of Neville Chamberlain's remarks about Czechoslovakia "a far away country about which we know little". The Luftwaffe, however, knew a great deal about Northern Ireland. Reconnaissance aircraft were over Belfast. The harbour and Lough were mined by German aircraft without hindrance in July 1940. The following month, more reconnaissance planes were sighted over the City; it was suspected that they used the Southern Irish coast to escape back to Germany. Heinkel He 111's and Dornier Do17's took detailed photographs of the City between July and October 1940. After the war, these photographs and intelligence assessments of the ease with which Belfast could be attacked, were captured by Allied troops.

When preparations were made to defend the City, it was too little and too late. By December 1940, recruitment in Civil Defence had risen to over 20,000 men and women, but air raid shelters and fire services were woefully inadequate. Out of a total of 70,000 school children in Belfast, less than 9,000 had been evacuated; the reason was belief that Belfast was safe from attack. Only 4,000 out of 6,000 households in the city had domestic shelter. A raid by the Luftwaffe was certain to spell disaster.

The fall of France in 1940 made Northern Ireland vital to the security of Britain. Ports on the Atlantic coastline were essential for the import of food and weapons. Moreover, they were vital sea bases in the battle of the Atlantic against German U boats. The historian Robert Fisk has read Hitler's directives for 1939 and has come to the conclusion that Hitler believed that "the occupation of Ireland might lead to the end of the war." The Governor of Northern Ireland told the War Office that he believed that the invasion of Eire "now seems certain." The result was that by June 1941 there were over 100,000 troops in Northern Ireland. Belfast, Larne and Londonderry were developed as refitting and refuelling centres for the Royal Navy. They were critical to the Allies in the defence of the shipping lanes in the North Atlantic and as naval bases to repel invasion. All this, ironically, made Northern Ireland the more likely to receive the attention of the Luftwaffe. It was not to be long before disaster struck.

In Belfast at that time were two former pupils of Wilson's Hospital. The first was William Ventin from County Cavan. He had joined Wilson's in September 1934 when he was thirteen. He left three years later, by which time he had presumably completed the Junior Certificate. The Warden records somewhat

Forbes Vigors

Forbes Vigors was something of a character, mischievous, inventive and full of fun. When on holiday, he was asked by his cousins where he had come in the class that term. "First, of course" young Forbes replied. What he did not immediately add was that, at nine years of age, he was the only boy in his class! Forbes brought home stories about the school; how they chased and rode the donkey round the fields; how they would play tricks on the lady who ran the Post Office in Bun Brosna.

As he grew older, Forbes Vigors developed a keen interest in crystal radios. He built his own, using Vim tubes with wire wrapped around. These were smuggled into the dormitory and hidden beneath the sheets for use after "lights out". In between times, Forbes must have done some work. When he left Wilson's in 1936 he had successfully passed the Inter Cert exams and went on to complete his education at Mountjoy. He joined his Local Defence Force in 1939.

Two years later, Forbes went to Belfast. There was no suitable night course available in Dublin and he wanted to study Ships' (naval) Engineering. This took Forbes to Belfast where he was apprenticed to Mackey's Foundry. He went to night school in Queen's University and by 1940 he had passed his first set of exams. He was well on his way to becoming a ship's engineer, which was where his heart was set. It was not all work for Forbes, though. He was a keen cyclist. At week-ends, he and a friend would ride a tandem all the way down to Carlow to see his family. It was here that he had incurred his father's wrath by chopping down part of a tree to make way for a radio aerial. He had a girl-friend in Greystones and would think nothing of cycling there and back from Belfast at week-ends to see her.

When Forbes was in Belfast during the early part of the war, the irony was that his parents did not worry unduly. They were far more concerned about his two sisters. Helen Vigors was a nurse in the Royal Buckinghamshire Hospital at a time when England was experiencing heavy raids by German bombers. His second sister, Myrtle, became a nurse, working behind the advance of the 8th Army. Neither of the girls ever came into any immediate danger throughout the war years.

cryptically that his "father removed him". In April 1941, William was in Belfast when the Luftwaffe mounted their attacks on the City.

The second Wilsonian in Belfast at that time was Patrick Forbes Vigors, from Bagenalstown in County Carlow. Forbes was 9 years and 6 months old when he joined Wilson's on September 11th 1930. He came under the care and guidance of Mr. James Gillespie, by then the Head Master of the School. James Gillespie was a legendary figure in the teaching profession. He was of a kind that has virtually disappeared; the "Mr. Chips", a bachelor who gave his life to the school and its pupils. Forbes Vigors fell very ill with dyptheria while at Wilson's. His sister, Mrs. Helen Kelly, attributes Forbes' survival to the care and attention which James Gillespie personally supervised.

The first air raids struck Belfast on the night of April 9th 1941. Led by pathfinder squadrons which dropped flares on the Belfast docks, the bombers showed an open contempt for the defences around the City. Back at base, they were later to report that opposition was "inferior in quality, scanty and insufficient". Damage was done in the docks area and to commercial and industrial premises. Thirteen people were killed. It was but a foretaste of what was to follow. On German radio, Irishman William Joyce, "Lord Haw-Haw", taunted over the air waves that there would be "Easter eggs for Belfast". Revelations have recently come to light that the I.R.A. aided and abetted German intelligence in its planning of the raids on Belfast.

On the night of April 15th/16th 1941, the Easter Tuesday raid by the Luftwaffe took place on Belfast. It was to cause widespread devastation and deaths, on a scale which brought shock and horror to all Irishmen, north and south. It was a wet April evening that Tuesday, but the Easter holiday spirit still prevailed. As night approached, the clouds cleared and a moon which was three-quarters full lit up the city. At 11.00pm, the ominous sound of enemy bombers was heard approaching Belfast from the south. Heinkel He111's and Junkers Ju88's led the attack. In the words of one German pilot, Paul Wiersbitzki, they took "visual checks" on their position by the lights of towns on the East coast of neutral Eire.

At 11.45pm the night sky over Belfast was lit up by flares, dropped as markers by German pathfinders. For the next five hours, 180 German aircraft dropped 674 bombs at a rate of two per minute. In addition, 2,900 incendiary bombs fell that night. The worst hit areas were the working class houses around the docks. Many bombs were designed to cause maximum blast damage; they had steel plates on their noses to stop them being buried on impact. Whole streets of houses collapsed like cardboard. Seventy-six land mines floated down on parachutes, falling onto the back-to-back terraced houses in Belfast's poorest districts. Each bomb created a terrifying roar, a huge dark red cloud, followed by a blast, which flattened whole streets.

The firestorm which was created did not come under control for 12 hours. The fire services in the north were totally

Belfast in the Blitz

inadequate to deal with the devastation. By 10.00am on the following morning, fire brigades began to arrive across the border from Drogheda and Dublin. An Taoiseach, Eamonn de Valera, had given permission for them to travel. He had been awakened at 4.35am to be told that an urgent appeal for help had come from Belfast. Thirteen fire engines and seventy firemen from neutral Eire went to assist in putting out the fires in Belfast. It was a breach of the neutrality which de Valera had declared but, he said later in Castlebar, "They are all our people". Subsequent to this, German bombs landed in the North Strand area of Dublin on May 31st 1941, killing 28 people and injuring 87. For years they were believed to be 'stray' bombs, accidentally jettisoned by Luftwaffe planes returning to base after attacking Britain. Recent evidence indicates they may in fact have been a warning by Nazi Germany to Eire not to interfere again.

No other city in Britain, except Liverpool and London, suffered such destruction and death on a single night during World War 2. The death toll was 950, with a further 650 seriously injured. Among these grim statistics lie the names of William Ventin and Forbes Vigors. Both were killed in the Luftwaffe raid that night on Belfast.

Forbes Vigors was in 'digs' near the docks. He had a room in a terraced, working class house in Ebenezer Street. A German land mine destroyed the entire street. The mine was one of those landed by parachute. The soft impact ensured that the blast would cause maximum carnage in a residential area. There was no air raid shelter in Ebenezer Street, let alone one inside the house. Forbes, his landlady and her small daughter, tucked themselves under the staircase as the bombs rained down for five terrible hours. When they were found the next day, Forbes was already dead. He was holding the little girl in his arms as if to protect her. She and her mother died later.

It was the dreadful duty of Forbes' brother, Stafford Vigors, also a Wilsonian, to travel from Carlow to Belfast to bring the body home for burial. When he arrived in the city, Stafford was appalled by what he saw. Whole streets had collapsed in piles of rubble. The pall of smoke hung over the city as fires crackled. Communications were destroyed. A small colony of ex-servicemen's homes in Messines Park, named after the joint action of the 36th (Ulster) and 10th (Irish) Divisions in the Great War, had suffered widespread damage. Forbes' body had been taken to the Royal Victoria Hospital to await collection. When Stafford got there, walking through the rubble-strewn streets, he found that the city had exhausted its supply of coffins. His brother, Forbes, lay in a makeshift cardboard box. Placing this on a borrowed wheelbarrow, Stafford made his way back through the smoke and dying embers of the firebombs to the railway station. Then began Forbes Vigors' last, long journey home for burial in his native County Carlow. He was 21 years of age.

Chapter 27

The Yanks are coming ! And the Brothers Grier

No less than eight former pupils of Wilson's Hospital served in the forces of the United States of America during the Second World War. Emigration has been a constant feature of Irish life for three centuries. Non-Conformists fled from religious discrimination in the eighteenth century. The Great Famine sent over a million into the emigration ships in the second half of the nineteenth century. In the last one hundred years, the rate of emigration can be measured alongside the state of the Irish economy. The 1920's, in particular, were decades which witnessed a high exodus of young people in search of a better standard of living - a new beginning.

Throughout these years, a steady stream of former pupils of Wilson's Hospital emigrated from these shores. Canada, Australia, South Africa, New Zealand and India -all the major dominions and colonies of the British Empire -offered opportunities of potential fame and fortune to those starved of opportunity at home. It was not until the 1920's, however, that the USA began to feature regularly as a destination for Wilsonians. There is clear evidence that these young men maintained contact with each other in the USA The foundation of the Wilsonian Club of America in 1935 pledged itself to maintain the bonds of friendship which had been forged in Multyfarnham. There must be good grounds for believing that Wilsonians in the USA were in regular contact with each other before the entry of the USA into the Second World War. It may never be known to what extent they encouraged each other to enlist, but that must be a distinct possibility.

After the end of the First World War, the USA had retreated into 'Splendid Isolation'. In spite of the fact that President Woodrow Wilson had set out the basic principles for a peace settlement in 1918, the USA did not join the League of Nations. The public sentiment was to leave Europeans to sort out Europe's problems. In the 1930's recession fuelled introspection. The rise of fascist dictatorships in Europe was distasteful to the burgeoning democracy of the USA The Nye Report in 1936 indicted Americans for being war profiteers during the Great War. In the same year, a Neutrality Act was passed forbidding the government from selling arms or giving financial aid to countries which were at war.

The election of Franklin D. Roosevelt brought a significant shift in this policy of isolationism. He took the pragmatic view that a European war was certain to affect the USA; the best method of avoiding this was to try to prevent it. Roosevelt did intervene, albeit without success, several times as the crises grew towards a climax in 1939. When war broke out, Roosevelt persuaded Congress to permit arms to be sold to the allies, the 'cash and carry' policy; the USA would sell arms, but the allies had to provide their own ships.

In 1940, in response to constant appeals from Churchill, Roosevelt gave 50 destroyers to the Royal Navy. All the time, the

Pearl Harbour

**Jack Grier (second from left) U.S. Army Paratroops, taken in Paris 1945.
The caption reads "Pigalle Raiders".**

USA was moving closer to direct involvement. Roosevelt was afraid of moving too far ahead of a largely pacifist American public. In this respect, the broadcasts by reporter Ed Murrow from London during the blitz did much to sway opinion in the USA. When the moment of entry came into the war, dramatic as the occasion was, it was historically inevitable. The USA had extensive economic investments in the Far East. The aggression of Japan was a threat which could not be averted. In 1941, Japan proclaimed a protectorate over French Indo-China (Vietnam) which led to immediate diplomatic hostility. The Japanese attack on Pearl Harbour at 1.15 p.m. on December 7th 1941 was a pre-emptive strike which aimed to cripple the American Pacific fleet.

When Roosevelt addressed Congress the following day, he described the attack as "unprovoked and dastardly". It was a day which would "live in infamy". Germany and Italy followed their treaty obligations with Japan and also declared war on the USA. For the next four years, America was once again committed to a World War. This time, however, it would be truly worldwide. From the Philippines to the beaches of Normandy; by land, sea and air, the USA was locked into a mortal combat.

One American to enlist who had been at Wilson's was James Pollock from Kells. He was born in 1905 and had entered the school in August 1918, just three months before the end of

The Great War. He was an able boy. After obtaining 5 honours at the Intermediate Certificate in 1924, he was awarded a scholarship to Mountjoy. From there he went on to Trinity College, Dublin, where he was awarded the 2nd Maths scholarship in 1926. There is a record of him enlisting briefly in the Irish Guards the same year before emigrating to the USA in 1927. His career is not known from that time until July 2nd 1943, when he enlisted in the U.S. Army Military Police. By this time he was 38 years of age, just under the maximum permitted age. James Pollock served until the end of the war and was discharged in November 1945.

David Ramsay from Longford and David Job from County Cavan both enlisted in the American army. David Ramsay was to be the oldest American whom Wilson's had in the war. He was born in 1901. When he left Wilson's after five years in August 1917, he was apprenticed as a shipwright to Mssrs Holloway, South Wall, Dublin. Nine years later he emigrated to the USA and served in the army for 2 years from 1942 to 1943. In that year, he would have achieved his fortieth birthday. It is probable that this brought his discharge before the war ended. David Job arrived in the USA aged 21. He served in the army for three years, being discharged on October 26th 1945.

John James Grier was born in Athboy, County Meath in August 1904. He entered Wilson's hospital on September 13th 1913, aged 9 years and 1 month. He left school six years when he was "put to business by his father in Birmingham", to quote the record of the Warden. Six years he emigrated to the USA. He served with the U.S. Merchant Marine from May 8th 1943 until his discharge on June 7th 1946.

Two Wilsonians served with the U.S. Army Air Corps during World War 11. The first was William Noble from Carigallan, County Leitrim. He was born in 1916 and emigrated to the USA in 1924, two years after leaving school. He served from March 1943 to November 1945. Two American Airborne Divisions, the 82nd and 101st were involved in Operation "Market Garden" at Arnhem in September 1944. Major General Maxwell Taylor's 101st Airborne Division, "The Screaming Eagles", had the task of capturing Eindhoven. This they had

Sgt. Frank E. Fetherston
U.S. Army Air Corps

**Sergeant Frank Fetherston,
U.S. Army Air Corps**

achieved, at no little cost, by 7.00pm on September 18th, the day after they were parachuted into Holland.

The second was Frank Edward West Fetherston from Newtownforbes, County Longford. He was the younger of two brothers who emigrated together to the USA on March 25th 1926. Both boys were born in Liverpool, but when their parents returned to Ireland, they were put to school in Multyfarnham. When Frank and his brother, Seward, arrived in the USA they both settled in New York City. Frank was a choirboy and soloist at St Anne's Church at 140th Street in the Bronx for thirteen years. During that time, his unusual and charming voice won him many friends. He was also connected with the Schola Cantorum Choral Society of New York, where he won distinctions. In August 1942, Frank Fetherston enlisted in the U.S. Army Air Corps "serving with valour and distinction in his outfit." The record continues "On October 10th 1943, Frank made the supreme sacrifice, offering his life on behalf of his country". After the war was over, The Wilsonian Club of America organised the dedication of memorial Hymn Boards to his name in St Anne's Church. This took place on Easter Day, March 28th 1948 at 11.00a.m. Among those present was Frank's elder brother, Seward Henry Lloyd. Seward had enlisted in the U.S.Navy in 1942 and served until the end of the war and his discharge in September 1945.

There were two more men from Wilson's who served in the forces in World War II, the Grier brothers from Granard in County Longford. The younger of the two was John Joseph, known as Jack, who attended Wilson's from 1924 to 1929. He attempted to enlist in the British Army when he was 17, but was disappointed to be rejected merely because he was too young. Jack then emigrated to the United States where he spent the next six years working in the grocery business. He had almost saved enough money to make a return trip to Ireland when a friend put

a more compelling idea to him. They put their funds together, bought a car, and set out to tour America. Jack was greatly taken by California and settled in Los Angeles. It was there that Jack's interest in cricket revived; he had been an enthusiastic player while at Wilson's. Amongst Jack Grier's fellow cricketers in California were well known stars of stage and screen, Boris Karloff, Erroll Flynn and Sir Henry Stevenson. Not content with this esteemed company, however, Jack decided that he must seek his fortune elsewhere. In 1938, he left Los Angeles for Alaska. On the sea voyage north, he met his future wife, Betty, who was on an adventure of her own. Jack Grier's dreams of striking it rich in Alaska never materialised. He panned for gold in the rivers of the North-West, but without the success for which he had hoped. He did, however, find plenty of work. Jack's time in Alaska was fuel for great stories which he loved to tell later in life. He stayed in Alaska until the Japanese attack on Pearl Harbour in December 1941.

In the same month, Jack Grier enlisted in the U.S. Army. After basic training near San Francisco, he volunteered for parachute training. On a fitness march in North Carolina, Jack broke his ankle and missed the despatch of U.S. troops to North America. He was fortunate. His regiment was overrun at Kasserine Pass and suffered heavy casualties. In the USA, Jack

U.S. Argosy from which Jack Grier made his record breaking parachute jump

Jim Grier's crew, RAF Stanton Harcourt, Oxford 1942. Left to right: Jim Grier (Irish), Calder (Scots), Mundell (skipper, Kiwi), Hart and Christie (Canadians)

was assigned to Airborne Command until 1944, where he tested parachute designs. In the course of this work, Jack Grier became the U.S. record holder for free jumps, with 102 successful landings. In 1944, he was sent to England to work with the British Airborne Division, comparing research on parachute development. In 1945, Jack Grier was attached to a British unit operating in Norway and participated in the German surrender of the Luftwaffe Base at Stavanger on May 9th 1945. Jack Grier received several decorations for his war service, of which the highest was the Legion of Merit. He was honourably discharged in December 1946.

James Frederick Grier was Jack's older brother. Born in Granard, County Longford in 1918, James came to Wilson's when he was ten years old. A photograph survives showing him in the Wilson's cricket team in 1934. In front of James, wearing pads and looking assertively towards the camera, is F.G. Calvert who was to lose his life in the RAF seven years later. James obtained Intercert with Honours in 1935 and entered the Provincial Bank in 1937. When war broke out, James Grier volunteered for the RAF and was called up for training in March 1941. In August that year, James found himself on the P & O

Liner Reina del Pacifico, bound for South Africa. The RAF disembarked at Cape Town and were sent 1,500 miles north to Bulawayo for training. Jim remembers only one stop on the three day journey. At Mafeking, dozens of ladies, with mountains of goodies were there to greet the troops. Fruit, cakes, biscuits and cigarettes galore; all gratefully received by men straight from shortages and rationing in Britain.

James Grier spent nearly nine months in Southern Rhodesia learning navigational skills and seeing the country when on leave. By June 1942, he was back in England at RAF Stanton Harcourt near Oxford. His crew was formed there to fly a two-engined Whitley, with two Canadians, one Scotsman, one Englishman and one Irishman (James). They were posted to Cornwall to join Coastal Command. Their duties were to patrol the Western approaches to Brittany in search of German submarines, for which they carried depth charges. At the end of August 1942, they met foul weather on their last patrol and were blown off course. Running short of fuel, the Captain made an emergency landing on a beach as the engines began to falter. The plane was surrounded by German troops who handed them over to the Luftwaffe for interrogation. James Grier now takes up the story in his own words:

"At Frankfurt we were held in solitary confinement for about a week while being questioned time and time again by German civilians who repeatedly asked the same questions in different wording - and with me, they wanted to know what part of Ireland I came from and why I joined the RAF. After a few days, they realised we were "Rookies" with little RAF experience and less information. They treated us quite well. My particular questioner told me he had worked on the Shannon Scheme (Power Station, I think) in 1937 and knew Longford town. He was very friendly, in fact he got me some books to read while in solitary confinement.

From Frankfurt we were moved by train to East Germany - Silesia - to a P.O.W. Camp (Stalag VIIIB, later to be Stalag 344). It was about 100 miles south-east of Breslau (now called Wroeclaw). The camp held between 12,000 & 15,000 British troops most of them taken P.O.W. at Dunkirk 1940, about 1,000

Postkarte from Jim Grier as Prisoner of War 27th September 1942

Canadian troops taken at Dieppe, August 1942, and roughly 1,000 RAF Aircrew. It was a huge camp and all of it sand, sand, sand and little or no grass. It was divided into compounds, each wired off from the next, each accommodating about 1,000 or more P.O.W.'s in 8 or 10 huts to each compound. We could communicate with the people in the next compound through the wire fencing but visiting was 'verboten' at first. Later we were given free access to all compounds and to a large playing field area - a big boost to camp morale. Administration of each compound was left to the senior British N.C.O. and an elected committee. The Germans held a head count morning and evening - there was no oppression, they were quite friendly. The food rations for us were meagre at best, but while the Red Cross parcels kept coming we were not too hungry. One big problem throughout the camp was security of water. It came through to each compound in a trickle. Water queueing was a daily and boring chore and sometimes a source of trouble between comrades. We survived life in the camp by forming little groups of 5 to 10 people, each pooling and sharing everything and looking after each other in sickness and in health."

As soon as he was permitted when taken prisoner, Jim Grier had written a Postkarte to his younger brother, George, then at school in England at Handsworth College: "27th

September 1942. Hello kid. Herewith a note from a Prisoner of War Camp somewhere in Germany. It must be hard to kill a bad thing, otherwise I would have been dead long since. I'm alive and kicking and unhurt. Life here is OK. Cigarette shortage is chief worry. Plenty comrades here. Moving again soon. Jim."

Jim Grier has retained several remarkable photographs from his P.O.W. days in Stalag V111B, Lamsdorf. They were taken in the summer of 1943. In one, the RAF prisoners are seen parading through the camp; a special occasion permitted by the German Camp Commandant. In the second, Jim Grier sits centre stage as Captain of The Irish International Rugby Team, the "Blarney Boys". That summer, the prisoners organised their own rugby competition between the nations represented in the camp. The Irish team were mostly army men, "Real tough guys", Jim writes. The only man whose name he can remember in the photograph (page 125) is "Pop" Press, the coach and physiotherapist "A great man". When the picture was taken, "Pop" was nearly 50 years of age. He was a Royal Marine who had served with Admiral Jackie Fisher in The Great War. The rugby teams were limited to twelve a side as the pitches were small. Included in the competition, in addition to the Home Countries, was a powerful Kiwi side. Rugby buffs will be disappointed to learn that the result of the competition was not an Irish Grand-Slam.

"The freedom of movement within the camp continued until October 1944 when there was a clamp-down following the Great Escape from Sagan - P.O.W. Camp for R.A.F. Officers. From Oct./Nov. 1944 conditions in the camp began to deteriorate when the German transport system collapsed and our Red Cross parcels stopped coming. We knew the situation on the East and West fronts from the illegal radios in camp. Hope kept us going on the decreasing German rations of rye-bread (blackbread), sauerkraut and watery soups.

Come the middle of January 1945, we were warned to prepare to evacuate camp next morning to begin marching westward - away from the Russians. Next day we left camp in compound groups of about 1,000 strong escorted by a "Dad's Army" type of German soldier. They were equally as unfit as we to undertake the journey ahead in dead of winter and intense cold. We had hope; they had none, and feared for their families left behind.

I have little recollection of that march westward, lasting 30 or 40 days. Many died on the way - most of us suffered from dysentry, all of us from hunger and cold but hope kept us going to reach the Elbe River and cross it near Dresden. I recovered consciousness later in a makeshift hospital building with hundreds of others, soldiers and R.A.F. - how we got there I don't know. We were being attended to by U.S. medical personnel of General Patton's Army. They dosed us with a mixture of Nestle's Sweetened Milk and Ovaltine which proved very acceptable to our tummies and an effective antidote to our common problem, dysentry. In time, 3 weeks or so, we were fit enough to be moved to a nearby airfield to await there, for a few days, a flight back to England, courtesy of U.S. Dakota aircraft. These aircraft did a great job flying thousands of ex-P.O.W's back to England from central Germany over a period of time.

There were several thousand of us at the airfield from which I was air lifted. Our flight landed somewhere in the Midlands. We were deloused, showered and reclothed in clean outfits. We smelt good and felt good! Sleeping in a clean, comfortable bed was luxury. A few days later we were bussed to R.A.F. Cosford near Wolverhampton for medical attention.

We were much underweight, very weak and had difficulty in holding down food. A month or so of special dieting and exercise worked wonders and the R.A.F. gave those of us recovering well the option of a month or two's leave at home or staying put in hospital awhile longer. I opted for home and on the Holyhead to Dublin Ferry as we entered Dublin Bay the words "Breathes there a man with soul so dead" kept recurring unbidden in my mind. I felt like crying and very foolish. It was my first return to Ireland since I left in March 1941.

Then back to the R.A.F. some months later and demobolization in 1946 with a new Demob Suit and £135 ex gratia payment - £1 for each week spent as a P.O.W. So endeth one chapter of my life, which I would not have missed for anything, despite the P.O.W. experience."

"The Blarney Boys" Rugby X11, Stalag V111B, Lamsdorf, 1943. James Grier (seated centre). Taken by the official German camp photographer. "Pop" Press, back row (left)

RAF Parade in POW Camp, Stalag V111B, Lamsdorf, 1943

Chapter 28

<u>Epilogue</u>

When the Second World War ended in 1945, vast tracts of Europe lay in ruins. Hitler's Third Reich, which was to last a thousand years, had ended after only twelve. Twenty million people had been killed. As weary soldiers celebrated their relief at being alive, the Gods of war continued to plot further destruction. An Iron Curtain descended on Europe from the Baltic to the Adriatic. The former allies, the U.S.A. and the U.S.S.R., confronted each other across this new front line. The World did not find peace in 1945. An unarmed conflict, the Cold War, gripped the two Superpowers. The line of confrontation extended from Berlin in the West to Korea in the Far East. It was not long before servicemen were called to arms once more.

In Wilson's Hospital, a new Warden, The Reverend Canon Isaac Mayne took over the reins. Three years later, in 1948, a service of Commemoration was held in the School Chapel in

Herbert Sharman

The Very Rev. Henry de Vere White

honour of those who had fallen in the Second World War. The Reverend Henry de Vere White was asked to make the address. One can imagine his feelings as he rose to speak. He and his father had served as Warden successively since 1879. Between them, they would have known all the boys who had fought and died in two European wars. As the casualties figures reached Multyfarnham for the second time in twenty years, they would have made grim reading. In the Second World War, 20.5% lost their lives, compared to 19.5% in The Great War. However, among those who enlisted in the Royal Air Force in 1939, the figure for those killed was 26%. In a small country school, the names would have been known to all. Those who died were not mere statistics but young men who, only a few years earlier, had run and laughed up and down the corridors and across the playing fields.

Herbert Sharman, for so many years the mainstay of the Past Pupils' Association, has left a graphic picture of the scene in the School Chapel when the Former Warden rose to speak. "As we watched him take up his old familiar stance with one elbow on the lectern and heard his voice, we were at once transported back through the years. He chose for his text these appropriate words, "I thank thee God for every remembrance of Thee". At first, as memories came crowding back, his words seemed tinged with sadness. It may have been the wistfulness of a man in the evening time of his years; regret that days of activity in these surroundings were over; sorrow born of the tragedy of War and the many young lives sacrificed."

"But, as he outlined what he termed "The glorious heritage of Wilson's Hospital", he seemed to rise above the sadness. There was much in the past to be proud of and thankful for. He bade us to cherish this heritage of ours of which many were jealous...... Wilson's Hospital was an honourable foundation and down through the years the former pupils had always upheld the fine tradition. We must, he continued, be worthy of that foundation and the sacrifices made by our comrades."

It is appropriate that the joint words of Herbert Sharman and The Reverend Henry de Vere White should lie side by side in the closing chapter of this book. The former Warden had not merely guided the school through some of the most troubled years in the history of this country, he had left for posterity a School Register, copiously maintained throughout his time. Its unique value lies not just in accurate records of former pupils, their parishes and dates of attendance, but in the subsequent notes. Within these lie the seeds from which this research has grown. Herbert Sharman founded the Old Boys' Association in 1929. He was its mainstay for over thirty years. He loved the

school and followed its fortunes with deep interest and concern. The records which he kept, on every aspect of life in the school, have formed the second foundation stone for this research. Many of the photographs come from his scrapbook.

It is not just Wilson's Hospital which owes a debt of gratitude to these two men. Their records shed light on a fragment of Irish history. The story of this school in the first half of the twentieth century helps to reveal truths about a forgotten corner of the history of our country. The soldiers of The Great War, together with those who served in World War 11, have been sidelined by Irish nationalism. The birth of the Irish Free State, transformation to Republic and emergence onto the international stage have produced a narrow concept of Irish history. It is one of the regrettable features of newly independent nations that traditions associated with the ancien regime are considered alien, if not disloyal. Such prejudices dishonour the Irish nation and hide the truth. The men from this country who fought and died in two World Wars were no less Irish than those who considered it their duty to stay at home. Loyalty has many traditions. It is a sign of strength and maturity when a nation recognises and proclaims its different cultures. It is to be hoped that, as the Irish Republic moves into the new millennium, it will grant parity of esteem to all those who espoused the common name of Irishman.

Wilson's Hospital enjoys a rich and colourful history. Moreover, it has the great fortune, almost unique among Church of Ireland schools in the Republic, of retaining the buildings which saw its foundation. The eighteenth century was one of the great eras of architecture. The splendours of this age are among the highlights of our heritage. The foundation by Andrew Wilson

WILSON'S HOSPITAL OLD BOYS' ASSOCIATION

of a Hospital at Multyfarnham for young boys and aged men is part of Irish history. Its architecture alone makes it worthy of note. But a building needs a living tradition to breath life into it.

This research has uncovered aspects of the lives of the young men from one small school in the Midlands of Ireland who served in two World Wars. Between 1891 and 1914, 205 boys were enrolled at Wilson's Hospital, of whom 33% (90) served in The Great War. Between 1919 and 1938, 355 boys enrolled in the school, of whom 30% (104) served in the Second World War. It is a remarkable story, one which forms part of Irish history. It was Herbert Sharman who chose the simple motto "Remember" as the hallmark of the Old Boys' Association which he founded. Today, Wilson's Hospital is a thriving, modern, coeducational school. The Irish Republic is a prosperous member of the European Union. As they move forward into the new millennium, it is to be hoped that neither school nor country will forget its heritage. History is not a burden to be dragged unwillingly into the future. History provides the roots from which a society draws its strength. The young men from Wilson's Hospital who fought and died in defence of freedom in two World Wars deserve a cherished place in the history of their school and their country. They served both well, following the precept learnt in their formative years in Multyfarnham; Res Non Verba - Deeds Not Words.

IN REMEMBRANCE

On 5th September 1933, four boys enrolled together in Wilson's Hospital

Tom Forster
William Hewitt
Brian Ronaldson
Anthony Tottenham

They all lost their lives during the course of World War II

Appendix 1A

<u>Roll Of Honour for the Great War 1914-1918</u>

ABRAHAM, John Richard (3914). Streete, Co. Westmeath.
Entered W.H. January 10th 1912, aged 10 years 6 months. Withdrawn by his mother. Joined Royal Air Force August 1918. (See Cap 14)

ALEXANDER, David I. (3721). Athboy, Co. Meath.
Entered W.H. November 2nd 1896, aged 9 years 10 months. Obtained Clerkship in Paymaster's Office G.S.W.R. War Service.

ANDERSON, Charles Sellery (3890). Clonfadforan, Co. Westmeath.
Entered W.H. July 1909 aged 8. Apprenticed to Belvedere Gardens June 15th 1916. Enlisted King's Royal Rifles January 1918. (See Cap 6)

ARMSTRONG, Frederick (3834). Co. Meath.
Entered W.H. August 14th 1905 aged 11 years. Gardener, Cloverhill, Co. Cavan. Joined Royal Navy 1913. On H.M.S. Majestic. Torpedoed Dardenelles 1915. In Battle of Jutland May 31st 1916. First Class Stoker. Visited School August 29th 1917. (See Cap 5,6,10)

W BAKER, Robert Corbett (3813). Ardluccan, Co. Meath.
Entered W.H. August 27th 1903 aged 10 years 2 months. Enlisted for war 1915. Wounded 1916.

W BARNARD, George R. (3755). Agher, Co. Meath.
Entered W.H. February 4th 1898 aged 10 years. His father undertakes to get him employment. Enlisted for war 1914.

* BARNARD, Thomas Sherwood (3796). Agher, Co. Westmeath.
Entered W.H. January 21st 1902, aged 11 years. Did not return after Christmas Vacation 1903. Enlisted for war 1914.

†* BELL, James William White (3677). Limerick.
Entered W.H. August 17th 1891 aged 10 yrs 5 months. Nominated by Bishop of Meath. Enlisted in Royal Munster Fusiliers. 2nd Lt. 3rd Btn. Leinster Rgt. Killed in France September 1917. (See Cap 5, 10)

W BOWER, Joseph (3713). Killucan, Co. Westmeath.
Entered W.H. January 22nd 1894 aged 10 years 10 months. To William Bower, Shoemaker, Killucan. Enlisted for war.

W BOWER, William (3735). Killucan, Co. Westmeath.
Entered W.H. July 6th 1896 aged 11 years. January 1898, his uncle, Colonel Clarke of Killucan undertook to provide for him. Captain (retired) 1929 in Christchurch, Hampshire.

BRADY, Frederick (3716). Moyne Co. Westmeath.
Entered W.H. January 22nd 1894 aged 10 years 7 months. Gardener, Clover Hill, Co. Cavan. Enlisted for War 1915. (See Cap 5)

W BULLICK, Robert (3621). Navan, Co. Meath.
Entered W.H. April 24th 1889 aged 10 years. General Merchant, Dungannon. Enlisted at War 1915.

W BYRNE, Henry (3823). Kells, Co. Westmeath.
Entered W.H. August 15th 1904 aged 11 years. Blacksmith, Moynalty, Co. Meath. Enlisted. Badly wounded June 1915.

† * CARLETON, Percy (3779). Delvin, Co. Westmeath.
Entered W.H. May 13th 1900 aged 7 years 8 months. Elected as free pupil of Masonic Orphan School, Dublin 1901. In War 1915-1918. Princess Patricia's Canadian Light Infantry. Died January 1919, result of exposure in France. (See Cap 6)

COX, George (3879). Almoritia, Co. Westmeath.
Entered W.H. November 9th 1908, aged 10 years 2 months. Apprenticed to Drapery Business, Belfast April 8th 1913. Enlisted for War 1915. (See Cap 6)

W ELLIOT, William G. (3835). Tunchoe, Queen's County.
Entered W.H. January 8th 1907, aged 11 years 5 months. Obtained Assisted Scholarship, Incorporated Society June 1908. Enlisted for War 1915.

ELLIS, Robert Alex (3718). Balbriggan, Dublin.
Entered W.H. April 26th 1894 aged 10 years 7 months. Obtained Clerkship in Civil Service. Enlisted for War 1915.

W FARLEY, Thomas (3815). Navan, Co. Meath.
Entered W.H. October 12th 1903 aged 9 years. Obtained an Assisted Scholarship, Incorporated Society. At Sligo Grammar School. Returned as Assistant Master Sept. 29th 1913. Enlisted Royal Dublin Fusiliers June 1916. 2nd Lieutenant Royal Irish Rifles 1st March 1917, 1st/4th Btn. On Tea Estate, Assam 1919. Visited school 1925, 1929. "Doing very well". (HVW) (See Cap 9)

W FRY, James (3712). Leney, Co. Westmeath,
Entered W.H. March 1893 aged 7 years. His father, having got a farm near Ardloghen, Co. Cavan, took him to live there in 1900. He was born at the Gate Lodge of Wilson's Hospital January 25th 1896 and baptised in School Chapel on April 12th 1886. Enlisted Royal Inniskilling Fusiliers November 1906. Wounded 1915 in Dardanelles. (See Cap 10)

GILMORE, Francis E. (3844). Derryhene, Co. Cavan.
Entered W.H. July 28th 1906 aged 11years. Mother undertook for him in England March 1908. Enlisted for war.
(See Cap 7)

GILMORE, William (3802). Derryhene, Cavan.
Entered W.H. August 15th 1904 aged 11 years 9 months. Left to be a gardener, June 30th 1907 Enlisted at war 1915. (See Cap 7)

W * HALL, Thomas Henry G. (3816). Bahallboyne, Co. Meath.
Entered W.H. January 9th 1904, aged 9 years 6 months. Obtained an Assisted Scholarship, Incorporated Society 1900. Ranelagh School. Enlisted 1915. Wounded and Missing at Dardanelles 1915. Safe in Dublin 1916. Went out again. Wounded second time, France. (See Cap 7)

W HALLIGAN, John (3880). Laracor, Meath.
Entered W.H. August 8th 1908. Went Kennans and sons, Fishamble St., Dublin, December 1913. Enlisted July 1917 Royal Artillery. Wounded in France 1918. In India 1920. Sergeant Indian police, Calcutta June 1923.

* HARVEY, Charles Dane (3659). Athboy, Co. Meath.
Entered W.H. January 14th 1891 aged 11.6 years. Nominated by Lord Primate. In Accountant General's Office, Bank of Ireland, Dublin 1901. Lt. Royal Dublin Fusiliers 1915. (Gallipoli) (See Cap 5, 10)

W HASSARD, Francis (3788). Moyne, Co. Westmeath.
Entered W.H. July 1901 aged 7 years. Gardener, Killegar August 25th 1908. Enlisted for War 1914 Royal Irish Rifles, Photograph Sharman Scrapbook. (See Cap 5)

† * HEGARTY, John (3681). Nobber, Co. Meath
Entered W.H. August 1891 aged 11. 2nd Btn Irish Guards. Died of wounds 15th September 1916. Husband of Anne Kate of Castlekiernan, Co. Meath. Grave No 11.D.64 in La Neuville Cemetery, Somme. (See Cap 6)

† HODGINS, Joseph Thomas (3737). Ardbraccan, Co. Meath.
Entered W.H. August 24th 1896 aged 10 years 10 months. Saddler, Killeshandra, Co. Cavan. Enlisted in Inniskilling Dragoons. Missing 1915. (See Cap 6)

HOURIGAN, Francis J. (3860). Mullingar, Co. Westmeath.
Entered W.H. February 1st 1907, aged 11 years. Sent as Gibson Hall Scholar to Ranelagh School, August 1909. Apprentice to Motor Garage, Mullingar. Enlisted Mechanical Transport, September 1916. (See Cap 5,6)

HOYSTED, Reginald.
Name on original Roll of Honour. No further Information

JONES, William James (3830). Cavan.
Entered W.H. August 14th 1905 aged 10 yrs 5 months. His father provided for him 1907. Visited school May 15th 1920. "Doing well in San Francisco" (Railway Clerk).(HVW)

W KELLS, George William (3808). Ballyconnell, Co. Cavan.
Entered W.H. August 20th 1903 aged 11 years. Obtained an Assisted Scholarship, Incorporated Society. In business in Athlone 1910. Enlisted at war 1915. Sergeant 1915. Wounded.

† KELLY, Austin (3866). Clonmellon, Co. Westmeath.
Entered W.H. September 12th 1907, aged 10 years 10 months. Went as Clerk to Lloyd's Shipping Co. Killed Suvla Bay, Dardanelles, August 16th 1915. Austin Kelly. "C" Coy. 7th Batt. Royal Dublin Fusiliers. Killed in action 16th August 1915 at Gallipoli, his unit held the line at Kiretch Tepe Sirth at Suvla. Name on Hellcs Memorial. (See Cap 10)

†* LAVERTY, Joseph. 2nd Lt. Home address unknown (Master).
Royal Irish Rifles. Enlisted in Dublin. Killed in action 16th August 1917. His unit was involved in heavy fighting at Hill 35 during the Battle of Langemarck, in France. The 13th Batt. were part of the 36th (Ulster Division).(See Cap 9,13)

LEAHEY, Jeremiah (3881). Kildrumferton, Cavan.
Entered W.H. Jan. 12th 1909 aged 10 years 4 months. Went Kildare Street club, December 11th 1913. "A very good boy!" (HVW) Enlisted Inniskilling Fusiliers, June 1915. Too young for active service. In Tramway Company, Burnley Dec. 1915. Enlisted R.F.A. Jan. 1917. In Army in India 1923.

W LEAHEY, John G. (3852). Kells, Co. Meath.
Entered W.H. January 8th 1907 aged 11 years. Provided for by friends who bound him to trade at home July 1st 1910. Enlisted for war 1914 Royal Dublin Fusiliers.

LEAHEY, Joseph (3882). Kildrumferton, Cavan.
Entered W.H. Jan 12th 1909, aged 10 years 4 months. Went to be trained as chauffeur September 1915. "Came back to me" (HVW) Feb 1916. Enlisted Motor Transport March 26th 1917. "A very reliable straightforward boy". (HVW) (See Cap 5,6)

LITTLE, William J. (3391). St. Peter's Athlone.
Entered W.H. Dec. 15th 1876 aged 8 years 6 months. Left January 1st 1882 to Porteus and Gibbs, Wicklow St., Dublin. In Australian Expeditionary Force in France September 1916. Visited School, August 29th 1917 on leave. (See Cap 6)

W LOUGHEED Walter Ellis (3877). Ballyboy, King's County.
Entered W.H. August 24th 1908. Went to hardware business, July 15th 1913. Went to England. On Midlands Railway, Sheffield, (in engine shed) August 1915. Enlisted 1915 Yorkshire Rgt. Wounded in action May 3rd 1917. Gains Military Medal 1918. Engine Driver, Midlands Railway 1920. (See Cap 7)

LOUGHEED, Richard (3856). Ballyboy, King's County.
Entered W.H. January 8th 1907, aged 10 years 6 months. Assisted scholarship June 1st 1910 Enlisted for War 1915 Royal Army Medical Corps. (See Cap 7)

MARTIN George (3866). Roscommon.
Entered W.H. Sept 12th 1907. Went to service February 17th 1912, Wm Gibbs, Co. Westmeath. Enlisted Royal Army Medical Corps 1915. M.S.M. (See Cap 5, 7)

MARTIN, Frederick (3839) Roscommon.
Entered W.H. August 22nd 1905 10 years 8 months Parents provided for him 1908. Enlisted for war 1914. Awarded D.C.M. March 1916. M.M. (See Cap 7)

MARTIN, William (3729). Roscommon.
Entered W.H. January 11th 1896 aged 11 years. In 1899 His father put him to business near him in Dublin. Enlisted for War 1915. (See Cap 7)

MC ALLISTER, Robert Arthur (3921). Mullingar, Co. Westmeath.
Entered W.H. Sept. 9th 1912 aged 10 yrs 3 months. Born 7/6/02. Went to H.M.S. Impregnable Training Ship, Royal Navy, Devonport, January 28th 1918. Got Advanced Gunnery. (See Cap 6)

W MC CORMACK, Harold R. (3841). Drumcree, Co. Westmeath.
Entered W.H. January 20th 1906 aged 9 years 6 months. Obtained Assisted Scholarship at Sligo Grammar School 1910. Enlisted in North of Ireland Horse 1916. Transferred 1st Btn. Royal Irish Rifles in France 1916. Gained Commission Royal Munster Fusiliers March 1918. Badly wounded October 1918. (See Cap 7)

W McCORMACK, J. Albert (3854) Drumcree, Co. Westmeath.
Entered W.H. January 8th 1907, aged 12 years 1 month. "Too delicate when first sent for". (HVW) Apprenticed to watchmaking business, Ballyboy, Co. Monaghan June 30th 1911. Enlisted for war 1915. Invalided home 1916. Out in France Oct. 1917-1918. Wounded April 1918. (See Cap 7)

W MCCREDDIN, Robert J. (3867). Longford.
Entered W.H. Sept. 12th 1907 aged 10 years 11 months. Provided for by parents who kept him back after holidays July 1913. Enlisted Royal Army Medical Corps 1915. Royal Irish Regiment 1917.

† * McMANUS, John J. (3859). Ballymachugh, Co. Cavan.
Entered W.H. January 28th 1907. Parents provided for him 1909. 2nd Btn. Leinster Rgt. Killed in Action aged 20 4th June 1918. Grave No. I, F, 24, Ebblingham Military Cemetery, Nord France.

McNEILL, William Albert (3847). Cloone, Leitrim.
Entered W.H. September 17th 1906, aged 10 years 5 months. Provided for by parents August 1911. In business in Liverpool 1914. Enlisted 1915 Lancashire Fusiliers.

MONTSERRAT, Edward Villiers. Tullamore, King's County.
Entered W.H. October 27th 1912 aged 12 yrs 1 month. Born 22/9/01 Left December 22 nd 1917. Joined H.M.S. Impregnable Training Ship, Royal Navy Feb. 4th 1918. Got Advanced Wireless Telegraphy. (See Cap 6)

W MORRIS Ernest.
Name on original Roll of Honour. No further Information

MORROW, Robert William (3875). Clonbroney, Longford.
Entered W.H. July 17th 1908 aged 11 years 3 months. Went to service Feb. 24th 1913. Outfit given. In service at Wilson's Hospital 1915. Left 1917. Enlisted 1918 (See Cap 5)

NEEDHAM, Henry (3895). Longford.
Entered W.H. July 1909, aged 9 years 5 months. Went to service to Miss Godley, Killegar House, Killeshandra, Co. Cavan, December 23rd 1914. Enlisted 1917 Royal Field Artillery. (See Cap 5)

† NELSON, Thomas William (3734). Mullingar, Co. Westmeath.
Entered W.H. July 6th 1896 aged 9 years 8 months. Obtained a Free Scholarship at Ranelagh School, Athlone. Clothing supplied by HWW. Gained clerkship G.S.G.R. by Open Competition 1903. Outfit presented by HWW. C.P.R. Stationmaster 1912. Sgt. Canadian 202 Rgt. 1916. Killed 1917. (See Cap 5,6)

† * NELSON, William George (3607). Edenderry.
Entered W.H. 1887 aged 9 years. Enlisted for war 1914, 9th Battalion Royal Inniskilling Fusiliers. Killed at the Somme, 1st July 1916. Name on Thiepval Memorial. (See Cap 11)

NERIN, Robert S. (3843). Longford.
Entered W.H. February 19th 1906 aged 9 years 4 months. Enlisted for war.

NERIN, William J. (3842). Longford.
Entered W.H. February 19th 1906, aged 10 years 8 months. Parents, who are changing their residence, removed boys. Travelling expenses defrayed (H.W.W.). Sept 8th 1906. Enlisted for war.

NORTH, Daniel (3793). Cloverhill, Cavan.
Entered W.H. Jan. 10th 1902 aged 8. Enlisted Royal Navy 1909. (See Cap 6)

NUMMY, Hugh (3948). Newry, Co. Down.
Entered W.H. August 13th 1914, aged 12years 5 months. Born 7/3/02. Went H.M.S. Impregnable Training Ship for Royal Navy, January 28th 1918 (Devonport) Passed for Wireless Telegraphy. (See Cap 6)

W PAKENHAM, George Henry (3794). Killucan, Co. Westmeath.
Entered W.H. January 21st 1902, aged 10 years 11 months. Went to service in Dunboden, August 1904. Enlisted in Leinster Regiment 1911. Badly wounded February 1915. (See Cap 5,10)

W * PATTON, Albert George (3792). Collinstown, Co. Westmeath.
Entered W.H. January 10th 1902 aged 11 years. Went to business, Ballymahon 1904. Went into R.I.C.

PATTON, Charles Nichols (3811). Collinstown, Co. Westmeath.
Entered W.H. August 12th 1903 aged 10 years 11 months. Obtained an Assisted Scholarship, Incorporated Society. Grange School 1905. Enlisted for war 1915.

* PATTON, Robert M. (3855). Collinstown, Co. Westmeath.
Entered W.H. January 8th 1907, aged 11 years 8 months. Mother provided for him August 1909. Enlisted for War 1915.

PIGOTT, John Drummond (3754). Kilkenny West, Co. Westmeath.
Entered W.H. February 3rd 1898 aged 11years. Gardener, Loughcrew, Co. Meath. Enlisted for War 1915. (See Cap 5)

* PRATT, David (3722). Agher, Co. Meath.
Entered W.H. March 1895 aged 11 years. Enlisted Royal Horse Artillery 1899.(See Cap 6)

W SAVAGE, Charles J. (3818). Donaghpatrick, Co. Meath.
Entered W.H. January 11th 1904 aged 11 years. Gardiner, Ballina, Co. Mayo. Enlisted for war 1915. (See Cap 5, 7)

†* SAVAGE, George (3786). Donaghpatrick, Co. Meath.
1st Batt. Royal Irish Rifles. Enlisted in Dublin. Home address Balrath Co. Meath. Killed in action France 4th March 1917, aged 26, formerly R.A.M.C. No further information. (See Cap 7)

† * SAVAGE, Robert (3739). Donaghpatrick, Co. Meath.
Entered W.H. August 24th 1896 aged 9 years 5 months. Merchant, Co. Carlow. 1st Batt. Royal Dublin Fusiliers. Killed in action, 8th August 1918, Age 31. Son of Robt. and Frances Savage of Co. Meath. Buried in Borre British Cemetery Nord France. Grave No. II.G.I3. (See Cap 7)

† SCHOALES, George (3769). Clara, King's County.
Entered W.H.October 19th 1899 aged 9 years. Gardener, Clover Hill, Co. Cavan. East Lancs. Rgt. Killed near Ypres May 10th 1915. (See Cap 5, 7, 13)

SCHOALES, William (3790). Clara, King's County.
Entered W.H. July 1901 aged 9 years. Unfit for school 1903. Enlisted 1915 Loyal North Lancashire Rgt. 2nd Lieutenant. (See Cap 7)

W SELVEY, Robert (3886). Ballyboy, King's County.
Entered W.H. July 1909 aged 11 years. Went to service June 21st 1913, Clover Hill, Co. Cavan. Enlisted 5th Lancers 1915. Discharged from army, unfit due to being gassed on active service 1917. (See Cap 14)

SMYTH, Charles Wilson (3916). St. Peter's, Dublin.
Entered W.H. April 1912 aged 9 years 11 months. Band Boy, 3rd Battalion, Royal Scots Guards, February 15th, 1918

W SOMERSETT, Isaiah (3820). Kilbixy, Co. Westmeath.
Entered W.H. January 16th 1904 aged 9 years 10 months. Went as clerk to land agent's office in Limerick, July 31st 1910. Clerk in Army Pay Depot 1914. At the Front 1915. Transferred to K.R.R. 1916, Sergeant. Commissioned on 26th April 1917 into the 9th West Belfast Service Batt., Royal Irish Rifles. 2nd Lieut. Gained Military Cross, France, 1918. Wounded 1916, 1917. Rich man in Stock Exchange, Johannesburg, S.A. (HVW) (See Cap 8, 11)

† **SOMERSETT, William Henry (3805). Kilbixy, Co. Westmeath.**
Entered W.H. August 8th 1902 aged 11 years. Obtained an Assisted Scholarship, Incorporated Society. Enlisted for War 1915. Listed as 'missing' on original Roll of Honour. (See Cap 8)

SOMERVILLE, William (3744). Clonfadforan, Co. Westmeath.
Entered W.H. November 21st 1896, aged 8 years 11 months Obtained Scholarship at Ranelagh School. Clerkship GSWR. Enlisted for War.

* **STOTESBURY, Thomas W. (3896). Almoritia, Co. Westmeath.**
Entered W.H. May 12th 1910, aged 9 years 5 months. Went to Mr. Sanderson, Cloverhill, 1916, outfit given. Joined Army September 1918. (See Cap 6)

W **STRONG, George Clarence (3801). Mount Nugent, Co. Cavan.**
Entered W.H. August 4th 1902, aged 10 years 8 months. Emigrated to Quebec 1908. £10 passage paid HWW. Enlisted for war 1915, 13th Canadian Highlanders. Gains Military Medal. Visited W.H. 1918. "Has own farm in Canada." (HVW)
(See Cap 6)

STRONG, Stephen Henry (3835). Mount Nugent, Co. Cavan.
Entered W.H. August 14th 1905 aged 9 years. Left for Canada November 26th 1910. Enlisted American Flying Corps 1918. Visited School May 15th 1920. "Doing well in San Francisco" (Railway Clerk).(HVW) (See Cap 6)

† * **TENNANT, Philip Eyre (3680). Tipperary.**
Entered W.H. August 17th 1891 aged 11 years 10 months. Nominated by Bishop of Kilmore. Sec. Lieut. Connaught Rangers. Son of Late John Tennant, Esq., Parkstown, Thurles, Co. Tipperary. (See Cap 12, 13)

† **THOMPSON, Edward (3831). Moate, Co. Westmeath.**
Entered W.H. March 20th 1905 aged 8 years 9 months. Father kept him to train for his work about horses, June 1907. Enlisted for war 1914. (See Cap 6)

THOMPSON, John Henry (3781). Moate, Co. Westmeath.
Entered W.H. August 18th 1900, aged 9 years 3 months. Enlisted Royal Horse Artillery 1908. (See Cap 6)

† **THOMPSON, William (3791). Moate, Co. Westmeath.**
Entered W.H. August 19th 1901, aged 8 years. Enlisted for war 1914. Killed 1916. (Not listed as killed on original Roll of Honour) (See Cap 6)

TILSON, Henry John (3895). Rathaspic, Co. Westmeath.
Entered W.H. May 12th 1910 aged 11 years. Apprenticed to Beleveder Gardens, January 6th 1912. Broke his apprenticeship June 1913. Joined Royal Artillery, August 1914. (See Cap 6)

W **VERE, Henry de, Lt.**
Science Master W.H. Died of Wounds after the war. (See Cap 9)

* **WACKETT, Arthur (3656). Navan, Co. Meath.**
Entered W.H. January 14th 1891 aged 11 years. Confirmed April 17th 1896. Stud Groom, Oakham, Rutland. 5th Lancers 1915-1918. Visited the school July 10th 1930. In Nottingham July 1930. (See Cap 5)

† **WALKER, William (3710). Kilkenny West, Westmeath.**
Entered W.H. March 1893 aged 9 years. Nominated by Colonel Magill. Domestic service Killucan. Enlisted 1915. (See Cap 5)

W **WEIR, Victor (3950). Tinahely, Wicklow.**
Entered W.H. August 15th 1914 aged 12 years 9 months, Born 3/11/01. Left school December 21st 1916. Went to Halleck and Best, plumbers, Lombard St., Dublin. Left, Master Plumber (Feb 1917). Enlisted Royal Field Artillery Sept. 1917. in France Sept. 1918. Wounded 1918. U.S. Navy, November 1919. (See Cap 5, 6)

†* **WILSON, Arthur William (3833). Kingstown, Dublin.**
Entered W.H. 14th August 1905 aged 11 years. Undertaken June 30th 1907. Enlisted 8th Btn. Royal Dublin Fusiliers. Killed in action 1916, aged 22 years. Son of Robert and Amy Clarence Wilson. No known grave. Name on the Special Memorial No. 45, Bois-Carre Military Cemetery, Pas de Calais, France. (See Cap 5)

WILSON, David (3673). Armagh.
Entered W.H. July 18th 1891 aged 9 years. In Kildare Street Club 1900. Had previously been employed in Adelaide Hospital. Enlisted for war. (See Cap 5)

WILSON, James (3870). St. Thomas, Dublin.
Entered W.H. July 7th 1908, aged 9 years. Got Clerkship, Millar's Wine Merchants, Thomas Street, Dublin. Left W.H. June 23rd 1915. Royal Navy 1918.

WILSON, Joseph Fitzwilliam (3807). Billis, Co. Cavan.
Entered W.H. August 11th 1903 aged 10 years 7 months. Obtained an Assisted Scholarship, Incorporated Society to Ranelagh School. Gained Clerkship W.R. 1910. Royal Dublin Fusiliers. Listed on original Roll of Honour with † (See Cap 5)

WILSON, Richard (3797). Temple Michael, Longford.
Entered W.H. 1st March 1902 aged 10 yrs. Apprenticed to saddler, Balturbet, Cavan 1905. No service details. Name on original Roll of Honour. Enlisted for War. (See Cap 5)

† WOODS, Ernest Victor (3846). Moyne, Co. Westmeath.
Entered W.H. August 13th 1906, aged 11 years 2 months. Father undertook for him 1910. 9th batt. Royal Dublin Fusiliers, died of wounds 20th August 1917, Age 22. Son of John Woods of Castlepollard Co. Westmeath. His unit was part of the 48 brigade in the assult at Langemarck, Third Ypres Offens. Buried in Lijssenthoek Military Cemetery Belgium. Grave No. XVII.H.20. Private Ernest Victor Woods, 11th Royal Dublin Fusiliers.

W   WOODS, James Thomas Harold (3872). Moyne, Co. Westmeath
Gained First Free Scholarship, Ranelagh School June 1st 1910. Got into bank 1914. Royal Dublin Fusiliers 1914. Sergeant 1917. Commission 1918. (See Cap 5, 13)

Total Numbers Enlisted 93
47 (50.5%) were killed or wounded.

*   -   Name not Listed on Original Roll of Honour (16).
W - Wounded in action (27).
†   -   Paid the Supreme Sacrifice (20).
The numbers (in brackets) refer to the computerised number on the School Register.

HVW: Reverend Henry de Vere White (Warden 1912-1945)
HWW: Reverend Hill Wilson White (Warden 1879-1912)

<u>Roll of Honour for the Great War 1914-1918</u>

	John Abraham.	†	Austin Kelly.		John Pigott.
	David Alexander.	† *	Joseph Laverty, Lt.	*	David Pratt.
	Charles Anderson		Jeremiah Leahey.	W	Charles Savage.
	Frederick Armstrong.	W	John G. Leahey.	†	George Savage.
W	Robert Baker.		Joseph Leahey.	† *	Robert Savage.
W	George Barnard.		William Little.	†	George Schoales.
*	Thomas Barnard.		Richard Lougheed.		William Schoales, Lt.
† *	James Bell, Lt.	W	Walter Lougheed, M.M.	W	Robert Selvey.
W	Joseph Bower.		Frederick Martin, D.C.M., M.M.		Charles Smyth.
W	William Bower, Captain.		George Martin, M.S.M.	W	Isaiah Somersett, Lt., M.C.
	Frederick Brady.		William Martin.	†	William Somersett.
W	Robert Bullick.		Robert Mc Allister.		William Somerville.
W	Henry Byrne.	W	Albert Mc Cormack.	*	Thomas Stotesbury.
† *	Percy Carleton.	W	Harold Mc Cormack, Lt.	W	George Strong, M.M.
	George Cox.	W	Robert Mc Creddin.		Stephen Strong.
W	William Elliot.	† *	John Mc Manus.	† *	Philip Tennant, Lt.
	Robert Ellis.		William Mc Neill.	†	Edward Thompson.
W	Thomas Farley, Lt.		Edward Montserrat.		John Thompson.
W	James Fry.	W	Ernest Morris.	†	William Thompson.
	Francis Gilmore.		Robert Morrow.		Henry Tilson.
	William Gilmore.		Henry Needham.	W	Henry de Vere, Lt.
W *	Henry Hall.	†	Thomas Nelson, Sgt.	*	Arthur Wackett.
W	John Halligan.	† *	William Nelson.	†	William Walker.
*	Charles Harvey, Lt.		Robert Nerin.	W	Victor Weir.
W	Francis Hassard.		William Nerin.	† *	Arthur William Wilson.
† *	John Hegarty.		Daniel North.		David Wilson.
†	Joseph Hodgins.		Hugh Nummy.		James Wilson.
	Francis Hourigan.	W	George Pakenham.		Wm. Joseph Wilson, 2nd Lt.
	Reginald Hoysted.	W *	Albert Patton.		Richard Wilson.
	William Jones.		Charles Patton.	†	Ernest Woods.
W	George Kells, Sgt.	*	Robert Patton.	W	Harold Woods, Lt.

* name not listed on original Roll of Honour.

W Wounded

† Paid the Supreme Sacrifice

Appendix 2A

Soldiers of The Great War listed by County of Birth

ARMAGH (1)
David Wilson

CAVAN (11)
Francis Gilmore
William Gilmore
William Jones
w   George Kells
Jeremiah Leahey
Joseph Leahey
*+   John McManus
Daniel North
w   George Strong
Stephen Strong
William Joseph Wilson

DOWN (1)
Hugh Nummy

DUBLIN (4)
Robert Ellis
Charles Smyth
*+   Arthur William Wilson
James Wilson

KING'S COUNTY (7)
Richard Lougheed
w   Walter Lougheed
Edward Montserrat
*+   William Nelson
+   George Schoales
William Schoales
w   Robert Selvey

LEITRIM (1)
William McNeill

LIMERICK (1)
*+   James Bell

LONGFORD (6)
w   Robert McCreddin
Robert Morrow
Robert Nairn
William Nairn
Henry Needham
Richard Wilson

MEATH (17)
David Alexander
Frederick Armstrong
w   Robert Baker
w   George Barnard
w   Robert Bullick
w   Thomas Farley
*w   Henry Hall
w   John Halligan
w   John G. Leahey
*   Charles Harvey
*+   Joseph Hegarty
+   Joseph Hodgins
*   David Patt
w   Charles Savage
*+   George Savage
+   Robert Savage
*   Arthur Wackett

QUEEN'S COUNTY (1)
w   William Elliot

ROSCOMMON (3)
George Martin
Frederick Martin
William Martin

TIPPERARY (1)
*+   Philip Tennant

WESTMEATH (34)
John Abraham
Charles Anderson
*   Thomas Barnard
w   Joseph Bower
w   William Bowers
w   Henry Byrne
Frederick Brady
*+   Percy Carleton
George Cox
w   James Fry
w   Francis Hassard
Francis Hourigan
+   Austin Kelly
William Little
Robert McAllister
w   James McCormack
w   Harold McCormack
+   Thomas Nelson
w   George Pakenham
w   George Patton
*   Charles Patton

Soldiers of The Great War listed by County of Birth contd.

*	Robert Patton		Henry Tilson	w	Ernest Morri
	John Piggott	+	William Walker	*+	Joseph Laverty
w	Isaiah Somersett	+	Ernest Woods	w	Henry de Vere
	William Somersett	+	Harold Woods		
	William Somerville				

WICKLOW (1)

w   Victor Weir

*   Robert Patton

John Piggott

w   Isaiah Somersett

William Somersett

William Somerville

*   Thomas Stotesbury

+   Edward Thompson

John Thompson

+   William Thompson

UNKNOWN (4)

Reginald Hoysted

Total: 93

+   (20) paid the supreme sacrifice.

w   (27) wounded.

*   (16) not listed on original

Soldiers of The Great War listed by Regiment

Australian Expeditionary Force
Pte William Little

Canadian 202 Regiment
+   Pte Thomas Nelson

13th Canadian Highlanders
+   Pte George Strong M.M.

Connaught Rangers
+   2nd Lt. Philip Tennant

East Lancs Regiment
+   George Schoales

Inniskilling Dragoons
+   Pte Joseph Hodgins

Irish Guards
+   Pte John Hegarty

King's Royal Rifles
Pte Charles Anderson

Lancashire Fusiliers
Pte William McNeill

Leinster Regiment
w   Pte Pte John McManus
+   Pte George Pakenham

Loyal North Lancs Regiment
2nd Lt William Schoales

Mechanical Transport
+   Pte Francis Hourigan
Pte Joseph Leahey

North of Ireland Horse
w   Pte Harold McCormack

Princess Patricia's Canadian Light Infantry
+   Percy Carleton

Royal Air Force
John Abraham

Royal Army Medical Corps
Pte Richard Lougheed
Ptd George Martin
+   Pte Robert McCreddin

Royal Dublin Fusiliers
w   Pte Thomas Halt
2nd Lt Charles Harvey
Pte Francis Hassard
+   Pte Austin Kelly
Pte John Leahey
+   Pte Robert Savage
2nd Lt. Harold Woods
+   Pte Ernest Woods

Soldiers of The Great War listed by Regiment contd.

+   Pte Arthur Wm Wilson
     2nd Lt. Joseph Wm Wilson

Royal Field Artillery

w   Pte John Halligan
     Pte Henry Needham
     Ptd Henry Tilson
     Pte Victor Weir

Royal Horse Artillery

     Pte David Pratt
     Pte John Thompson

Royal Inniskilling Fustiliers

w   Pte James Fry
     Pte Jeremiah Leahey
+   Pte William Nelson

5th Royal Irish Lancers

     Pte Robert Selvey
     Pte Arthur Wackett

Royal Irish Regiment

     Pte Robert McCreddin

Royal Irish Rifles

     2nd Lt Thomas Farley
+   2nd Lt Joseph Laverty
+   Pte George Savage
w   2nd Lt Isaiah Somerett M.C.

Royal Munster Fusiliers

+   Capt James Bell
     Pte John Piggott
w   Lt Harold McCormack

Royal Navy

     A/B Frederick Armstrong
     A/B Robert McAllister
     A/B Edward Montserrat
     A/B Daniel North
     A/B Hugh Nummy
     A/B James Wilson

Royal Scots Guards

     Pte Charles Smyth

The West Yorkshire Regiment

     Pte Walter Lougheed M.M.

U.S. Flying Corps

     Stephen Strong

Appendix 3

Analysis by date and age on enlistment

YEAR OF ENLISTMENT	NUMBER ENLISTMENT	AVERAGE AGE
Before 1914	12	18. 5
1914	15	22. 5
1915	32	24. 7
1916	3	21. 0
1917	5	18. 2
1918	11	17.4*
not known		16 not known
TOTALS	93	22.4

* those enlisting in 1918 include 5 boys sailors/soldiers

Appendix 4

Analysis of killed and wounded in The Great War

90 boys and 3 staff enlisted for The Great War

W 27 (29%) were wounded in action

+ 20 (21.5%) paid the supreme sacrifice

Roll of Honour for the Second World War 1939-1945

ABBOTT, James Richard (4091). Mohill, Co. Leitrim.
Entered W.H. May 24th 1924 aged 12 years 5 months Left July 1927 to go into business.British Army 1929.

ANDERSON, L.E. (Master).
Royal Inniskilling Fusiliers.

BEACOM, William J.C. (4300). Aughnacloy, Co. Tyrone.
Entered W.H. September 1935 aged 12. Left July 1936. Royal Signals Radion Security Service 1939-1945. (See Cap 25)

BEALE, Eric Edward (4175). Athboy, Co. Meath.
Entered W.H. Sept 7th 1929 aged 10 yrs 5 months. Entered King's Hospital 1931. R.A.F. 1940

BLACKBURN R.H.N. (4381). Co. Tyrone.
Entered W.H. September 6th 1938 aged 11.10 years. Left July 1941. Services.

† BOUMPHREY, Arnold (4153). St. George's, Dublin
Entered W.H. Nov. 26th 1927, aged 10 yrs. Left Xmas 1933. R.A.F. 1939 Killed evacuation of B.E.F. June 17th 1940 aged 23, flying a Lancaster. Member of 73 Squadron R.A.F. Name on Runnymede Memorial to R.A.F. Panel 24. Son of William and Gertrude Boumphrey. The Runnymede Memorial overlooks the River Thames on Cooper's Hill, four miles from Windsor. (See Cap 18)

BROWNE, Dudley Patrick (4319). Co. Westmeath
Entered W.H. Sept 2nd 1936. Born 26/8/24. Honours Intercert 78% June 1940. R.A.F. 1942 B.A. (Mod) TCD 1950.

BUTLER, Percival George (4126). Streete, Co. Westmeath.
Entered W.H. Sept 10th 1928 aged 10 yrs 2 months. Left July 1931. Royal Field Artillery. Major. Dorset Regiment. (See Cap 25)

† CALVERT, Frederick George Mountjoy (4157). St. Ann's, Dublin.
Entered W.H. March 27th 1928 aged 10 yrs. Entered TCD 1936. R.A.F. 1941. Severely injured in plane crash 1941. (See Cap 19)

CALVERT, Thomas Church (4156). St. Ann's, Dublin.
Entered W.H. Feb. 14th 1928 aged 8 yrs 4 months. Left Dec 1935 to Pollock & Co., Dublin. R.A.F. 1940. (See Cap 19)

CASTLES, Charles (4182). Ahuscragh, Galway.
Entered W.H. Jan 15th 1930 aged 9. 10 years. Intercert Honours (83%) 1936. Went to Mountjoy. Junior Exhibition T.C.D. 1938. R.A.F. December 1943 - March 1947. (See Cap 25)

CHALONER, Gerald H. (3952). Waterford.
Entered W.H.Sept 4th 1916 aged 10yrs 7 months. Born 18/1/06. Got clerkship in London in the firm Downey & Co in which his late father had been employed. Left July 1922. "Active Service in the Mediterranean theatres of war". Royal Engineers. (See Cap 25)

CHRISTIE, David Hamilton (Master).
Appointed to Colonial Service. Wrote from Gibraltar on way to Malay. War Service.

COCHRANE, W. Leslie (4278). Rathconnell, Co. Westmeath.
Entered W.H. September 14th 1934 aged 13.6 years. Left Xmas 1936. Intercert with honours. 1941 in Belfast. Royal Air Force.

COLEMAN, James (4226). Bailieborough, Co. Cavan.
Entered W.H. Sept 1932 aged 13 years. Intercert Hons. 1936. Went to Mountjoy. Commission L.D.F. 1939. Chief Radio Officer Merchant Navy 1939/45. First troopship into Java. (See Cap 25).

† **DINEEN, Robert Lewis (4360). Ballinamore, Leitrim.**
Entered W.H. September 2nd 1937 aged 13 years 8 months. Left 1940. Royal Air Force. Killed in plane crash in York 5th march 1945. Buried at Harrogate, Yorkshire.

DIXON, W.S. (not listed). Royal Ulster Rifles.
(Not listed in school register. However, he is listed in the School magazine (1940) as in the Services.)

DOBBS, F.J.J. (4415). Athlone, Co. Westmeath.
Entered W.H. September 6th 1939 aged 13.1 years. Left June 1943.British Army.

DOHERTY, Donald Albert (4240). Mullingar, Co. Westmeath.
Entered W.H. September 8th 1941 aged 10 years 3 months. Intercertificate Honours July 1937. Bank of Ireland 1941.Warrant officer, R.A.F.

DOUGLAS, Benjamin (4114). Ballivor, Co. Meath.
Entered W.H. January 27th 1926 aged 11.1 years. Father kept him at home (delicate) July 1926. Royal Air Force.

DOWDALL, Thomas (4327). Co. Westmeath.
Entered W.H.Sept 2nd 1936. Born 4/9/20. Intercert Honours June 1937. R.A.F 1941. (See Cap 16)

ECHLIN, James (4106). Moyliscar, Co. Westmeath.
Entered W.H. 5th September 1925 aged 12 years 9 months. Left 22nd March 1929 to Millar and Beatty, Grafton Street, Dublin. Royal Air Force, 17 Squadron, C flight.

ELDON, William George (4171). Streete, Co. Westmeath.
Entered W.H. April 6th 1929 aged 10yrs 6 months. Went into motor work Dublin, January 1934 R.A.F. 1940.

EVANS, Walter John (4305). Mullingar, Co. Westmeath.
Entered W.H. 4th September 1935 aged 11.8 years. Left July 1938. R.A.F.

FARRAR, John Joseph (4090). Kilbixy, Co. Westmeath.
Entered W.H. 12th May 1924 aged 12 years. Left July 1927. British Army 1929. Irish Guards, No. 7063.

† **FETHERSTON, Frank Edward West (4058).**
Newtownforbes, Longford. Entered W.H. October 16th 1922, aged 10 years, 2 months. Emigrated to USA 1926. Sgt. U.S. Army Air Corps. Photo Sharman Scrapbook. Killed in action August 10th 1942 aged 32. (See Cap 27)

FETHERSTON, Seward Henry Lloyd (4057). Newtownforbes, Co. Longford.
Entered W.H. October 16th 1922 aged 12 years. Born 4/10/10. Left W.H. March 25th 1926 to go to U.S.A. Married in New Jersey, April 18th 1942. Enlisted in U.S. Navy May 21st 1942. Discharged September 1st 1945. (See Cap 16,27)

† **FORSTER, Thomas Noble (4248). Clonbroney, Co. Longford.**
Entered W.H. Sept. 5th 1933. Born 8/8/21. Left July 1938. Got Intercert with Honours. Went to Mountjoy School.

F/Off.: Thomas Noble Forster (Foster) 78 sqdn.
RAF VR. 3rd April 1943. Age 21. Son of Thomas Elliott and Frances Maria Forster of Ballinalee, Co. Longford. No known grave. Name on the RAF Memorial at Runnymede, Surrey, on panel No. 124. His squadron was part of 4 group based at Dishforth, Middleton and St. George Crofton, Linton-on-Ouse and Breighton. On the night of 3/4th of April 1943, 348 aircraft were sent to Essen and 23 aircraft lost. (See Cap 21)

GARDINER, William Henry (4210). Athlone, Co. Westmeath.
Entered W.H. October 10th 1931 aged 9 years 11 months. Left 1936 to Masonic School. Merchant service 1939. Royal Air Force. Pilot with Aer Lingus after War.

GRAY, Desmond Samuel (4293). Drumcondra.
Entered W.H. Sept 4th 1935. Born 2/5/23 Left July 1940. Honours Intercert Exam June 1940.Joins R.A.F. 1941.

GREER, George (4053). Swords, Co. Dublin
Entered W.H. January 20th 1922, aged 10 years. Entered TCD June 1930 Left to live in Dublin to attend TCD July 1931 Passed Junior Freshman May 1931 Journalism in London. Enlisted for War 1941, Commission 1942.

GRIER, James Frederick (4164). Granard, Co. Longford.
Entered W.H. Sept 10th 1928 aged 10 yrs 4 months. Intercert with Honours 1935. Provincial Bank 1937. Enlisted for War 1940. Prisoner of War (RAF) 1942. Ft / Sergeant. (See Cap 16, 27)

GRIER, John James (3916). Athboy, Co. Meath.
Entered W.H.Sept 13th 1913, aged 9 years 1 month. Born 22/8/04. Put to business by his father in Birmingham July 1919. Arrived in U.S.A. 1925. Entered U.S. Merchant Marine Service May 8th 1943. Discharged June 7th 1946.(See Cap 16, 17,27)

GRIER, John Joseph (4096). Granard, Co. Longford.
Born 25/2/12 Entered W.H. Sept 8th 1924, aged 11 years 7 months. Left Xmas 1929 to go to America. Sailed for New York, January 1930. U.S. Army Paratroops March 7th 1942 - Dec. 23rd 1946. Sergeant. (See Cap 27)

† GRIFFIN, Robert G.G. (4232). Edgeworthstown, Co. Longford.
Entered W.H. Sept. 11th 1932. Born 24/4/21. Went to Sligo School July 1934. Robert Grattan Gurney Griffin, son of H.G. and Daphne F.I. Griffin of Greystones, Co. Wicklow. 103 Squadron R.A.F. Voluntary Reserve. Killed 5th August 1941 aged 21. Service No. 947898. Rank - Sergeant. Buried in Calais at Canadian War Cemetery, No. 3.D.5

HARVEY, Eric John (4180) Moyliscar, Co. Westmeath.
Entered W.H. October 7th 1929 aged 9 years 6 months. (Cousin of Charles Castles 4182). Left July 1935 to go to business. Royal Air Force.

HARVEY, Richard H. (4269). Moyliscar, Co. Westmeath.
Entered W.H. September 14th 1934 aged 10 years 4 months. Left June 1939. Army Glider Pilot.Military Police.

HARVEY-KELLY, William. Clonhugh, Co. Westmeath.
Entere dW.H. 1932 aged 8. Left 1933. Enlisted 1943. Commissioned Irish Guards Sept 1943. Wounded, October 1944. Chevalier of Order Leopold II avec Palme, Croix de Guerre 1940 avec Palme. Retired 1969, Colonel. M.B.E. 1998. (See Cap 25)

HASSELL, George Thomas (4302). Killucan Co. Westmeath.
Entered W.H. Sept 4th 1935. Born 27/5/25. Intercert June 1942 and left. Irish Guards.

HATTON, George Albert (4179). Mount Temple, Westmeath.
Entered W.H. October 2nd 1929 aged 11 yrs 2 months. Went to business June 1935. R.A.F. 1942-1983. Squadron Leader. (See Cap 16,20)

† HEWITT, William (4239). Kildallon, Co. Cavan.
Entered W.H. Sept 5th 1933. Born 16/9/20. Left July 1935. On Mountjoy Roll of Honour. William Herbert Hewitt, Pioneer Corps. Service No. 7667701. Son of David and Anna Hewitt, Belfast. Killed 12th October 1945. Buried in Padua War Cemetery, Italy. Grave No. 11.A.10. The cemetery is 3.5 kilometres West of Padua on N11 towards Vicenza. (See Cap 25)

HICK,Benjamin John (4067). Killeshea, Longford.
Entered W.H. February 24th 1923 aged 8 yrs. 2 months. Went to Mountjoy School July 1930. In North of Ireland from 1934. Enlisted for war 1940 in Royal Artillery. Missing Singapore 1942. Reported prisoner of War 1943. (See Cap 25)

HOOD, K.H. (Master).
Joined the staff at W.H. November 1936 to teach Geography and History. War Service.

† HUGHES, Albert O. (4276). Kells, Co. Meath.
Entered W.H. September 14th 1934 aged 11 years 3 months. Left June 1940. Rear Gunner R.A.F. Killed in action.

HUNT, William Samuel (4043). Navan, Co. Meath.
Entered W.H. August 17th 1921, aged 11 years 2 months. Left May 4th 1925 to Kennan and sons. Tank Corps 1928. British Expeditionary Force 1940. Royal Field Artillery. (See Cap 18)

JOB, David Henry (4010). Gowra, Co. Cavan.
Entered W.H. January 11th 1919 aged 10 yrs 6 months. Kept at home by mother January 1925. Arrived in U.S.A. October 1929. Enlisted in U.S. Army October 6th 1942. Discharged October 26th 1945.

† JONES, Griffith (4216). Rathvilly, Co. Carlow.
Entered W.H. January 13th 1932 aged 10 yrs 6 months. Left July 1935. Sgt. Richard G. Jones RAF VR. Age 21. Son of William and Jane A. Jones of Rathvilly Co. Carlow. Grave No. 6.C.I3. in Abbeville Communal Cem. Extension - Somme

† KELLS, Lionel George Hosford (4151). Killeshandra, Co Cavan.
Entered W.H. October 15th 1927 aged 9 years 9 months. Left July 1931 to join father in India. Killed in R.A.F. 1942

KELLS, Norman Cyril Fredrick (4181). Killeshandra, Co Cavan.
Entered W.H. 15th January 1930 aged 9 years 10 months. Left July 1931 to go to his father in India, Joined Army. 54 Ordnance Field Depot , India Command. (See Cap 25)

KEOWN, Richard Henry (4021) Easkey, Co. Sligo.
Entered W.H. August 23rd 1919 aged 12.7. Left January 21st 1922 for Mssrs Thompson Engines, Grafton Street, Dublin. Irish Guards.

† KERR, James Noel (4198). Athboy Co. Meath.
Entered W.H. April 11th 1931 aged 11yrs. 1 month. Intercert Honours 1936. Went to Armstrong Siddely, Coventry 1936. R.A.F. 1939. P/O 81041 RAF (V.R) Lost his life aged 21 on service with 144 Squadron, 10th April 1941. Son of John and Marie, Athboy, Co. Meath. Buried in Adegem Canadian war Cemetery, Belfast, No 111.AA.5. This cemetery is on the N9 midway between Brugge and Ghent. (See Cap 16, 23)

KILROY, William George (4150). Tullamore, Co. Offaly.
Entered W.H. September 12th 1927 aged 13 years 5 months. Left July 1929 for father's business, Tullamore. Enlisted for war 1940. Royal Field Artillery.

LLOYD, Charles Holmes (4192). Streete, Co. Westmeath.
Entered W.H. Sept 27th 1930 aged 12 yrs. 1 month. Left July 1933 R.A.F. 1940. Discharged two years later due to ill health.

† LOCKHART, Godfrey Morgan (4128). St. Bartholomew's, Dublin.
Entered W.H. Sept. 14th 1926 aged 11 yrs. 2 months. Left December 1929. Killed serving Royal Navy, 5th December 1942. Served on board H.M.S. Kelt as Able Seamen. Part of Royal Naval Patrol Service. Service No. Lt/JX 228112. His name is on Lowestoft Naval Memorial, Suffolk, Panel 9, Column 1. This Memorial commemorates men of The Royal Naval Service who have no grave but the sea. (See Cap 18)

LYONS, Charles Alfred (4142). Drumcree, Co. Westmeath
Entered W.H. Sept 12th 1927. Left July 1933 R.A.F. 1940

MARRAH, Robert (4169) Cahir, Co. Tipperary.
Entered W.H. 12/1/29 aged 12 years and 10 months. Left summer 1933 to go to business in Tipperary. King's Royal Rifles.

† MARTIN, William (4100). Shandon, Co. Cork.
Entered W.H. January 13th 1925, aged 14 years 6 months. Left July 1927, "a promising boy." In Fords Factory Cork 1930 Died as a prisoner in Germany 1942, aged 31. (See Cap 17)

MATTHEWS, Arthur Edward (4026). Tyrrellspass, Co. Westmeath
Entered W.H. October 7th 1919 aged 11 yrs. 3 months. Royal Ulster Rifles, India 1930. Major. M.B.E. (See Cap 25)

MATTHEWS, George William (4312). Drogheda, Co. Louth.
Entered W.H. September 1936 aged 15 years. Intercert Hons. 1937. To Mountjoy. Fleet Air Arm.

MILLS, James N. (4428). Kilbixy, Co. Westmeath.
Entered W.H. 6th September 1939 aged 13.2. Dayboy. Royal Army Service Corps.

MONTSERRAT, Edward Villiers (3937). Tullamore, Co. Offaly.
Entered W.H. October 27th 1912 aged 12 years 1 month. Left December 1917. Joined H.M.S. Impregnable Training Ship, Royal Navy, February 4th 1918. Advanced Wireless Tetegraphy. Served in the Royal Navy in Second World War. Submarines. P.O.W. (See Cap 17, 18)

MONTSERRAT, Ernest Frederick (3985). Tullamore, Co. Offaly.
Entered W.H. 11/8/1917 aged 11 years 3 months. Left July 1922. Motor Garage, Tullamore. Enlisted Royal Artillery December 1925. Royal Army Service Corps. British Army Expeditionary Force 1939.

MORGAN, George Foster (4136). Monaghan.
Entered W.H. Jan. 12th 1926 aged 11 years 3 months. Left March 1932 to join Wireless Class in Dublin. Enlisted Army. Dragoon Guards. Manpower Planning Directorate, G.H.Q. India. (See Cap 25)

MORRISON, Frederick Lancelot (4288). Ballinlough, Roscommon.
Entered W.H. January 16th 1935 aged 12.7 Intercert Hons. June 1934. Went to Mountjoy. Royal Navy.

† MORROW, Robert (4223). Cruddum, Co. Cavan.
Entered W.H. Sept 10th 1932. Born 29/10/17. Got pupil teachership. Passed Intercert with Honours. Left July 1934. Fusilier. Robert John Morrow. No. 6 Commando and The Royal Inniskilling Fusiliers. Killed in action 23rd March 1945. Age 31. Grave No. 62.A.6 in Reichwald Forest war Cemetery near Cleves. (See Cap 17)

NELSON, William.
Not listed in school register, but named in Past Pupils' memoranda as in the Royal Air Force.

NOBLE, William Irvine (3987). Carigallan, Co. Leitrim.
Entered W.H. August 18th 1917 aged 11 years 1 month. Born 18/7/16. Left July 1922. Arrived in U.S.A. October 1924.

Enlisted U.S. Army Air Corps March 15th 1943. Discharged November 16th 1945. (See Cap 27)

NUMMY, Hugh (3948). Howth, Dublin.
Entered W.H. August 13th 1914 aged 12.5. Joined H.M.S. Impregnable Training Ship, Royal Navy, January 25th, 1918. Wireless Telegraphy. Served in Royal Navy in World War II. (See Cap 17)

OGDEN, Leslie (4029). Cork.
Entered W.H. April 19th 1920 aged 8 years 11 months. Left Nov. 1925 for Band of 1st Dragoon Guards. (O.G.S.) Egypt 1927, India 1930. (See Cap 25)

PAKENHAM, Charles Albert S. (4186). Killucan, Co. Westmeath.
Entered W.H. Sept. 15th 1930 aged 11 yrs. Left July 1934 Pilot R.A.F. 1939 . (See Cap 17)

PARKER, Richard Thomas (4089). Killeshandra, Co. Cavan.
Entered W.H. May 2nd 1924. Left July 1928 to go to Canada. 1st Royal Tank Corps, January 1931, Dunkirk. (See Cap 18)

PARKER, Robert Frederick (3981). Killeshandra, Co. Cavan.
Entered W.H. 10th January 1917 aged 10 years 9 months. Left school July 1922. Enlisted Royal Artillery August 1924. India 1927. Joined Tea Planters Brigade, reached rank of Lieutenant Colonel. (See Cap 25)

AYNE, G. Herbert (4267). Tullamore, Co. Offaly.
Entered W.H. 14/9/34. Born 5/5/22. Taken home by mother to go to day school. Royal Air Force.

POLLOCK, James (4003). Kells, Co. Meath.
Entered W.H. Aug. 16th 1918 aged 12 years 11 months. Passed middle grade Inter 1924, 5 honours. Scholarship to Mountjoy. 2nd Maths Scholarship TCD 1926. Irish Guards 1926. Arrived in USA 1927. Enlisted U.S. Army Military police, July 2nd 1943. Discharged 24/11/45. (See Cap 27)

POWER, Antony Grattan (4108). Kingstown, Dublin.
Entered W.H. October 1st 1925 aged 8 years 1 month. Left July
1927. "Left very well off." Inherited baronetcy. Going to school
in England at Cheam Park. In Lloyds Insurance, London, 1928.
Lincoln Rgt.

RAMSAY, David (3919). Longford.
Entered W.H. August 30th 1912 aged 11 years. Born
10/8/01. Left August 1917. Shipwright business, Mssrs
Holloway, Southwall, Dublin. Arrived in U.S.A. 1926. U.S.
Army November 24th 1942 to May 19th 1943. (See Cap
27)

EDPATH, Charles (4098). Kells, Co. Meath.
Entered W.H. October 1924. Left July 1930 to Chetwoods.
R.E.M.E., B.A.O.R.

REID, Michael (4080). Killucan, Co. Westmeath.
Entered W.H. September 26th 1923 aged 8 years. Left December
1930. R.A.F.

**† RIGGS, Albert Victor (4160). Clara, King's
County.**
Entered W.H. Sept 10th 1928 aged 12 yrs. 3 months. Left Xmas
1931. 1386921: Sgt (Air Gunner). Albert Victor Riggs. RAF VR.
9 Sqdn. Killed in air operations, 24th Sept 1942, age 26. Son of
Thos. and Ann Riggs of Tullamore Co. Offaly. Buried in Berlin
War Cemetery, Grave No. 9J.23.26. His squadron was part of No.
5 group, based at Waddington and Boardney. On the night of 23-
24 Sept 1942, 83 Lancasters were despatched to attack a Dornier
factory at Wismar, 4 aircraft were lost. The attack was judged as
successful. (See Cap 19)

ROBINSON, W. J. (4273). Mount Nugent, Cavan
Entered W.H. Sept 14th 1934. Born 10/11/23. Joins Royal Navy
April 1939. H.M.S. Ganges

ROE, Alfred John (4457). Boyle, Co. Roscommon.
Entered W.H. 16/9/40. Born 21/6/26. Left June 1944. Royal
Air Force.

**† RONALDSON, Brian Sidney (4244). Moyliscar, Co.
Westmeath.**
Entered W.H. Sept 5th 1933. Born 13/3/21. Left July 1938.
Junior Intercert with Honours 1935. Sgt. Sidney Bryan
Ronaldson, 150 Sqdn. RAF VR. Age 21. Killed on air operations
3rd Sept 1942. Son of Sidney and Olive Ronaldson of Milltown
Pass, Co. Westmeath. No known grave. Name on panel 92 R.A.F.
Memorial at Runnymede Egham Surrey. His Sqdn. was part of
No.I.Group B.C. They were based at Newton, Snaith and
Kirmington, and flew mostly Blenheims. On the night of
3/4th Sept 1942, 11 aircraft were despatched to attack a target in
Emden and 2 Wellingtons were lost. Sgt Ronaldson was a
Navigator. Plaque to his memory presented to WH by Mrs Nora
Johnston and Mrs. May Flower. (See Cap 16,19)

**SAMUEL, John Augustine (4243) Boyle, Co.
Roscommon.**
Entered W.H. 5th September 1933. Born 31st December 1919.
Left July 1936 to go to Scotland to his people. War Service.

SCANLON, Charles (not listed).
Royal Air Force. P.O.W. Son of stationmaster, Multyfarnham.
(Not listed in school register. However, He is listed in the School
magazine (1940) as in the Services.)

SCARGILL, Walter (4087). Aghadoe, Co. Kerry.
Entered W.H. April 3rd 1924 aged 13 yrs. born 28/4/11. Left July
1927 to go to Canada with his brothers - but did not go - at home
May1928. R.A.F. Served in India. (See Cap 25)

SEAMAN, George Henry (4317). Kildare.
Entered W.H. September 2nd 1936. Born 27/12/22. Left June
1938. Elvery & Co. 1940. Enlisted in Omagh, Royal Artillery,
2nd October 1941 to 22nd July 1945. Royal Army Service Corps
23rd July 1945 to 18th January 1949. Army service No.
S/11410007. Lance Bombardier.

SHARPE, Ronald Keith (4289) Westmeath.
Entered W.H. 3rd September 1936. Born 29/3/23. Left June
1939. R.A.F.

STUBBS, Richard Thomas (4125) Glasnevin, Dublin
Entered W.H. Sept 14th 1926 aged 10 yrs 7 months. Left July 1931 to St Alban's School. R.A.F. Commission 1939. Squadron Leader 1941. Awarded D.F.C. 1941. (See Cap 16)

† TATE, Stanley O'Connor (4103). Ardbraccan, Co. Meath.
Entered W.H. January 31st 1925 aged 14 years 5 months. Left June 12th 1927 for grocery business, Dublin. His name is on the panel 133 on the RAF War Memorial at Runnymede. Pilot Officer No.138889 R.A.F. (V.R.) 467 Squadron 13th of July 1943 aged 31 years. Son of William and Marie-Louise Tate (née O'Connor). Husband to Alice Catherine Tate (Dunmore, Co. Waterford). Youngest brother of Irene Rennicks (née Tate), Grandmother to Richard, Stephen and Helen. (See Cap 19)

TAYLOR, N. A. D. (4282). Kells Co. Meath.
Entered September 16th 1934. Born 17/12/20. Left July 1937. In Royal Air Force May 1938. Died 1943.

THOMPSON, Geoffrey Jack (4339). Co. Offaly.
Entered W.H. Sept. 2nd 1936. Left 1942. Royal Air Force. (See Cap 25)

THOMPSON, George Langen (4197). Ferbane, King's County.
Entered W.H. January 16th 1931 aged 10 yrs 1 month. Left July 1937. In Watson and Sons, Dublin. Enlisted Irish Guards 1941. Captain in Irish Fusiliers. Saw service in Egypt, India and Gibraltar (See Cap 25)

† THORPE, Charles James (4105). Mullingar, Co. Westmeath.
Entered June 2nd 1925 aged 11 years 1 month. Assisted scholarship, Ranelagh School July 1926. No. 1800350: Sgt. (Air Gunner). Charles James Thorpe. RAF VR. 115 Sqdn. Killed in air operations over Duisburg Germany, 27th April 1943 age 29. Buried in Reichwald War Cemetery, near the town of Cleves on the Dutch/German border, Grave No. 9.D.13. His Squadron was part of 3 group Bomber Command. They were based at Mildenhall and East Wretham. On the night of 27th April 1943, 561 aircraft were sent to attack targets in Duisburg. A total of 17 aircraft were lost on the raid. (See Cap 19)

† TOTTENHAM, Anthony B.L. (4249). Moyliscar, Co. Westmeath
Entered W.H. Sept 5th 1933. Born 11/9/23. Left Jan 1939 to go to Australia. F/Lieut.: Anthony Bowen Loftus Tottenham. D.F.C. RAAF. Killed in air operations, 26th Sept. 1944. age 21. Son of Harold Wm. and Veronica Mary Bower Tottenham of Mullingar Co. Westmeath.Buried in Coll. grave no 3 in Wissant Communal Cemetery, Pas de Calais, France. Aircraft lost in attacking target in the Calais area, 722 aircraft involved, 2 lost. (Lancasters) (See Cap 24)

TOTTENHAM, Nicholas L. (4217). Moyliscar, Co. Westmeath.
Entered W.H. Jan 18th 1932 aged 9 yrs 11 months Went to uncle in Australia, April 8th 1939. In Australian Imperial Forces 1940. Taken prisoner in Syria and released 1941. Missing March 1942. (Java) Prisoner of War 1942. (See Cap 24)

TRAILL, Alexander Frederick William (4262). Kells, Co. Meath.
Entered W.H. Jan. 1934 aged 10.9. Left July 1940. R.N.V.R. 1942. Service No. DJX614613.

† TRAILL, Daniel Anthony (4289). Kells, Co. Meath.
Entered W.H. Feb. 17th 1935. Born 14/4/20. Left Easter 1937 to go to business in Belfast. R.A.F. Killed in Duisburg Raid 13th May 1943. Member of 466 Squadron, Royal Australian Air Force. Service No 657379. Son of Alexander and Margaret Traill of Newburgh, Fife, Scotland. Buried in Driffield Cemetery, Yorkshire, Grave No. 6218. (See Cap 19)

TURNER, John Cyril (4141). St. George's, Dublin.
Entered W.H. September 12th 1927 aged 12. Left September 1931 to go into Ferrier, Pollock and Co, Dublin. R.A.F.

† VENTIN, William (4283). Cavan.
Entered W.H. 14th September 1934 aged 13.3. Left July 1936. Father removed him. Killed in air raid on Belfast 16th April 1941. (See Cap 26)

† **VIGORS, Patrick Forbes (4178). Bagenalstown, Co. Carlow.**
Entered W.H. September 11th 1929 aged 9.6 years. Intercert (pass) June 1936. Local Defence Force 1939. Killed in an air raid on Belfast 16th April 1941.(See Cap 26)

WHITTAKER, John Bindon (4354). Greystones, Co. Wicklow.
Entered W.H. September 2nd 1937 aged 12.4 years. Entered Imperial Services College July 1940. Royal Naval Auxiliary Service.

WHITTLE, Edward Gordon (4144). Sandyford, Dublin
Entered W.H. Sept 12th 1927 aged 9 years 5 months. R.A.F. 1942. (See Cap 22)

WILLIAMS, George Alexander (4201). Portnashangan, Multyfarnham, Co. Westmeath.
Entered W.H. September 9th 1931 aged 13.4. Left 1934 to work in Dublin. Royal Air Force. Served in Hong Kong.

WILLIAMS, George Elliot Cecil (4187). Raphoe, Donegal.
Entered W.H. Sept 15th 1930 aged 11yrs 6 months. Born 12/3/19.

Left July 1936 to go to Mountjoy School. R.A.F. served in Hong Kong. (See Cap 16)

WILLOUGHBY, Desmond (4265). Clones, Co. Monaghan.
Entered W.H. February 9th 1934. Born 6th June 1923. Left February 1940. Royal Air Force.

WILLOUGHBY, Harold (4239). Co. Meath.
Entered W.H. September 2nd 1936. Born 23 Mearch 1925. Left July 1941. Royal Air Force.

WILSON, William (4256). Kilkenny.
Entered W.H. September 1934 aged 13. Ft. Lieutenant R.A.F. Air H.Q. India. (See Cap 25)

WRIGHT, Robert (4219). Newtownforbes, Longford.
Entered W.H. Sept 10th 1932. Born 28th April 1919. Left July 1935 "owing to delicate health". Royal Air Force 1939-1946. Wireless Operator, based in France, Northern Ireland and Australia. Demobilized 1946, rank Corporal. Defence Medal. France/Germany Star. 1939/1945 Star. Returned home after the War and bought his own farm at Coolarty, Co. Longford. Married Letty Gilpin; four children, 1 boy and 3 girls. (See Cap 17).

† **Paid the Supreme Sacrifice (22)**

Total Numbers Listed (107)

The numbers (in brackets) refer to the computerised Nos. of entry on the School Register.

Appendix 5B

<u>Roll of Honour for the Second World War</u>

James Abbott.
L.E. Anderson.
William Beacon
Eric Beale.
R.H.N. Blackburn.
† Arnold Boumphrey, P/O
Dudley Browne
Percival Butler, Major.
† Frederick Calvert, P/O.
Thomas Calvert.
Charles Castles.
Gerald Chaloner.
David Christie.
Leslie Cochrane.
James Coleman.
† Robert Dineen.
W.S. Dixon.
F.J.J. Dobbs.
Donald Doherty, W/O.
Benjamin Douglas.
Thomas Dowdall.
James Echlin.
William Eldon.
Walter Evans.
John Farrar.
† Frank Fetherston, Sgt.
Seward Fetherston.
† Thomas Forster, P/O.
Henry Gardiner.
Desmond Gray.
George Greer.
James F. Grier, Sgt.
John James Grier.
John Joseph Grier, Sgt.
† Robert Griffin, Sgt.
Eric Harvey.

Richard. Harvey.
William Harvey-Kelly, Lt.
George Hassell.
George Hatton, P/O.
† William Hewitt.
Benjamin Hick.
K.H. Hood.
† Albert Hughes.
William Hunt.
David Job.
† Griffith Jones, Sgt.
† Lionel Kells.
Norman Kells.
Richard Keown.
† Noel Kerr, P/O.
William Kilroy.
Charles Lloyd.
† Godfrey Lockhart.
Charles Lyons.
Robert Marrah.
† William Martin.
Arthur Mathews, Major.
George Matthews.
James Mills.
Edward Montserrat.
Ernest Montserrat.
George Morgan.
Frederick Morrison.
† Robert Morrow.
William Nelson.
William Noble.
Hugh Nummy.
Leslie Ogden.
Charles Pakenham.
Richard Parker.
Robert Parker, Lt. Col.

Herbert Payne.
James Pollock.
Anthony Power.
David Ramsay.
Charles Redpath.
Michael Reid.
† Albert Riggs, Sgt.
W. J. Robinson.
Alfred Roe.
† Brian Ronaldson, Sgt.
John Samuel.
Charles Scanlon.
Walter Scargill.
George Seaman.
Ronald Sharpe.
Richard Stubbs, Sqn. Ldr. D.F.C.
† Stanley Tate, P/O.
N. A. D. Taylor.
George Thompson, Capt.
Jack Thompson.
† Charles Thorpe, Sgt.
† Anthony Tottenham, P/O D.F.C.
Nicholas Tottenham.
Alexander Traill.
† Daniel Traill.
John Turner.
† William Ventin.
† Forbes Vigors.
John Whittaker.
Edward Whittle, Sgt.
George C. Williams.
George Williams.
Desmond Willoughby.
Harold Willoughby.
William Wilson, P/O.
Robert Wright, Cpl.

Enlistment for the Second World War - Royal Air Force

Eric Beale
† Arnold Boumphrey
Dudley Browne
† Frederick G.M. Calvert
Thomas C. Calvert
Charles Castles
Leslie Cochrane
† Robert Dineen
W.S. Dixon
Donald Doherty
Thomas Dowdall
Benjamin Douglas
James Echlin
William Eldon
Walter Evans
† Thomas Forster
Henry Gardiner
Desmond Gray
James F. Grier
† Robert Griffin
Eric Harvey
George Hatton
† Albert Hughes
† Griffith Jones
† Lionel Kells
† Noel Kerr
Charles Lloyd
Charles Lyons
William Nelson
Charles Pakenham
Herbert Payne
Michael Reid
Alfred Roe
† Albert Riggs
† Brian Ronaldson
Walter Scargill

Charles Scanlon
Ronald Sharpe
Richard Stubbs
† Stanley Tate
N.A.D. Taylor
Jack Thompson
† Charles Thorpe
† Anthony Tottenham
† Daniel Traill
John Turner
Edward Whittle
George A. Williams
George C. Williams
Desmond Willoughby
Harold Willoughby
William Wilson
Robert Wright
(53)

ARMY (29)

L.E. Anderson
James Abbott
William Beacon
Percy Butler
Gerald Chaloner
F.J.J. Dobbs
John Farrar
Richard Harvey
William Harvey-Kelly
George Hassell
† William Hewitt
Benjamin Hick
William Hunt
K. Hood
Norman Kells
William Kilroy

Robert Marragh
Arthur Matthews
James Mills
Ernest Montserrat
George Morgan
† Robert Morrow
Leslie Ogden
Richard Parker
Robert Parker
Anthony Power
Charles Redpath
George Seaman
George Thompson

ROYAL NAVY (7)

+ Godfrey Lockhart
Edward Montserrat
Frederick Morrison
Hugh Nummy
W. R. Robinson
John Whitaker
Alexander Traill

AUSTRALIAN ARMY (1)

Nicholas Tottenham

ROYAL AUSTRALIAN AIR FORCE (2)

† Anthony Tottenham
† Daniel Traill

U.S ARMY (6)

† Frank Fetherston
John Joseph Grier
David Job
William Noble

<u>Enlistment for the Second World War - Royal Air Force contd.</u>

James Pollock
David Ramsay

U.S. NAVY (1)
Seward Fetherston

U.S. MERCHANT MARINE (1)
John James Grier

MERCHANT NAVY (1)
James Coleman

FLEET AIR ARM (1)
George Matthews

CIVILIAN (2)
†   William Ventin
†   Forbes Vigors

NOT KNOWN (5)
    David Christie
    George Greer
†   William Martin
    John Samuel
    R.H.N Blackburn

† **Paid supreme Sacrifice:**

22 (+ 2 civilians)
Total: 107 (+ 2 civilians) =109

Appendix 6B

<u>World War II - Enlistment in the Army: Analysis by Regiment</u>

<u>Dorset Regiment</u>

Percy Butler

<u>Dragoon Guards</u>

George Morgan
Leslie Ogden

<u>King's Royal Rifles</u>

Robert Marrah

<u>Irish Guards</u>

John Farrar
George Hassell
Richard Keown
James Pollock
George Thompson

<u>Lincolnshire Regiment</u>

Sir Anthony Power

<u>Pioneer Corps</u>

† William Hewitt

<u>Royal Army Service Corps</u>

James Mills

<u>Royal Signals Corps</u>

William Beacom

<u>Royal Engineers</u>

Gerald Chaloner
Charles Redpath

<u>Royal Field Artillery</u>

Benjamin Hick
William Hunt
William Kilroy
Ernest Montserrat
Robert Parker

George Seaman

<u>Royal Inniskilling Fusiliers</u>

L.E Anderson
† Robert Morrow

<u>Royal Tank Corps</u>

Richard Parker

<u>Royal Ulster Rifles</u>

W.S Dixon
Arthur Matthews

<u>Not Known</u>
5

Total: 29
† 2

Appendix 7

Analysis By County 1939/45

CAVAN (10)
  James Coleman
† William Hewitt
  David Job
† Lionel Kells
† Robert Morrow
  Richard Parker
  Robert Parker
  W.J. Robinson
† William Ventin
  Norman Kells

CARLOW (2)
† Griffith Jones
† Forbes Vigors

CORK (2)
† William Martin
  Leslie Ogden

DONEGAL (1)
  George C. Williams

DUBLIN (11)
† Arnold Boumphrey
† Frederick Calvert
  Thomas Calvert
  Desmond Gray
  George Greer
† Godfrey Lockhart
  Hugh Nummy
  Anthony Power
  Richard Stubbs
  John Turner
  Edward Whittle

GALWAY (1)
  Charles Castles

KERRY (1)
  Walter Scargill

KILDARE (1)
  George Seaman

KILKENNY (1)
  William Wilson

LEITRIM (3)
  James Abbot
  William Noble
† Robert Dineen

LONGFORD (10)
† Frank Fetherston
  Seward Fetherston
† Thomas Forster
  James Grier
  John Joseph Grier
  John James Grier
† Robert Griffin
  Benjamin Hick
  David Ramsay
  Robert Wright

LOUTH (1)
  George W. Matthews

MEATH (12)
  Eric Beale
  Benjamin Douglas

† Albert Hughes
  William Hunt
† Noel Kerr
  James Pollock
  Charles Redpath
† Stanley Tate
  N.A.D. Taylor
  Alexander Traill
† Daniel Traill
  Harold Willoughby

MONAGHAN (2)
  George Morgan
  Desmond Willoughby

OFFALY (7)
  William Kilroy
  Edward Montserrat
  Ernest Montserrat
  Herbert Payne
† Albert Riggs
  George Thompson
  Jack Thompson

ROSCOMMON (3)
  Fredrick Morrison
  Alfred Roe
  John Samuel

SLIGO (1)
  Richard Keown

TIPPERARY (1)
  Robert Marrah

Analysis By County 1939/45 contd.

TYRONE (1)
R.H.N. Blackburn
William Beacon

WATERFORD (1)
Gerald Chaloner

WICKLOW (1)
John Whittaker

WESTMEATH (29)
Dudley Browne
Percy Butler
Leslie Cochrane
F.J.J. Dobbs
Donald Doherty
Thomas Dowdall
James Echlin
George Eldon
Walter Evans
John Farrar
William Gardiner
Richard Harvey
William Harvey-Kelly
Eric Harvey
George Hassell
George Hatton
Charles Lloyd
Charles Lyons
Arthur Matthews
Arthur Mills
Charles Pakenham
Michael Reid

† Brian Ronaldson
Charles Scanlon
Ronald Sharpe
† Charles Thorpe
† Anthony Tottenham
Nicholas Tottenham
George A. Williams

UNKNOWN (5)
L.E Anderson
David Christie
W.S Dixon
K.Hood
William Nelson

Total: 107 + 2 civilians = 109

Analysis By Age On Enlistment for World War 11 1939/45

Age:	Nos. Enlisting
18	35
19	6
20	10
21	10
22	3
23	3
24	6
25	3
26	2
27	5
28	4
29	2
30	1
31	2
32	1
33	3
34	0
35	0
36	0
37	1
38	0
39	2
Not Known	7
Not Applic.	2
TOTAL	107

Average Age = 20.7

A Select Bibliography

Martin Gilbert; First World War Atlas
Martin Gilbert: First World War
Henry Harris: The Irish Regiments of the First World War
Tom Johnstone: Orange, Khaki and Green
John Laffin: Damn the Dardanelles; The Agony of Gallipoli
Lynn MacDonald: They called it Passchendaele
Philip Orr: The Road to the Somme
John Terraine: The Great War
Denis Winter: Death's Men. Soldiers of the Great War
Leon Wolff: In Flanders Fields

Brian Barton : The Belfast Blitz
L.E.O. Charlton : The RAF and the USAAF
Horace D. Cherrington : Winged Chariot
R.F. Foster : Modern Ireland
M. Garbett & B. Goulding : The Lancaster at War
John Keegan : The Second World War
F.S.L. Lyons : Ireland Since the Famine
R.D.A. Ltd. : The World at Arms
Ivan Rendall : Reaching for the Skies

Wilson's Hospital School 1998